TOO
COOL
to be
Forgotten

For the *loners*, *losers* and *outcasts*.

May you show them all someday.

TOO COOL

to be

Forgotten

ALEX ROBINSON

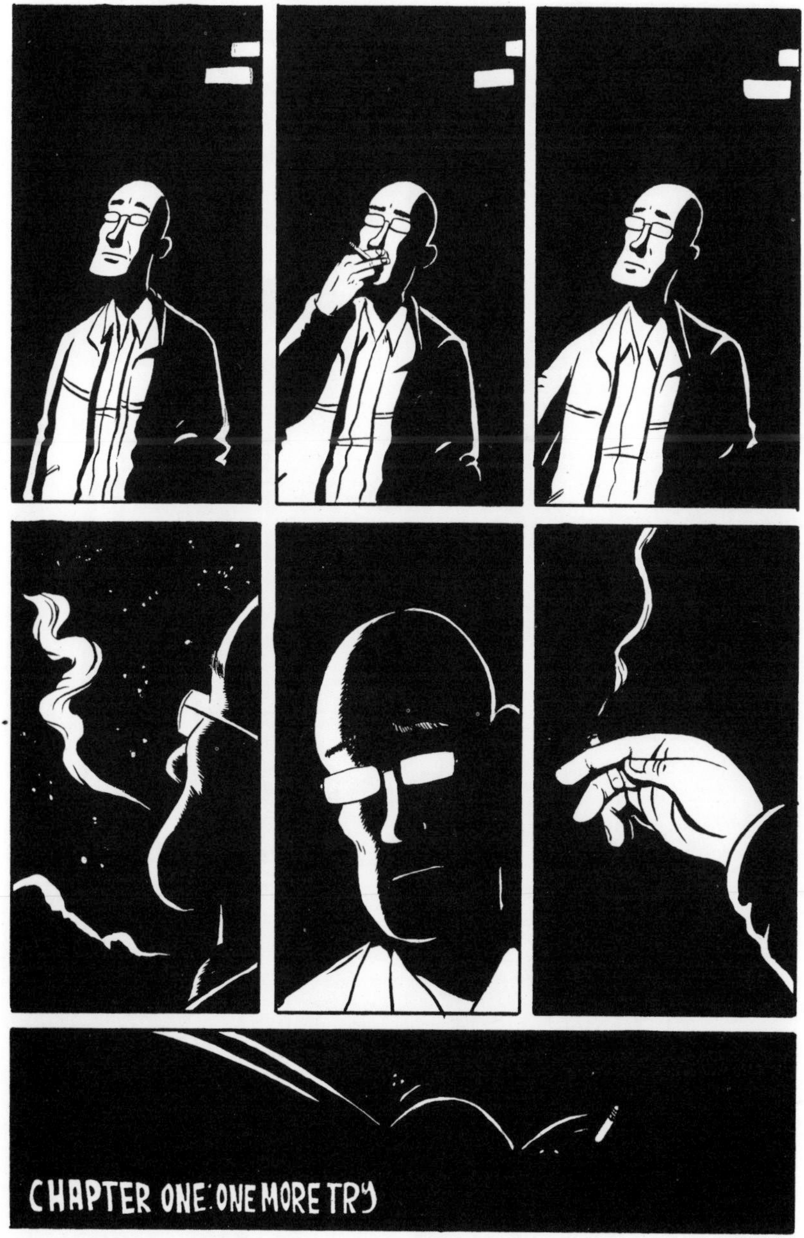
CHAPTER ONE: ONE MORE TRY

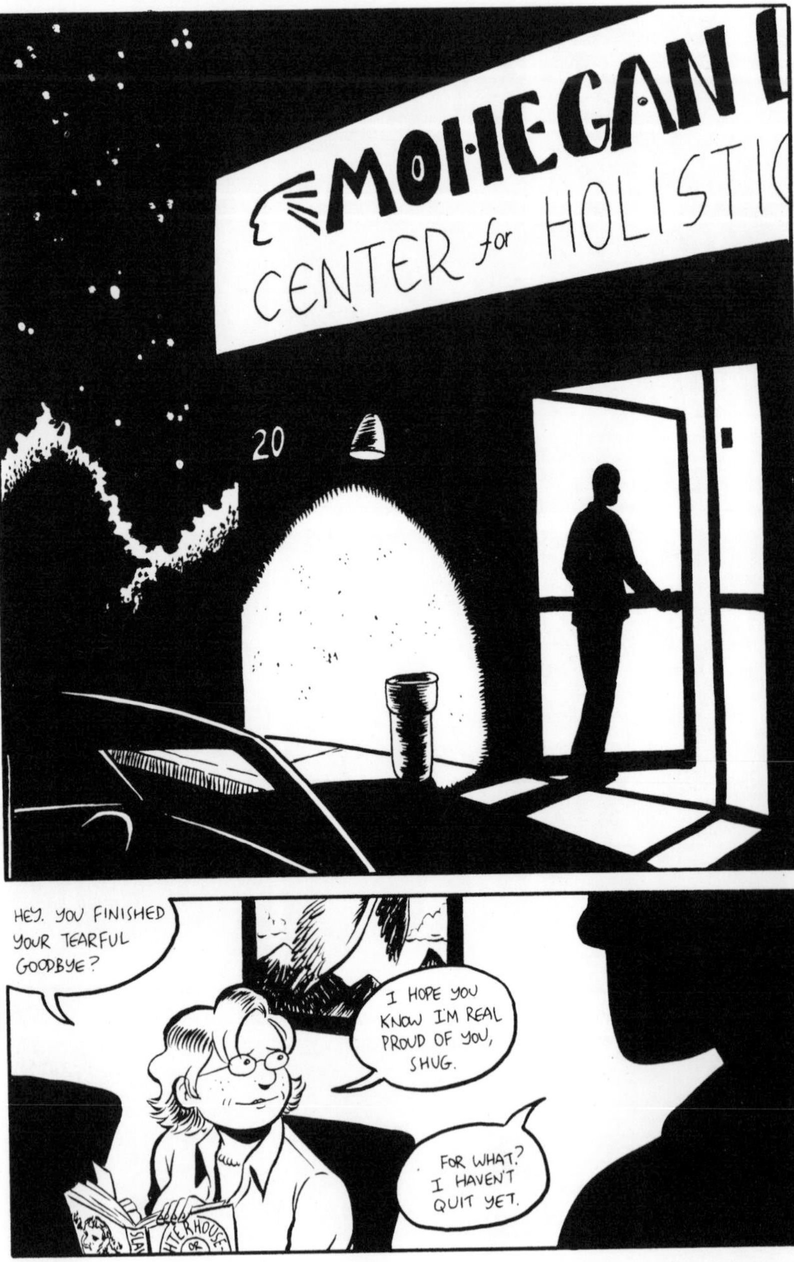
MOHEGAN
CENTER for HOLISTI
20
HEY. YOU FINISHED YOUR TEARFUL GOODBYE?
I HOPE YOU KNOW I'M REAL PROUD OF YOU, SHUG.
FOR WHAT? I HAVEN'T QUIT YET.

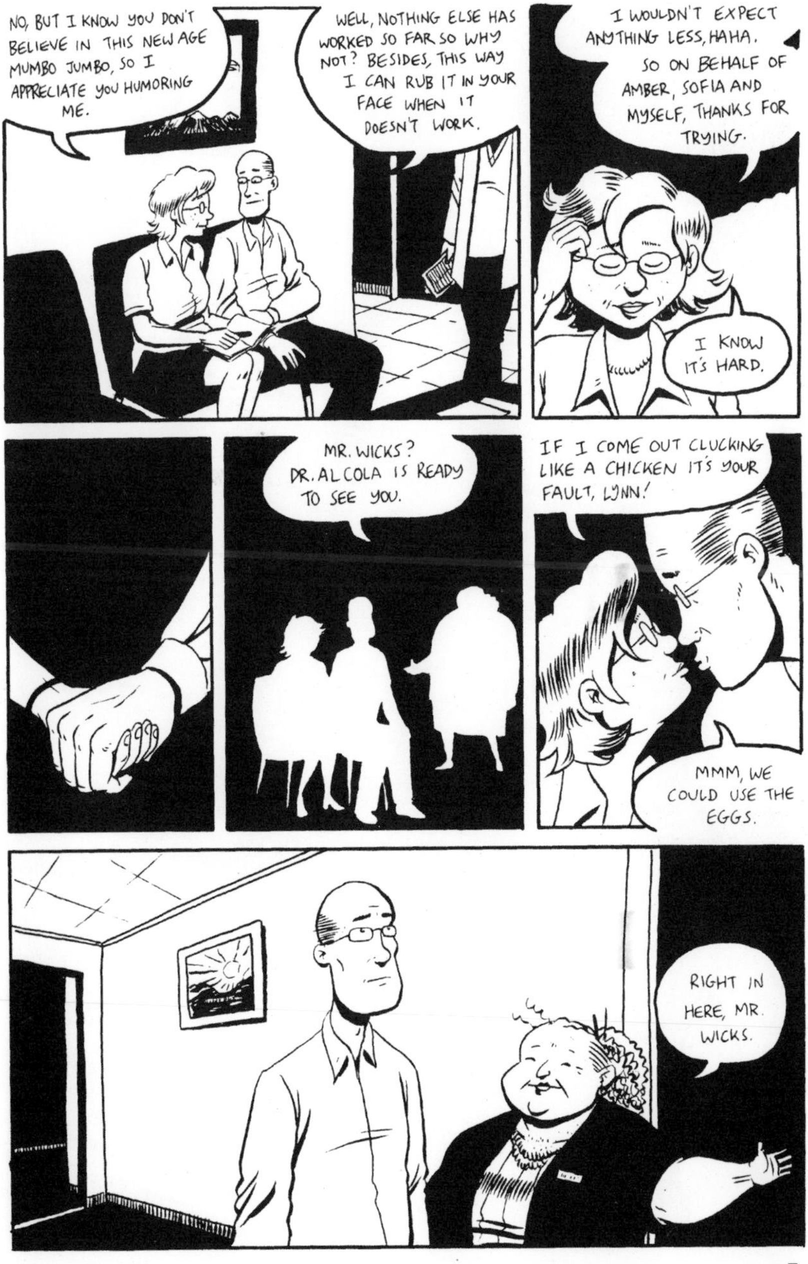

NO, BUT I KNOW YOU DON'T BELIEVE IN THIS NEW AGE MUMBO JUMBO, SO I APPRECIATE YOU HUMORING ME.
WELL, NOTHING ELSE HAS WORKED SO FAR SO WHY NOT? BESIDES, THIS WAY I CAN RUB IT IN YOUR FACE WHEN IT DOESN'T WORK.
I WOULDN'T EXPECT ANYTHING LESS, HAHA.
SO ON BEHALF OF AMBER, SOFIA AND MYSELF, THANKS FOR TRYING.
I KNOW IT'S HARD.
MR. WICKS? DR. ALCOLA IS READY TO SEE YOU.
IF I COME OUT CLUCKING LIKE A CHICKEN IT'S YOUR FAULT, LYNN!
MMM, WE COULD USE THE EGGS.
RIGHT IN HERE, MR. WICKS.

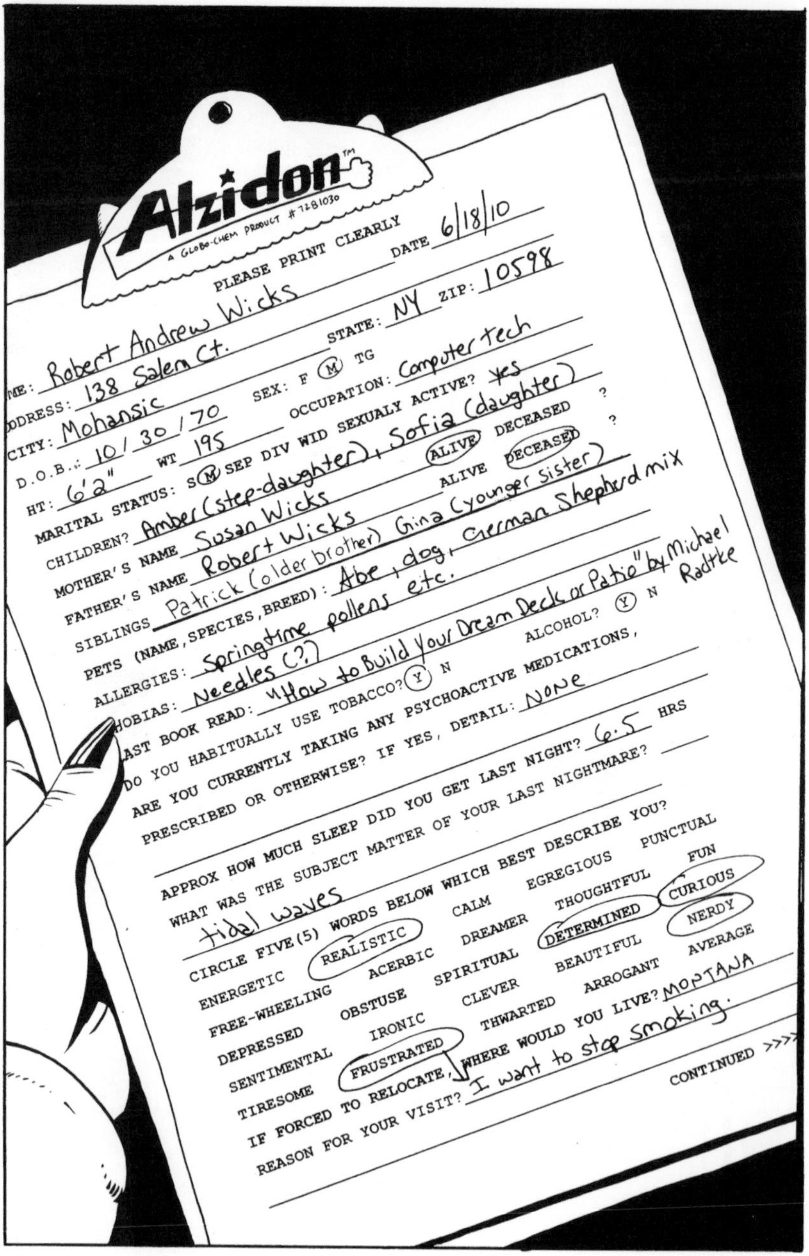
Alzidon™
A GLOBO-CHEM PRODUCT #7281030
PLEASE PRINT CLEARLY
DATE 6/18/10
ME: Robert Andrew Wicks
DDRESS: 138 Salem Ct. STATE: NY ZIP: 10598
CITY: Mohansic SEX: F M TG
D.O.B.: 10/30/70 OCCUPATION: Computer tech
HT: 6'2" WT 195 SEXUALY ACTIVE? yes
MARITAL STATUS: S M SEP DIV WID
CHILDREN? Amber (step-daughter), Sofia (daughter)
MOTHER'S NAME Susan Wicks ALIVE DECEASED ?
FATHER'S NAME Robert Wicks ALIVE DECEASED ?
SIBLINGS Patrick (older brother) Gina (younger sister)
PETS (NAME, SPECIES, BREED): Abe, dog, German Shepherd mix
ALLERGIES: Springtime pollens etc.
HOBIAS: Needles (?)
AST BOOK READ: "How to Build Your Dream Deck or Patio" by Michael Radtke
DO YOU HABITUALLY USE TOBACCO? Y N ALCOHOL? Y N
ARE YOU CURRENTLY TAKING ANY PSYCHOACTIVE MEDICATIONS, PRESCRIBED OR OTHERWISE? IF YES, DETAIL: NONE
APPROX HOW MUCH SLEEP DID YOU GET LAST NIGHT? 6.5 HRS
WHAT WAS THE SUBJECT MATTER OF YOUR LAST NIGHTMARE? tidal waves
CIRCLE FIVE (5) WORDS BELOW WHICH BEST DESCRIBE YOU?
ENERGETIC REALISTIC CALM EGREGIOUS PUNCTUAL
FREE-WHEELING ACERBIC DREAMER THOUGHTFUL FUN
DEPRESSED OBSTUSE SPIRITUAL DETERMINED CURIOUS
SENTIMENTAL IRONIC CLEVER BEAUTIFUL NERDY
TIRESOME FRUSTRATED THWARTED ARROGANT AVERAGE
IF FORCED TO RELOCATE, WHERE WOULD YOU LIVE? MONTANA
REASON FOR YOUR VISIT? I want to stop smoking.
CONTINUED >>>>

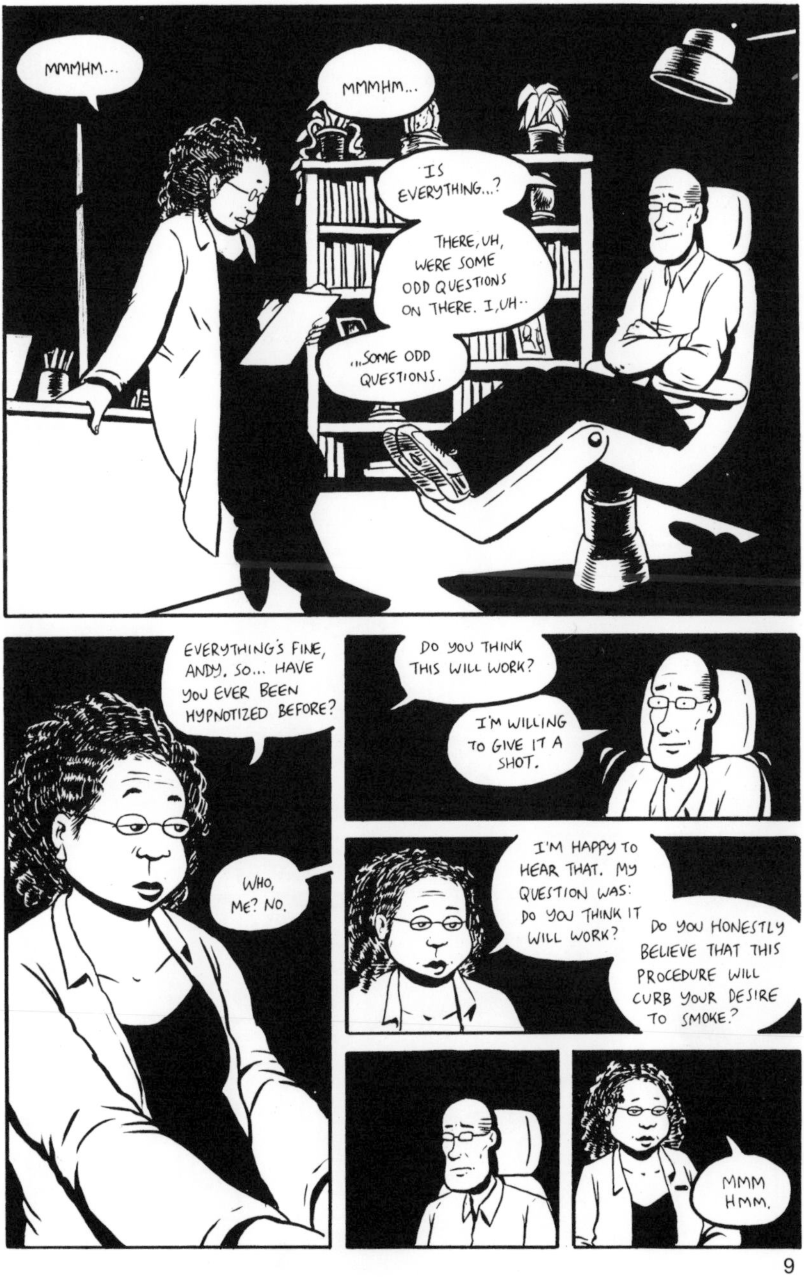
MMMHM...
MMMHM...
IS EVERYTHING...?
THERE, UH, WERE SOME ODD QUESTIONS ON THERE. I, UH..
...SOME ODD QUESTIONS.
EVERYTHING'S FINE, ANDY. SO... HAVE YOU EVER BEEN HYPNOTIZED BEFORE?
WHO, ME? NO.
DO YOU THINK THIS WILL WORK?
I'M WILLING TO GIVE IT A SHOT.
I'M HAPPY TO HEAR THAT. MY QUESTION WAS: DO YOU THINK IT WILL WORK?
DO YOU HONESTLY BELIEVE THAT THIS PROCEDURE WILL CURB YOUR DESIRE TO SMOKE?
MMM HMM.

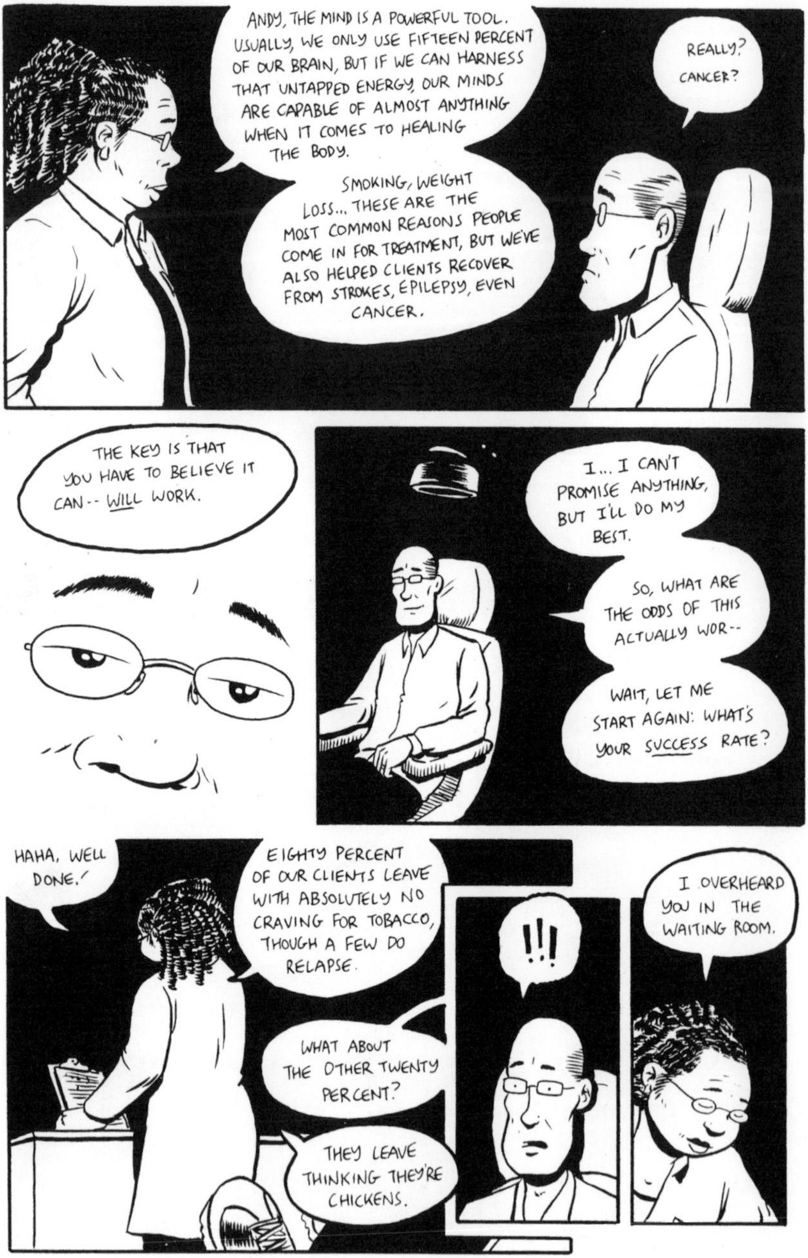
ANDY, THE MIND IS A POWERFUL TOOL. USUALLY, WE ONLY USE FIFTEEN PERCENT OF OUR BRAIN, BUT IF WE CAN HARNESS THAT UNTAPPED ENERGY, OUR MINDS ARE CAPABLE OF ALMOST ANYTHING WHEN IT COMES TO HEALING THE BODY.
SMOKING, WEIGHT LOSS... THESE ARE THE MOST COMMON REASONS PEOPLE COME IN FOR TREATMENT, BUT WE'VE ALSO HELPED CLIENTS RECOVER FROM STROKES, EPILEPSY, EVEN CANCER.
REALLY? CANCER?
THE KEY IS THAT YOU HAVE TO BELIEVE IT CAN-- WILL WORK.
I... I CAN'T PROMISE ANYTHING, BUT I'LL DO MY BEST.
SO, WHAT ARE THE ODDS OF THIS ACTUALLY WOR--
WAIT, LET ME START AGAIN: WHAT'S YOUR SUCCESS RATE?
HAHA, WELL DONE.
EIGHTY PERCENT OF OUR CLIENTS LEAVE WITH ABSOLUTELY NO CRAVING FOR TOBACCO, THOUGH A FEW DO RELAPSE.
WHAT ABOUT THE OTHER TWENTY PERCENT?
THEY LEAVE THINKING THEY'RE CHICKENS.
!!!
I OVERHEARD YOU IN THE WAITING ROOM.

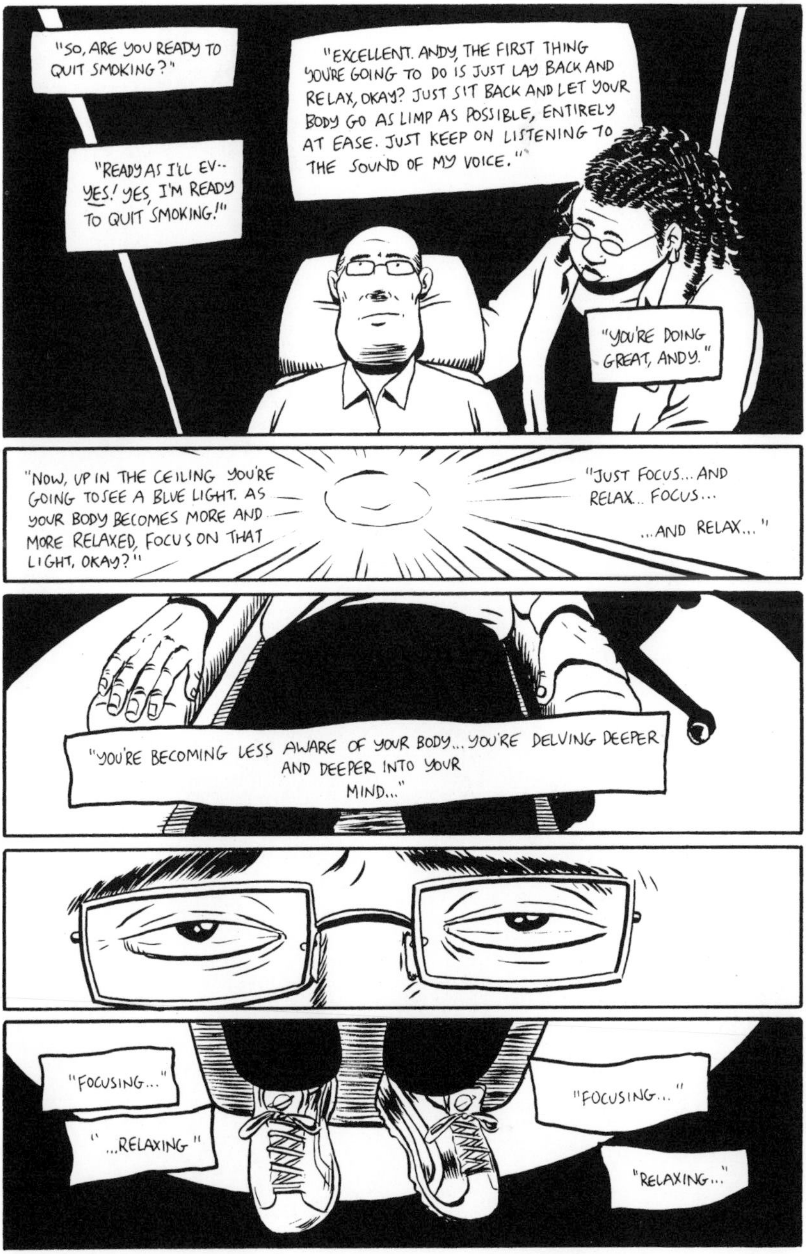
"SO, ARE YOU READY TO QUIT SMOKING?"
"READY AS I'LL EV-- YES! YES, I'M READY TO QUIT SMOKING!"
"EXCELLENT. ANDY, THE FIRST THING YOU'RE GOING TO DO IS JUST LAY BACK AND RELAX, OKAY? JUST SIT BACK AND LET YOUR BODY GO AS LIMP AS POSSIBLE, ENTIRELY AT EASE. JUST KEEP ON LISTENING TO THE SOUND OF MY VOICE."
"YOU'RE DOING GREAT, ANDY."
"NOW, UP IN THE CEILING YOU'RE GOING TO SEE A BLUE LIGHT. AS YOUR BODY BECOMES MORE AND MORE RELAXED, FOCUS ON THAT LIGHT, OKAY?"
"JUST FOCUS... AND RELAX.. FOCUS...
...AND RELAX..."
"YOU'RE BECOMING LESS AWARE OF YOUR BODY... YOU'RE DELVING DEEPER AND DEEPER INTO YOUR MIND..."
"FOCUSING..."
"...RELAXING"
"FOCUSING..."
"RELAXING..."

FOCUS...AND
RELAX...FOCUS AND
RELAX...FOCUS AND...
RELAX... I WILL NOT
SMOKE...FOCUS... I WILL
NOT SMOKE...RELAX...I WILL
NOT SMOKE...FOCUS...RELAX...
I WILL NOT SMOKE... RELAX...
IS IT WORKING?...FOCUS... I WILL
NOT SMOKE...RELAX... I CAN'T TELL
IF IT'S WORKING. I DON'T FEEL ANY
DIFFERENT. FOCUS/RELAX! BUT HOW
CAN I FOCUS AND RELAX? THIS ISN'T
WORKING. SHE PROBABLY JUST LULLS
PEOPLE TO SLEEP, WAKES THEM UP
AND CHARGES $300. THE WHOLE THING
IS A PLACEBO, IF IT WORKS AT ALL.
PEOPLE ARE PROBABLY TOO SCARED TO
ADMIT **IT DOESN'T WORK.** I SHOULD
UP AND **SAY "CUT THE CRAP, DOC!"**

DO IT! I SHOULD JUST SIT
BUT I DON'T WANT TO MAKE

A SCENE. I PROMISED LYNN I'D AT
LEAST GIVE IT   A TRY.
NOW I'M NOT   MONICA
WELL JUST RESIGN   EVEN DOING THAT.   MYSELF
TO A LIFE OF   SMOKING.

O'CONNOR. I MIGHT AS

NOTHING HAS WORKED, THE PATCH, COLD TUR-
KEY, GUM, NEGATIVE STIMULATION, NONE OF
IT. I CAN ONLY HOPE THE GIRLS ARE ALL
GROWN UP BEFORE I ·· WAIT, WHY DID
I SUDDENLY THINK OF MONICA JUST
THEN? GOD, I HAVEN'T THOUGHT OF
HER IN YEARS.' BUT I HAVE
TO KEEP TRYING. I WANT
TO SEE AMBER GRADUATE
FROM YALE AND I WANT
TO DANCE AT SOFIA'S WED-
DING. I DON'T WANT TO BE LIKE HIM.
SO, COME ON ANDY! YOU PROMISED
LYNN YOU'D GIVE IT A SHOT. GIVE
THIS STUPID HYPNOSIS A TRY...
FOCUS...RELAX... RELAX...YOU ARE GETTING SLEEPY...
SLEEPY! WHEN YOU AWAKE YOU
WILL NO LONGER CRAVE NICOTINE.'
AND YOU WILL HAVE A THICK HEAD
OF BEAUTIFUL HAIR! HAHA!
DON'T LAUGH! IF YOU LAUGH SHE'LL
KNOW YOU AREN'T FOCUSED...
AND RELAXED... FOCUSED,...
AND RELAXED... I WILL NOT
SMOKE... I WILL NOT SMOKE
... FOCUSED AND RELAXED...
I WILL NOT...NOT...OH,
FORGET IT.

12

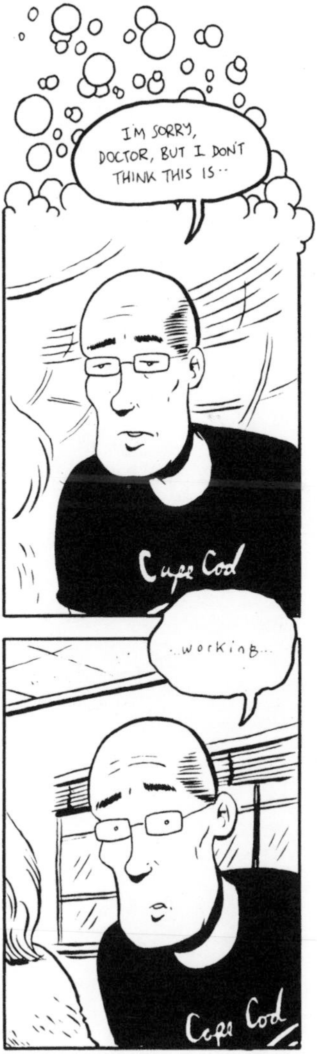

I'M SORRY, DOCTOR, BUT I DON'T THINK THIS IS…
…working…
Cape Cod
Cape Cod

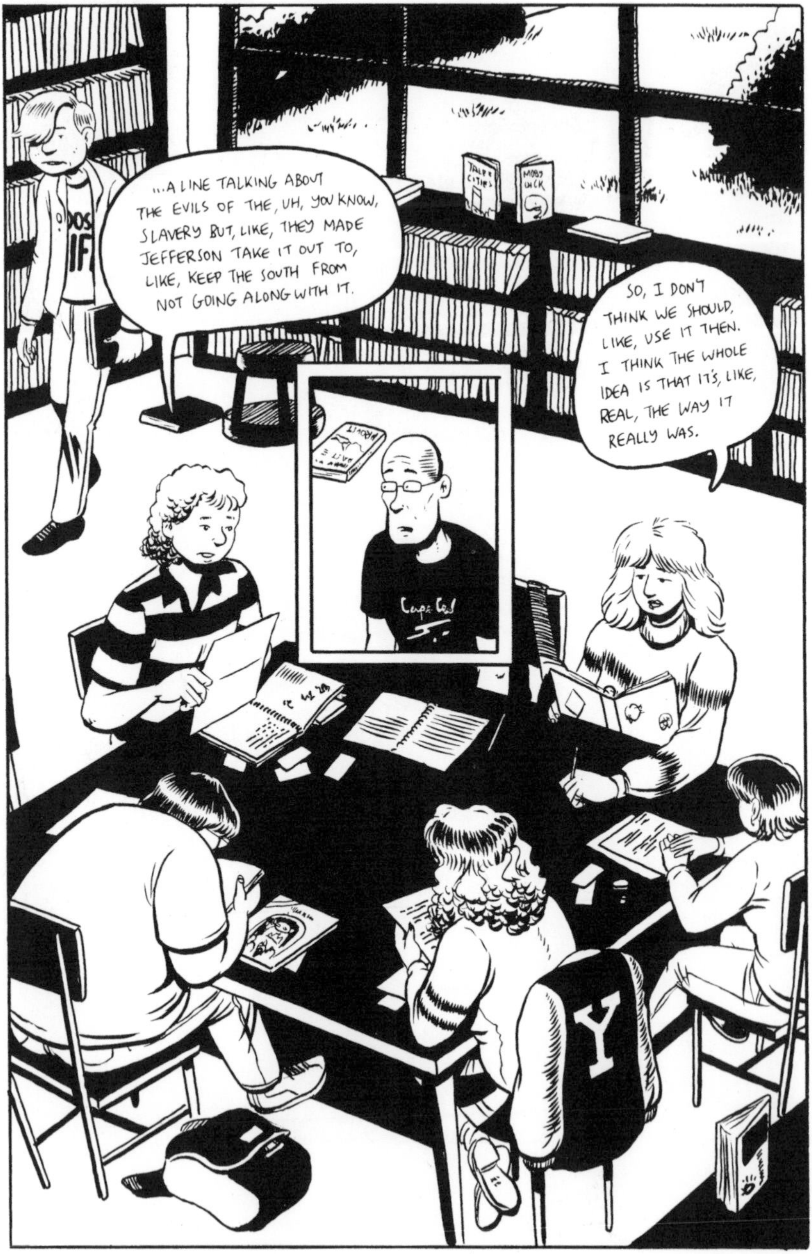
...A LINE TALKING ABOUT THE EVILS OF THE, UH, YOU KNOW, SLAVERY BUT, LIKE, THEY MADE JEFFERSON TAKE IT OUT TO, LIKE, KEEP THE SOUTH FROM NOT GOING ALONG WITH IT.
SO, I DON'T THINK WE SHOULD, LIKE, USE IT THEN. I THINK THE WHOLE IDEA IS THAT IT'S, LIKE, REAL, THE WAY IT REALLY WAS.

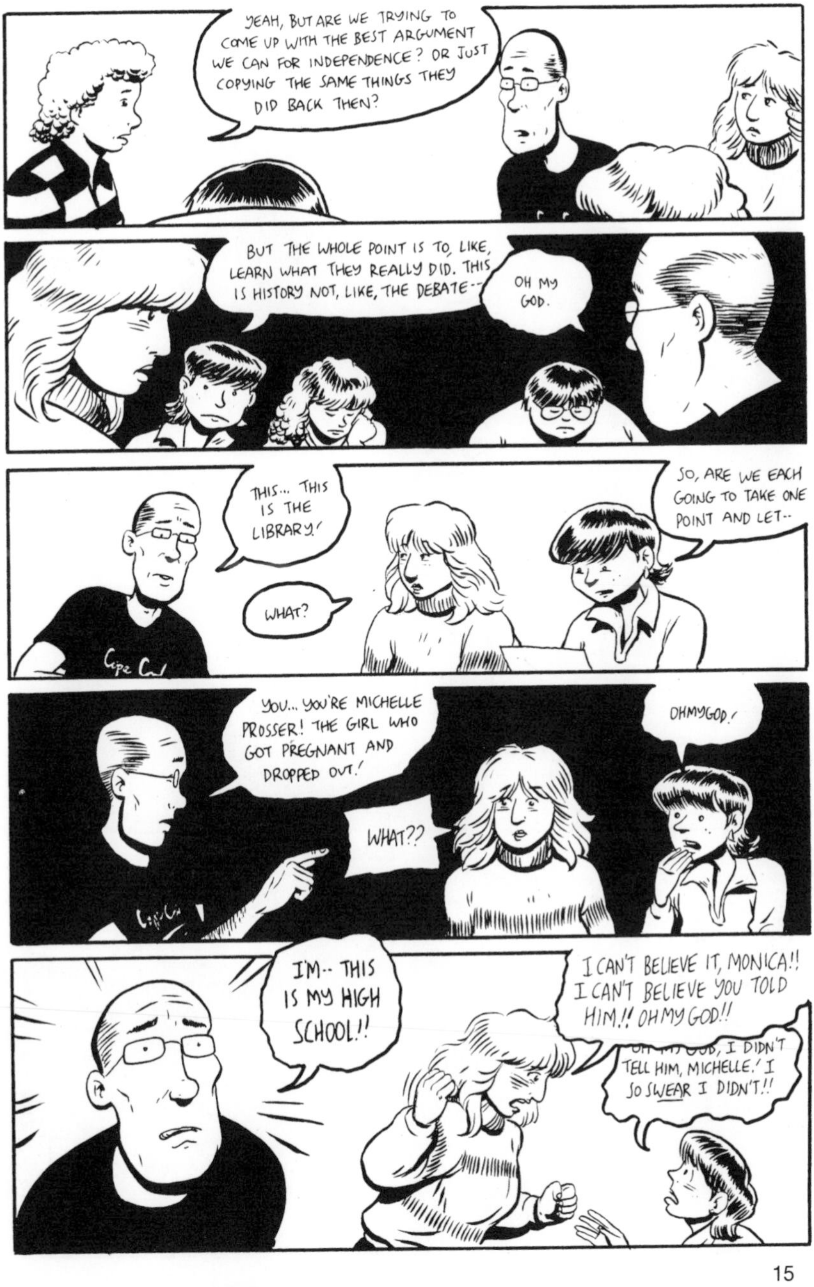
YEAH, BUT ARE WE TRYING TO COME UP WITH THE BEST ARGUMENT WE CAN FOR INDEPENDENCE? OR JUST COPYING THE SAME THINGS THEY DID BACK THEN?
BUT THE WHOLE POINT IS TO, LIKE, LEARN WHAT THEY REALLY DID. THIS IS HISTORY NOT, LIKE, THE DEBATE--
OH MY GOD.
THIS... THIS IS THE LIBRARY!
WHAT?
SO, ARE WE EACH GOING TO TAKE ONE POINT AND LET--
YOU... YOU'RE MICHELLE PROSSER! THE GIRL WHO GOT PREGNANT AND DROPPED OUT!
WHAT??
OHMYGOD!
I'M-- THIS IS MY HIGH SCHOOL!!
I CAN'T BELIEVE IT, MONICA!! I CAN'T BELIEVE YOU TOLD HIM!! OHMYGOD!!
I DIDN'T TELL HIM, MICHELLE! I SO SWEAR I DIDN'T!!

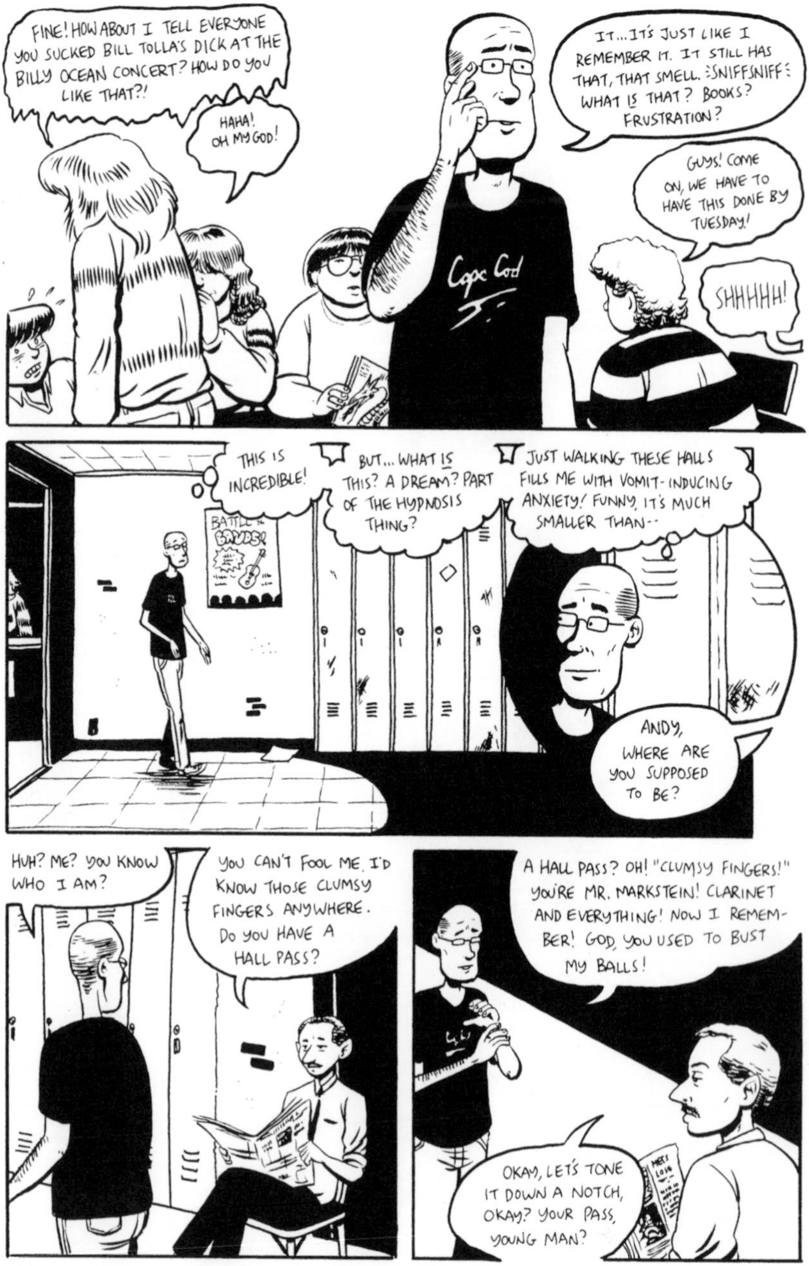

FINE! HOW ABOUT I TELL EVERYONE YOU SUCKED BILL TOLLA'S DICK AT THE BILLY OCEAN CONCERT? HOW DO YOU LIKE THAT?!
HAHA! OH MY GOD!
IT... IT'S JUST LIKE I REMEMBER IT. IT STILL HAS THAT, THAT SMELL. SNIFFSNIFF WHAT IS THAT? BOOKS? FRUSTRATION?
GUYS! COME ON, WE HAVE TO HAVE THIS DONE BY TUESDAY!
SHHHHH!
Cape Cod
THIS IS INCREDIBLE!
BUT... WHAT IS THIS? A DREAM? PART OF THE HYPNOSIS THING?
JUST WALKING THESE HALLS FILLS ME WITH VOMIT-INDUCING ANXIETY! FUNNY, IT'S MUCH SMALLER THAN--
ANDY, WHERE ARE YOU SUPPOSED TO BE?
HUH? ME? YOU KNOW WHO I AM?
YOU CAN'T FOOL ME. I'D KNOW THOSE CLUMSY FINGERS ANYWHERE. DO YOU HAVE A HALL PASS?
A HALL PASS? OH! "CLUMSY FINGERS!" YOU'RE MR. MARKSTEIN! CLARINET AND EVERYTHING! NOW I REMEMBER! GOD, YOU USED TO BUST MY BALLS!
OKAY, LET'S TONE IT DOWN A NOTCH, OKAY? YOUR PASS, YOUNG MAN?

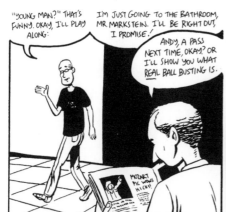

"YOUNG MAN?" THAT'S FUNNY. OKAY, I'LL PLAY ALONG:
I'M JUST GOING TO THE BATHROOM, MR. MARKSTEIN. I'LL BE RIGHT OUT, I PROMISE.
ANDY, A PASS NEXT TIME, OKAY? OR I'LL SHOW YOU WHAT REAL BALL BUSTING IS.
MOZART PIC WOWS HICKS!
YOU GOT IT. AND THANKS A--
BOY
OH, UH, HEY, FELLAS. I WAS JUST TALKING TO MR. MARKSTEIN OUT THERE.
I HOPE I'M NOT INTER--
WAS HE TELLING YOU HOW GOOD YOUR NUT-SACK TASTED LAST NIGHT?
PHAHAHA!
WHOA! HAHA, OKAY, LET'S TONE IT DOWN A NOTCH, OKAY? YOU--
YEAH, I HEARD HE GAVE YOU FIFTY BUCKS TO LET HIM GIVE YOU A BLOW JOB AT DOWNING LAST NIGHT.
Cape Cod
WH--?? YOU GUYS DON'T EVEN KNOW ME. WHAT THE HELL IS YOUR--
SURE I KNOW YOU. WE'RE IN THE SAME GYM CLASS. YOUR NAME IS GAYLORD, RIGHT?
YEAH, GAYLORD QUEERBAIT, RIGHT?

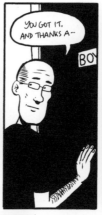

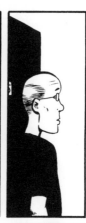

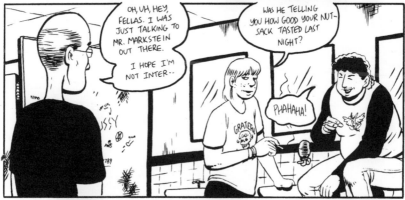

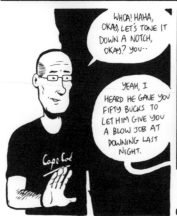

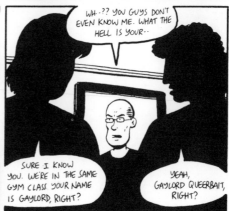

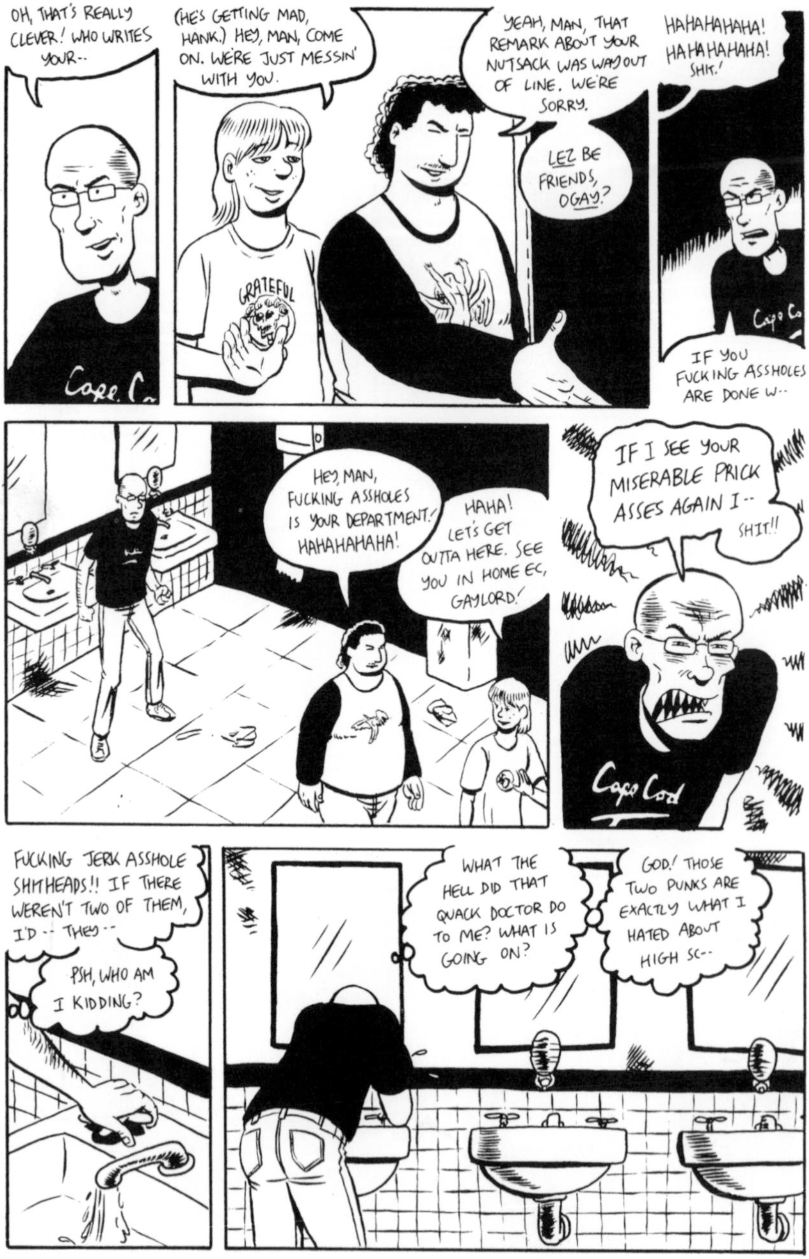
OH, THAT'S REALLY CLEVER! WHO WRITES YOUR--
(HE'S GETTING MAD, HANK.) HEY, MAN, COME ON. WE'RE JUST MESSIN' WITH YOU.
YEAH, MAN, THAT REMARK ABOUT YOUR NUTSACK WAS WAY OUT OF LINE. WE'RE SORRY.
LEZ BE FRIENDS, OGAY?
HAHAHAHAHA! HAHAHAHAHA! SHK!
IF YOU FUCKING ASSHOLES ARE DONE W--
HEY, MAN, FUCKING ASSHOLES IS YOUR DEPARTMENT! HAHAHAHAHA!
HAHA! LET'S GET OUTTA HERE. SEE YOU IN HOME EC, GAYLORD!
IF I SEE YOUR MISERABLE PRICK ASSES AGAIN I-- SHIT!!
FUCKING JERK ASSHOLE SHITHEADS!! IF THERE WEREN'T TWO OF THEM, I'D -- THEY --
PSH, WHO AM I KIDDING?
WHAT THE HELL DID THAT QUACK DOCTOR DO TO ME? WHAT IS GOING ON?
GOD! THOSE TWO PUNKS ARE EXACTLY WHAT I HATED ABOUT HIGH SC--

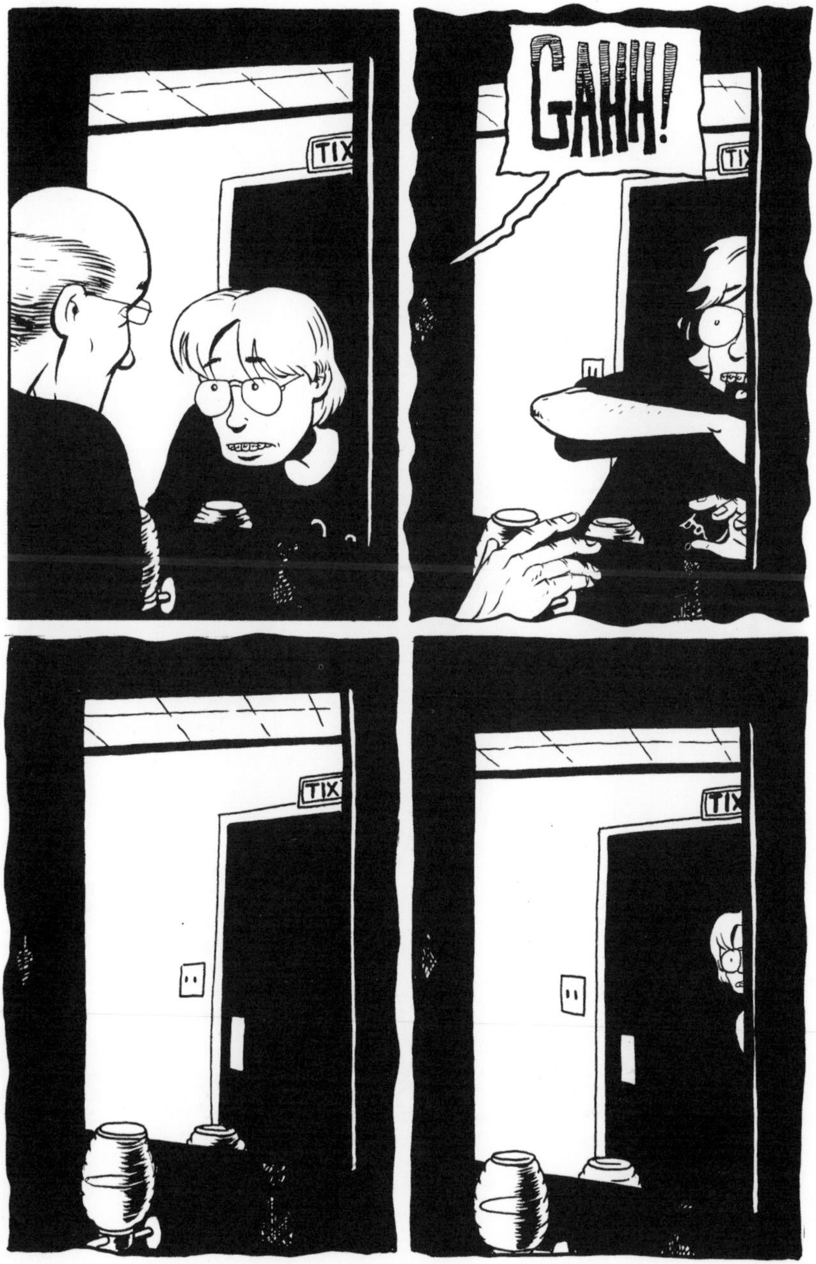
GAHH!
TIX

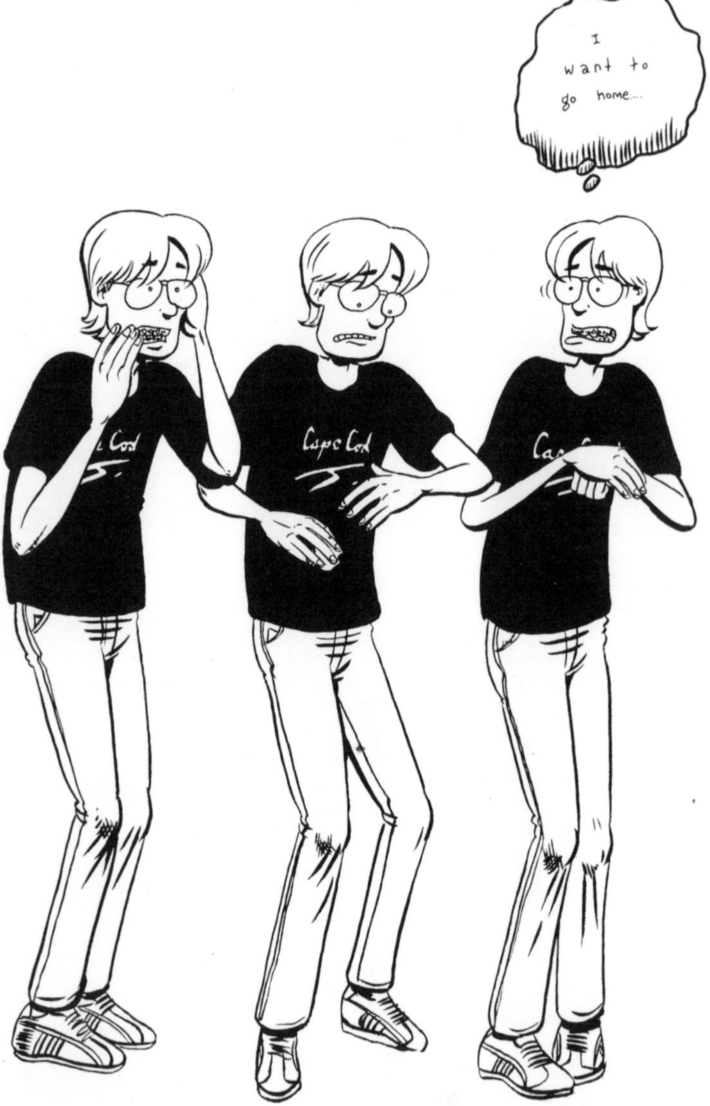
I want to go home....
Cape Cod

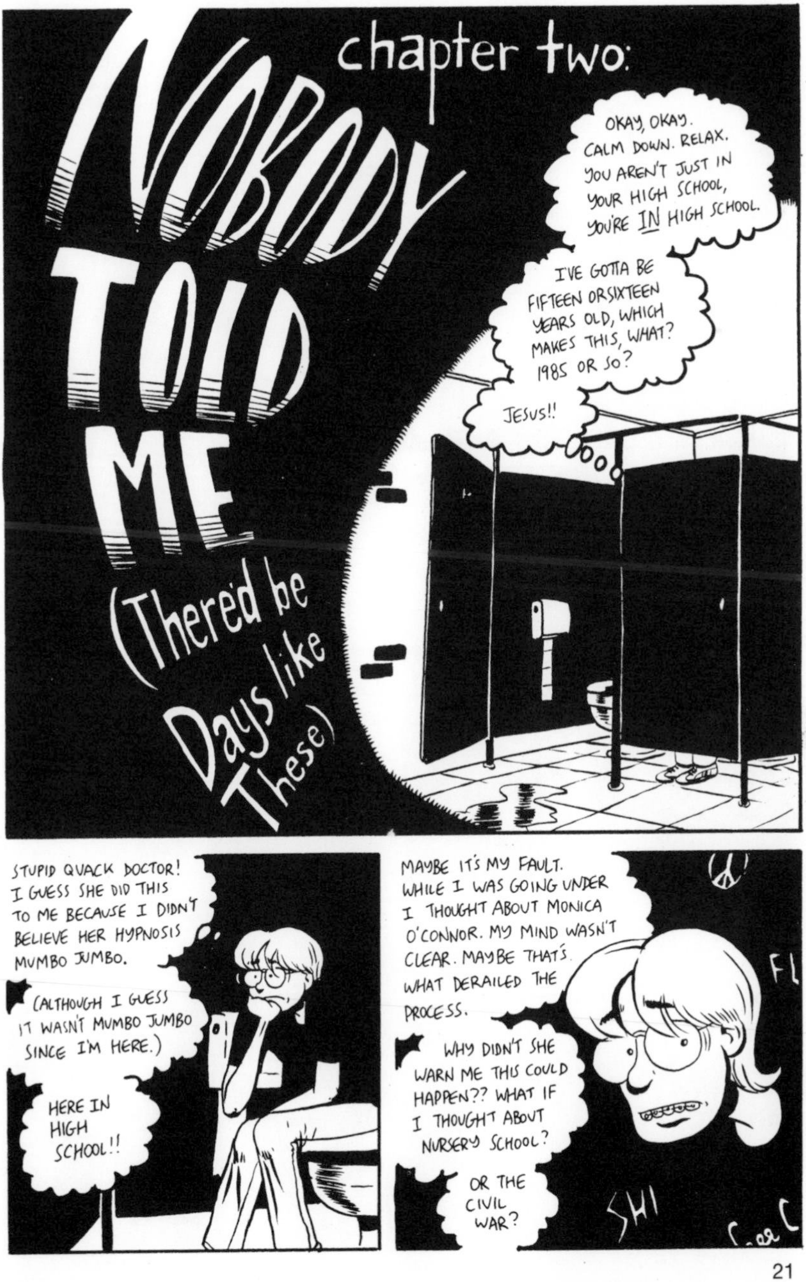
chapter two:
NOBODY TOLD ME (There'd be Days like These)
OKAY, OKAY. CALM DOWN. RELAX. YOU AREN'T JUST IN YOUR HIGH SCHOOL, YOU'RE IN HIGH SCHOOL.
I'VE GOTTA BE FIFTEEN OR SIXTEEN YEARS OLD, WHICH MAKES THIS, WHAT? 1985 OR SO?
JESUS!!
STUPID QUACK DOCTOR! I GUESS SHE DID THIS TO ME BECAUSE I DIDN'T BELIEVE HER HYPNOSIS MUMBO JUMBO.
(ALTHOUGH I GUESS IT WASN'T MUMBO JUMBO SINCE I'M HERE.)
HERE IN HIGH SCHOOL!!
MAYBE IT'S MY FAULT. WHILE I WAS GOING UNDER I THOUGHT ABOUT MONICA O'CONNOR. MY MIND WASN'T CLEAR. MAYBE THAT'S WHAT DERAILED THE PROCESS.
WHY DIDN'T SHE WARN ME THIS COULD HAPPEN?? WHAT IF I THOUGHT ABOUT NURSERY SCHOOL?
OR THE CIVIL WAR?
FL
SHI

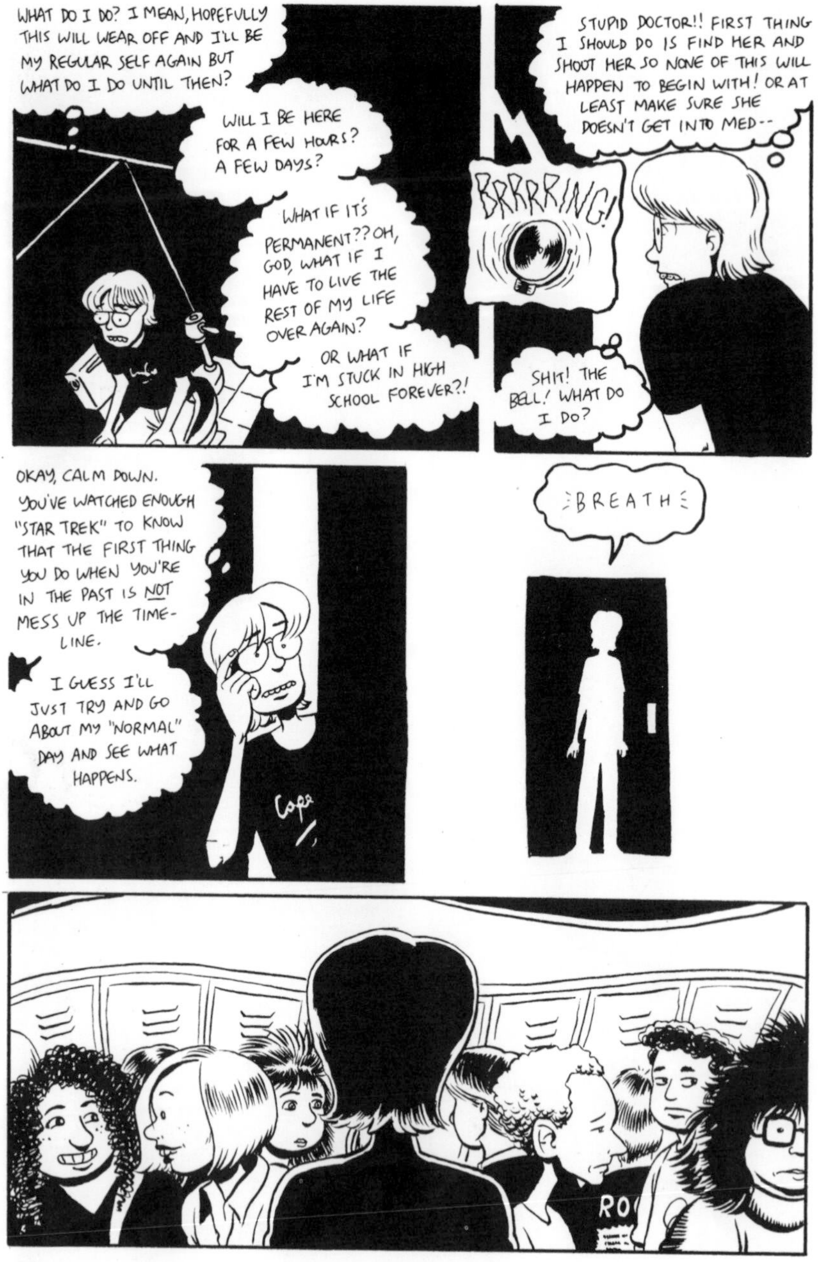
WHAT DO I DO? I MEAN, HOPEFULLY THIS WILL WEAR OFF AND I'LL BE MY REGULAR SELF AGAIN BUT WHAT DO I DO UNTIL THEN?
WILL I BE HERE FOR A FEW HOURS? A FEW DAYS?
WHAT IF IT'S PERMANENT?? OH, GOD, WHAT IF I HAVE TO LIVE THE REST OF MY LIFE OVER AGAIN?
OR WHAT IF I'M STUCK IN HIGH SCHOOL FOREVER?!
STUPID DOCTOR!! FIRST THING I SHOULD DO IS FIND HER AND SHOOT HER SO NONE OF THIS WILL HAPPEN TO BEGIN WITH! OR AT LEAST MAKE SURE SHE DOESN'T GET INTO MED--
BRRRRING!
SHIT! THE BELL! WHAT DO I DO?
OKAY, CALM DOWN. YOU'VE WATCHED ENOUGH "STAR TREK" TO KNOW THAT THE FIRST THING YOU DO WHEN YOU'RE IN THE PAST IS NOT MESS UP THE TIME-LINE.
I GUESS I'LL JUST TRY AND GO ABOUT MY "NORMAL" DAY AND SEE WHAT HAPPENS.
BREATH

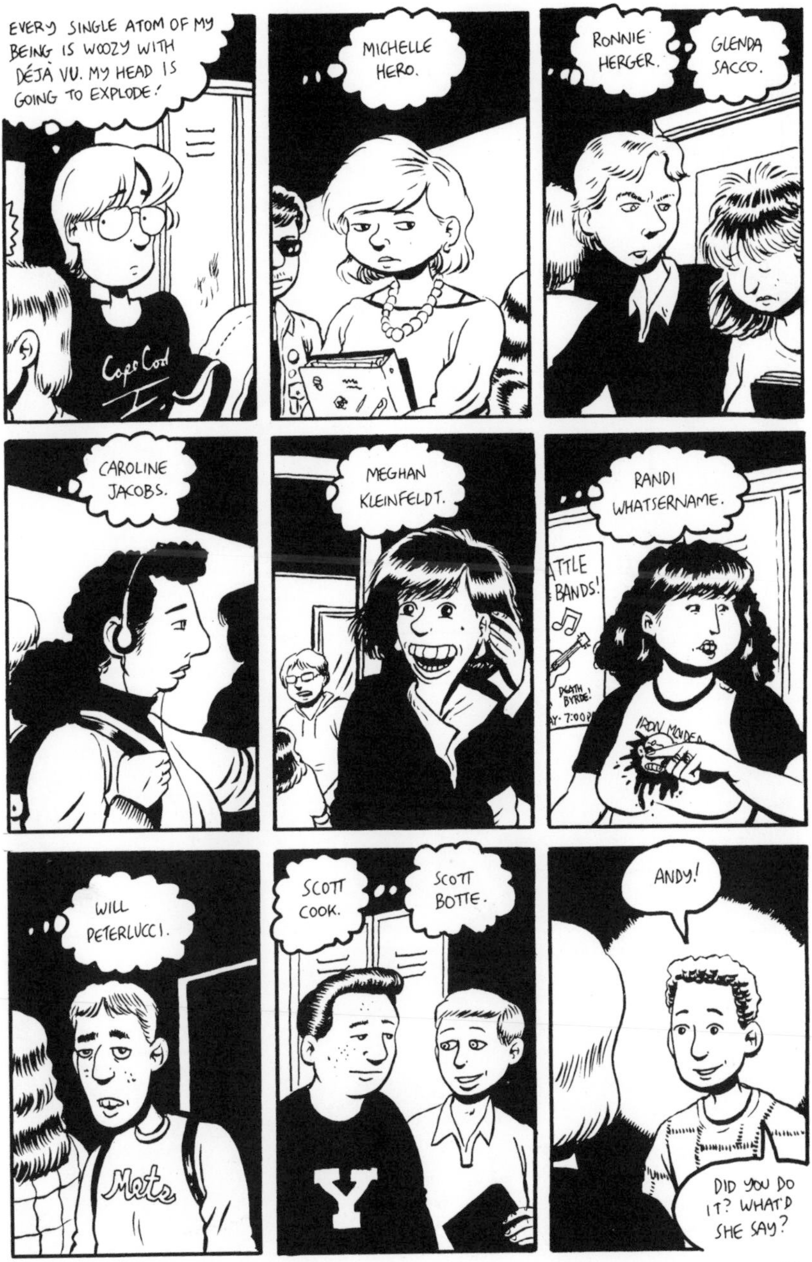
EVERY SINGLE ATOM OF MY BEING IS WOOZY WITH DÉJÀ VU. MY HEAD IS GOING TO EXPLODE!
Cape Cod
MICHELLE HERO.
RONNIE HERGER.
GLENDA SACCO.
CAROLINE JACOBS.
MEGHAN KLEINFELDT.
RANDI WHATSERNAME.
DEATH BYRDE!
IRON MAIDEN
WILL PETERLUCCI.
Mets
SCOTT COOK.
SCOTT BOTTE.
Y
ANDY!
DID YOU DO IT? WHAT'D SHE SAY?

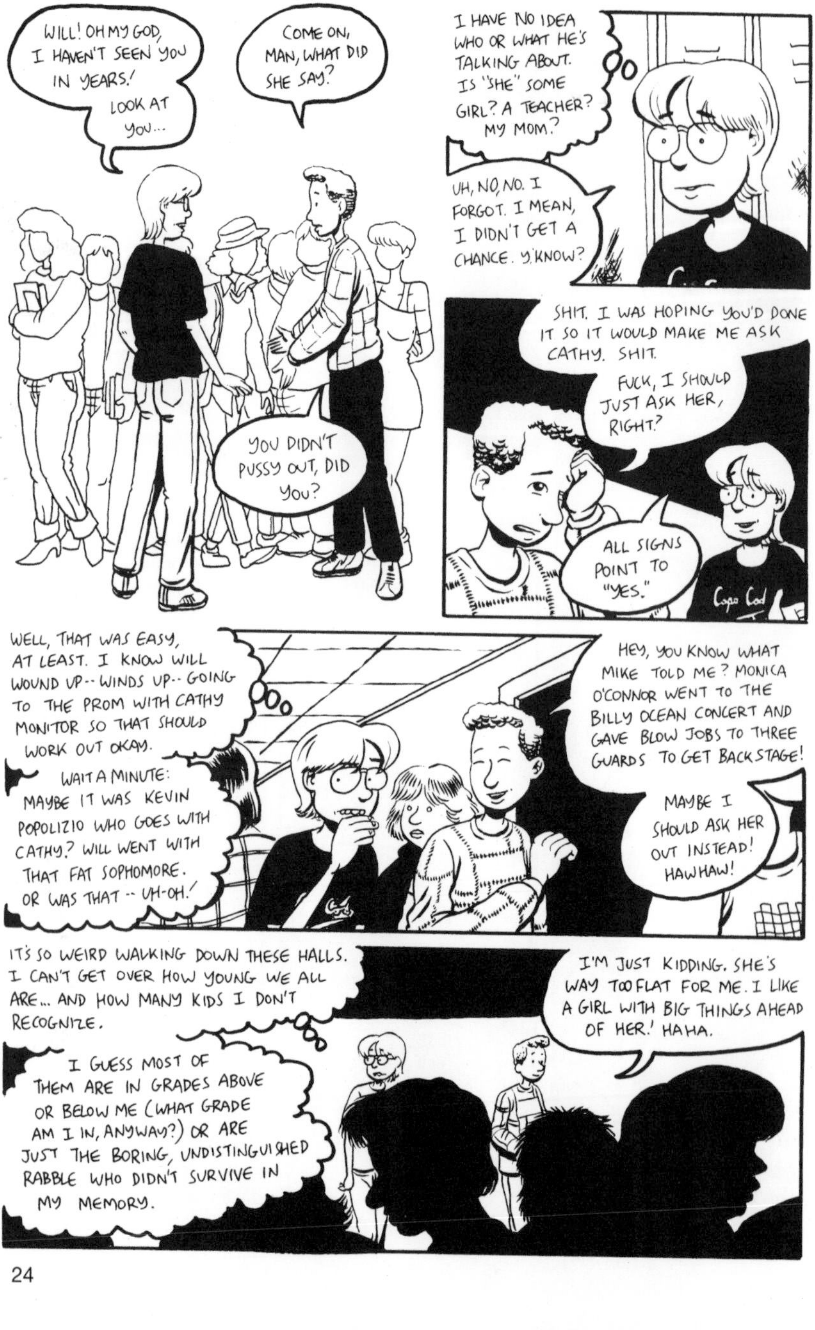
WILL! OH MY GOD, I HAVEN'T SEEN YOU IN YEARS! LOOK AT YOU...
COME ON, MAN, WHAT DID SHE SAY?
YOU DIDN'T PUSSY OUT, DID YOU?
I HAVE NO IDEA WHO OR WHAT HE'S TALKING ABOUT. IS "SHE" SOME GIRL? A TEACHER? MY MOM?
UH, NO, NO. I FORGOT. I MEAN, I DIDN'T GET A CHANCE. Y'KNOW?
SHIT. I WAS HOPING YOU'D DONE IT SO IT WOULD MAKE ME ASK CATHY. SHIT.
FUCK, I SHOULD JUST ASK HER, RIGHT?
ALL SIGNS POINT TO "YES."
WELL, THAT WAS EASY, AT LEAST. I KNOW WILL WOUND UP-- WINDS UP-- GOING TO THE PROM WITH CATHY MONITOR SO THAT SHOULD WORK OUT OKAY.
WAIT A MINUTE: MAYBE IT WAS KEVIN POPOLIZIO WHO GOES WITH CATHY? WILL WENT WITH THAT FAT SOPHOMORE. OR WAS THAT -- UH-OH!
HEY, YOU KNOW WHAT MIKE TOLD ME? MONICA O'CONNOR WENT TO THE BILLY OCEAN CONCERT AND GAVE BLOW JOBS TO THREE GUARDS TO GET BACKSTAGE!
MAYBE I SHOULD ASK HER OUT INSTEAD! HAWHAW!
IT'S SO WEIRD WALKING DOWN THESE HALLS. I CAN'T GET OVER HOW YOUNG WE ALL ARE... AND HOW MANY KIDS I DON'T RECOGNIZE.
I GUESS MOST OF THEM ARE IN GRADES ABOVE OR BELOW ME (WHAT GRADE AM I IN, ANYWAY?) OR ARE JUST THE BORING, UNDISTINGUISHED RABBLE WHO DIDN'T SURVIVE IN MY MEMORY.
I'M JUST KIDDING. SHE'S WAY TOO FLAT FOR ME. I LIKE A GIRL WITH BIG THINGS AHEAD OF HER! HAHA.

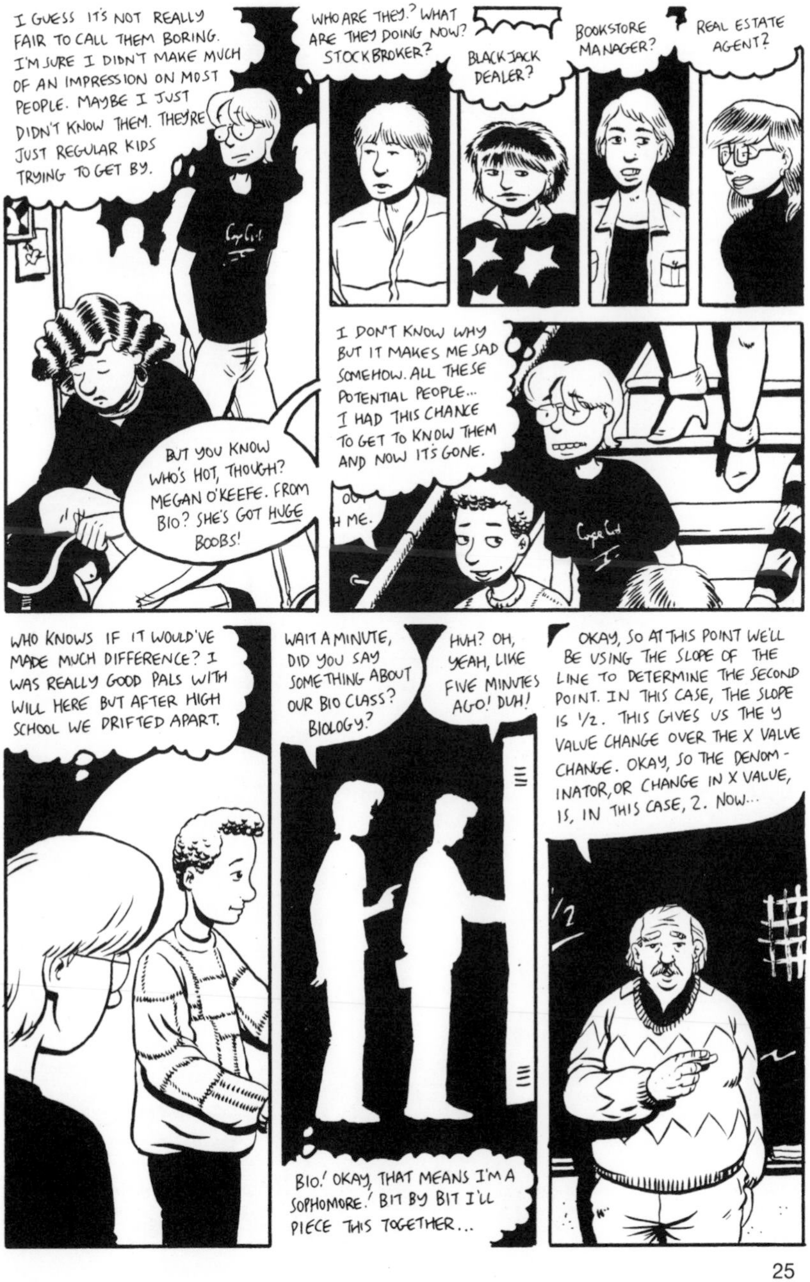
I GUESS IT'S NOT REALLY FAIR TO CALL THEM BORING. I'M SURE I DIDN'T MAKE MUCH OF AN IMPRESSION ON MOST PEOPLE. MAYBE I JUST DIDN'T KNOW THEM. THEY'RE JUST REGULAR KIDS TRYING TO GET BY.
WHO ARE THEY? WHAT ARE THEY DOING NOW? STOCKBROKER?
BLACKJACK DEALER?
BOOKSTORE MANAGER?
REAL ESTATE AGENT?
BUT YOU KNOW WHO'S HOT, THOUGH? MEGAN O'KEEFE. FROM BIO? SHE'S GOT HUGE BOOBS!
I DON'T KNOW WHY BUT IT MAKES ME SAD SOMEHOW. ALL THESE POTENTIAL PEOPLE... I HAD THIS CHANCE TO GET TO KNOW THEM AND NOW IT'S GONE.
WHO KNOWS IF IT WOULD'VE MADE MUCH DIFFERENCE? I WAS REALLY GOOD PALS WITH WILL HERE BUT AFTER HIGH SCHOOL WE DRIFTED APART.
WAIT A MINUTE, DID YOU SAY SOMETHING ABOUT OUR BIO CLASS? BIOLOGY?
HUH? OH, YEAH, LIKE FIVE MINUTES AGO! DUH!
BIO! OKAY, THAT MEANS I'M A SOPHOMORE! BIT BY BIT I'LL PIECE THIS TOGETHER...
OKAY, SO AT THIS POINT WE'LL BE USING THE SLOPE OF THE LINE TO DETERMINE THE SECOND POINT. IN THIS CASE, THE SLOPE IS 1/2. THIS GIVES US THE Y VALUE CHANGE OVER THE X VALUE CHANGE. OKAY, SO THE DENOMINATOR, OR CHANGE IN X VALUE, IS, IN THIS CASE, 2. NOW...

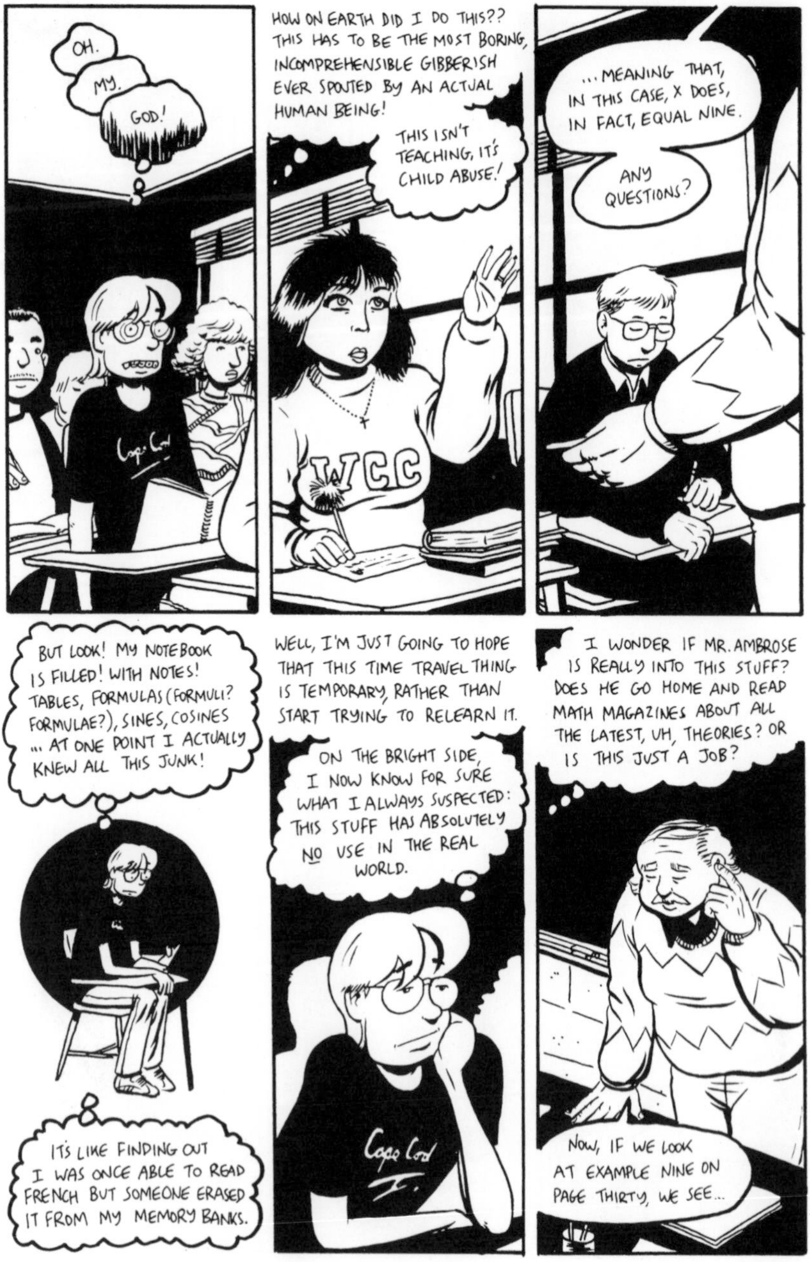
OH.
MY.
GOD!
HOW ON EARTH DID I DO THIS?? THIS HAS TO BE THE MOST BORING, INCOMPREHENSIBLE GIBBERISH EVER SPOUTED BY AN ACTUAL HUMAN BEING!
THIS ISN'T TEACHING, IT'S CHILD ABUSE!
... MEANING THAT, IN THIS CASE, X DOES, IN FACT, EQUAL NINE.
ANY QUESTIONS?
WCC
Cape Cod
BUT LOOK! MY NOTEBOOK IS FILLED! WITH NOTES! TABLES, FORMULAS (FORMULI? FORMULAE?), SINES, COSINES ... AT ONE POINT I ACTUALLY KNEW ALL THIS JUNK!
IT'S LIKE FINDING OUT I WAS ONCE ABLE TO READ FRENCH BUT SOMEONE ERASED IT FROM MY MEMORY BANKS.
WELL, I'M JUST GOING TO HOPE THAT THIS TIME TRAVEL THING IS TEMPORARY, RATHER THAN START TRYING TO RELEARN IT.
ON THE BRIGHT SIDE, I NOW KNOW FOR SURE WHAT I ALWAYS SUSPECTED: THIS STUFF HAS ABSOLUTELY NO USE IN THE REAL WORLD.
Cape Cod
I WONDER IF MR. AMBROSE IS REALLY INTO THIS STUFF? DOES HE GO HOME AND READ MATH MAGAZINES ABOUT ALL THE LATEST, UH, THEORIES? OR IS THIS JUST A JOB?
NOW, IF WE LOOK AT EXAMPLE NINE ON PAGE THIRTY, WE SEE...

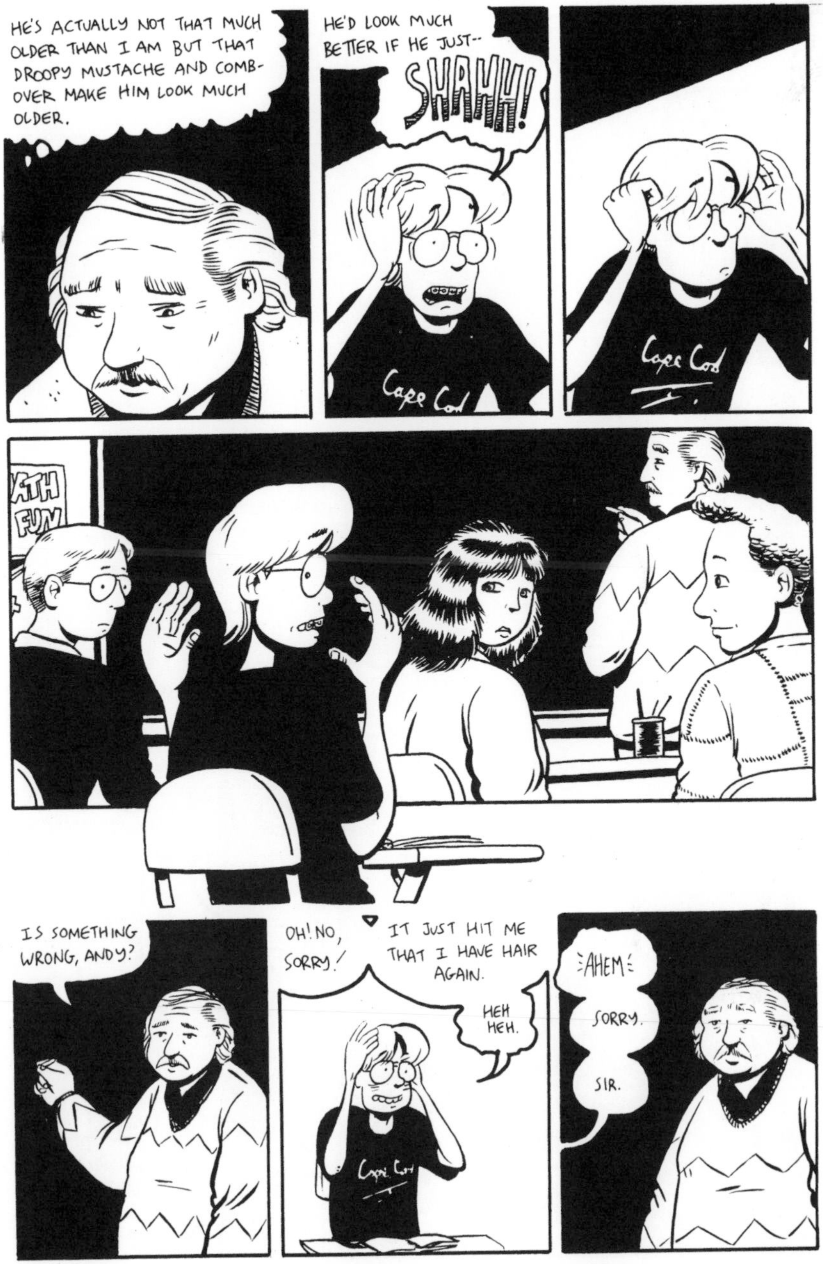
HE'S ACTUALLY NOT THAT MUCH OLDER THAN I AM BUT THAT DROOPY MUSTACHE AND COMB-OVER MAKE HIM LOOK MUCH OLDER.
HE'D LOOK MUCH BETTER IF HE JUST--
SHAHH!
Cape Cod
Cape Cod
ATH FUN
IS SOMETHING WRONG, ANDY?
OH! NO, SORRY!
IT JUST HIT ME THAT I HAVE HAIR AGAIN.
HEH HEH.
Cape Cod
AHEM
SORRY.
SIR.

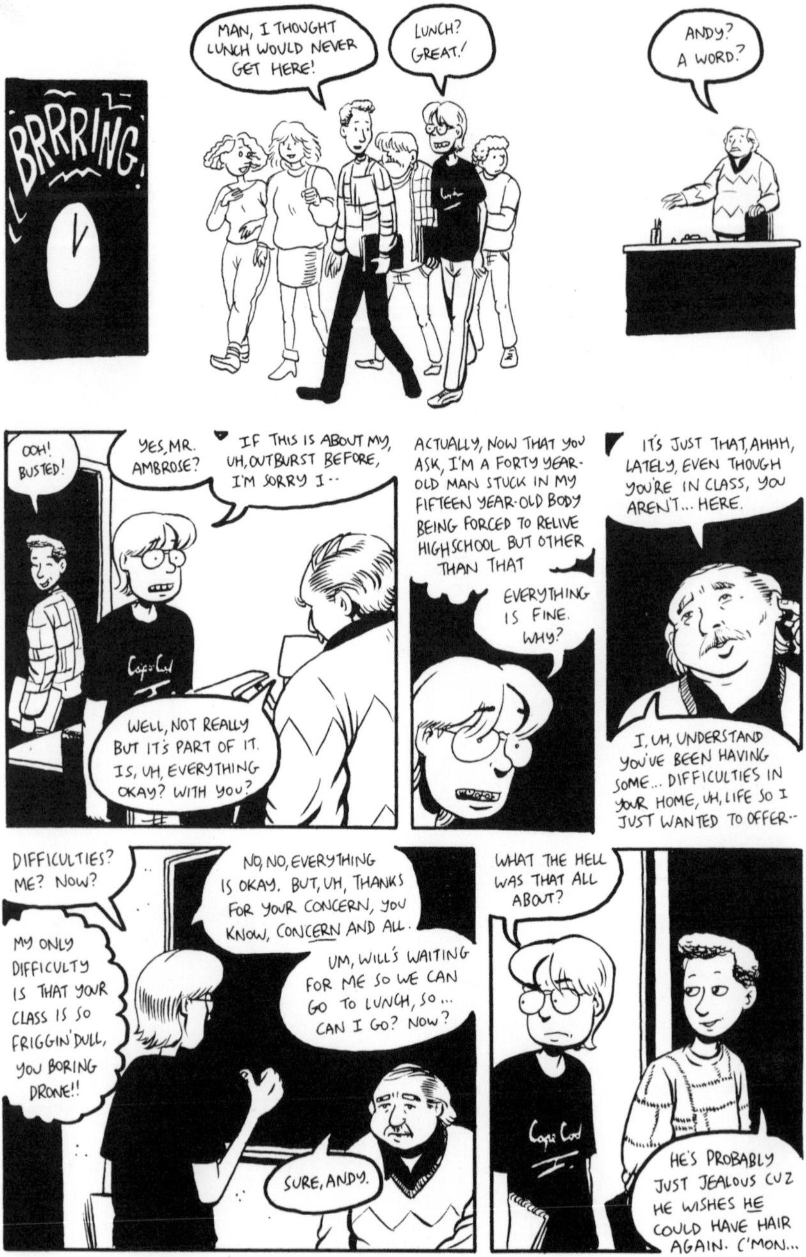
BRRRING!
MAN, I THOUGHT LUNCH WOULD NEVER GET HERE!
LUNCH? GREAT!
ANDY? A WORD?
OOH! BUSTED!
YES, MR. AMBROSE?
IF THIS IS ABOUT MY, UH, OUTBURST BEFORE, I'M SORRY I--
WELL, NOT REALLY BUT IT'S PART OF IT. IS, UH, EVERYTHING OKAY? WITH YOU?
ACTUALLY, NOW THAT YOU ASK, I'M A FORTY YEAR-OLD MAN STUCK IN MY FIFTEEN YEAR-OLD BODY BEING FORCED TO RELIVE HIGHSCHOOL BUT OTHER THAN THAT
EVERYTHING IS FINE. WHY?
IT'S JUST THAT, AHHH, LATELY, EVEN THOUGH YOU'RE IN CLASS, YOU AREN'T... HERE.
I, UH, UNDERSTAND YOU'VE BEEN HAVING SOME... DIFFICULTIES IN YOUR HOME, UH, LIFE SO I JUST WANTED TO OFFER--
DIFFICULTIES? ME? NOW?
MY ONLY DIFFICULTY IS THAT YOUR CLASS IS SO FRIGGIN' DULL, YOU BORING DRONE!!
NO, NO, EVERYTHING IS OKAY. BUT, UH, THANKS FOR YOUR CONCERN, YOU KNOW, CONCERN AND ALL.
UM, WILL'S WAITING FOR ME SO WE CAN GO TO LUNCH, SO... CAN I GO? NOW?
SURE, ANDY.
WHAT THE HELL WAS THAT ALL ABOUT?
HE'S PROBABLY JUST JEALOUS CUZ HE WISHES HE COULD HAVE HAIR AGAIN. C'MON...

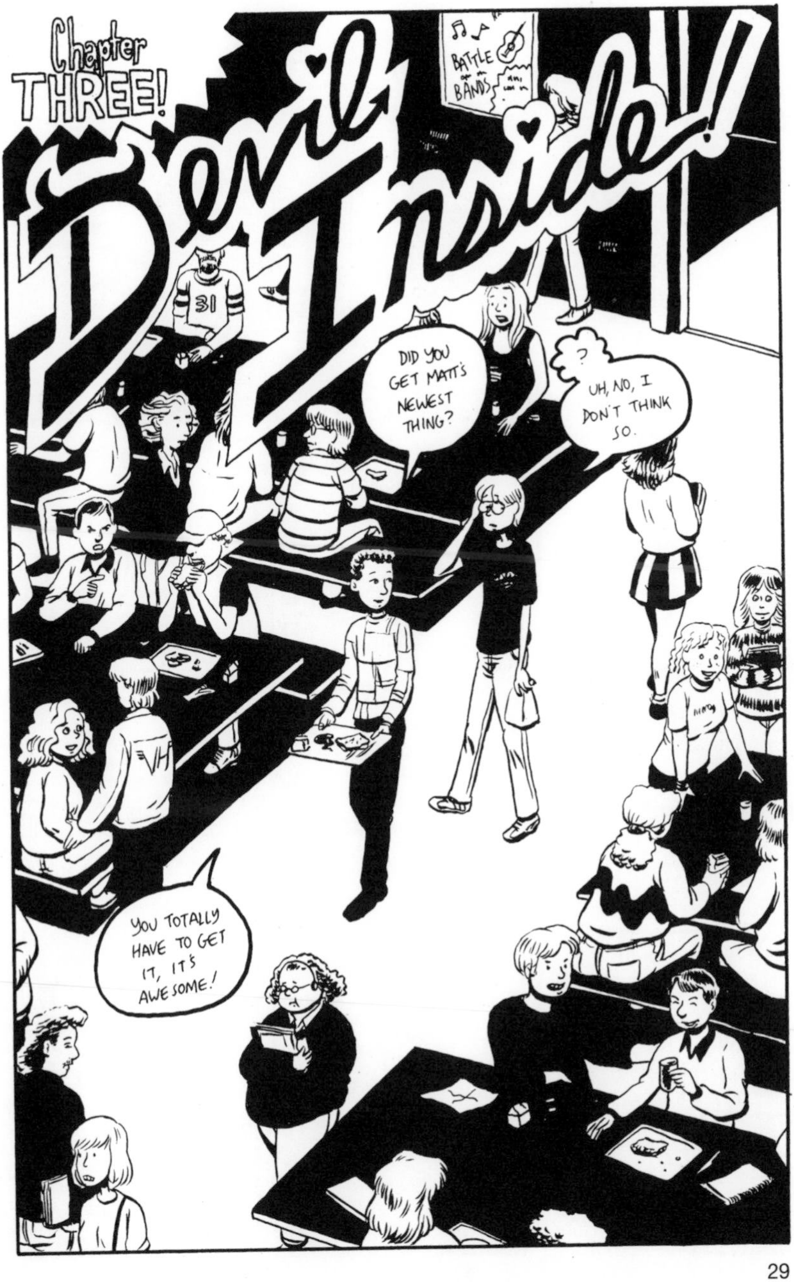
Chapter THREE!
Devil Inside!
BATTLE of the BANDS
DID YOU GET MATT'S NEWEST THING?
?
UH, NO, I DON'T THINK SO.
YOU TOTALLY HAVE TO GET IT, IT'S AWESOME!

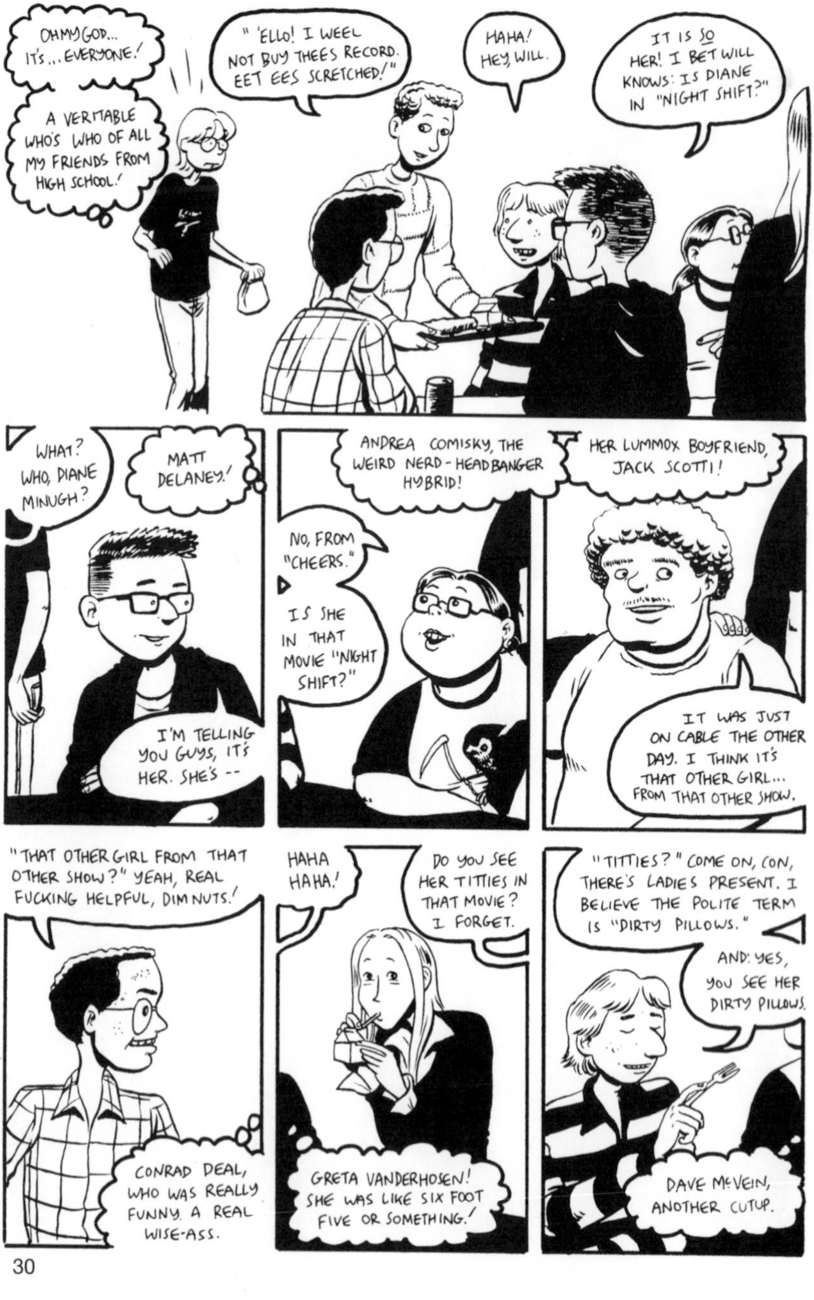

OHMYGOD... IT'S... EVERYONE!
A VERITABLE WHO'S WHO OF ALL MY FRIENDS FROM HIGH SCHOOL!
" 'ELLO! I WEEL NOT BUY THEES RECORD. EET EES SCRETCHED!"
HAHA! HEY, WILL.
IT IS SO HER! I BET WILL KNOWS: IS DIANE IN "NIGHT SHIFT?"
WHAT? WHO, DIANE MINUGH?
MATT DELANEY!
I'M TELLING YOU GUYS, IT'S HER. SHE'S --
ANDREA COMISKY, THE WEIRD NERD-HEADBANGER HYBRID!
NO, FROM "CHEERS."
IS SHE IN THAT MOVIE "NIGHT SHIFT?"
HER LUMMOX BOYFRIEND, JACK SCOTTI!
IT WAS JUST ON CABLE THE OTHER DAY. I THINK IT'S THAT OTHER GIRL... FROM THAT OTHER SHOW.
"THAT OTHER GIRL FROM THAT OTHER SHOW?" YEAH, REAL FUCKING HELPFUL, DIM NUTS!
CONRAD DEAL, WHO WAS REALLY FUNNY. A REAL WISE-ASS.
HAHA HAHA!
DO YOU SEE HER TITTIES IN THAT MOVIE? I FORGET.
GRETA VANDERHOSEN! SHE WAS LIKE SIX FOOT FIVE OR SOMETHING!
"TITTIES?" COME ON, CON, THERE'S LADIES PRESENT. I BELIEVE THE POLITE TERM IS "DIRTY PILLOWS."
AND: YES, YOU SEE HER DIRTY PILLOWS.
DAVE McVEIN, ANOTHER CUTUP.

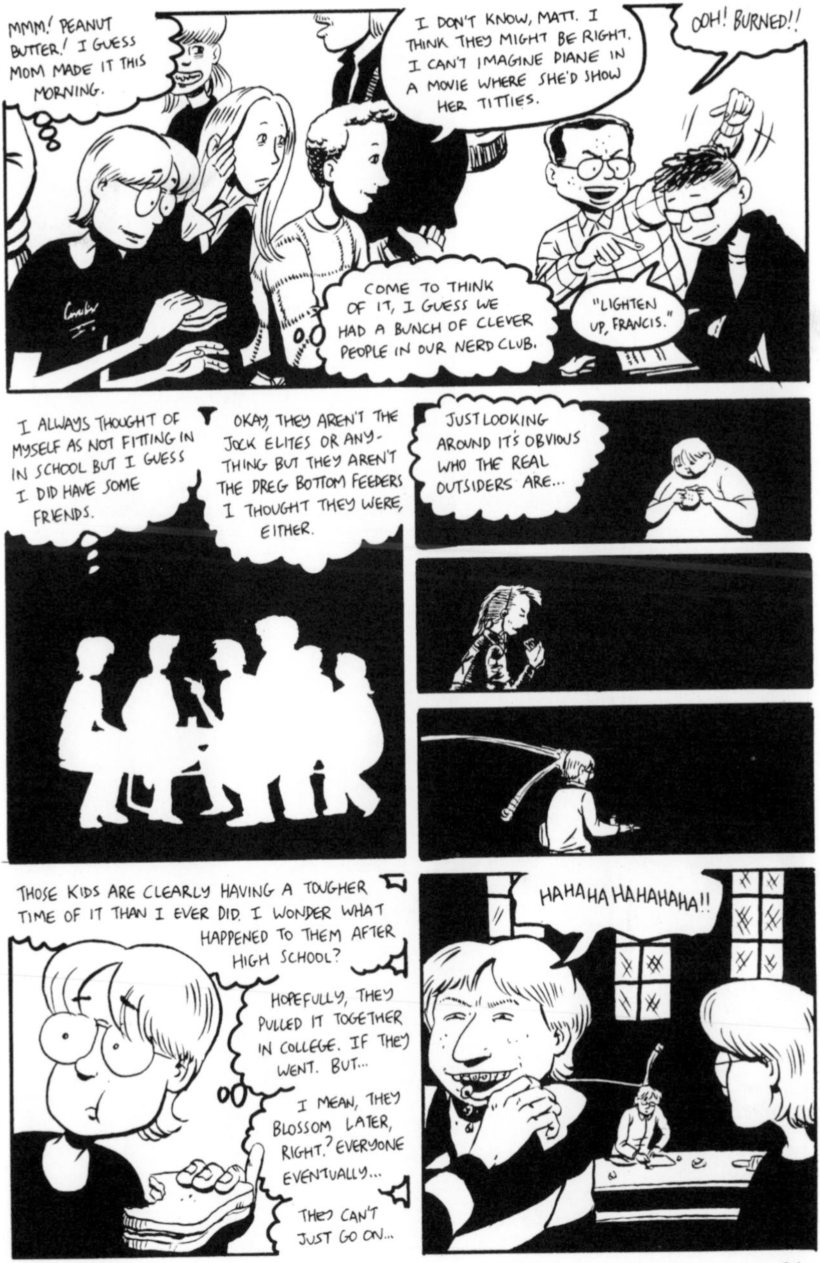
MMM! PEANUT BUTTER! I GUESS MOM MADE IT THIS MORNING.
I DON'T KNOW, MATT. I THINK THEY MIGHT BE RIGHT. I CAN'T IMAGINE DIANE IN A MOVIE WHERE SHE'D SHOW HER TITTIES.
OOH! BURNED!!
COME TO THINK OF IT, I GUESS WE HAD A BUNCH OF CLEVER PEOPLE IN OUR NERD CLUB.
"LIGHTEN UP, FRANCIS."
I ALWAYS THOUGHT OF MYSELF AS NOT FITTING IN IN SCHOOL BUT I GUESS I DID HAVE SOME FRIENDS.
OKAY, THEY AREN'T THE JOCK ELITES OR ANYTHING BUT THEY AREN'T THE DREG BOTTOM FEEDERS I THOUGHT THEY WERE, EITHER.
JUST LOOKING AROUND IT'S OBVIOUS WHO THE REAL OUTSIDERS ARE...
THOSE KIDS ARE CLEARLY HAVING A TOUGHER TIME OF IT THAN I EVER DID. I WONDER WHAT HAPPENED TO THEM AFTER HIGH SCHOOL?
HOPEFULLY, THEY PULLED IT TOGETHER IN COLLEGE. IF THEY WENT. BUT...
I MEAN, THEY BLOSSOM LATER, RIGHT? EVERYONE EVENTUALLY...
THEY CAN'T JUST GO ON...
HAHAHA HAHAHAHA!!

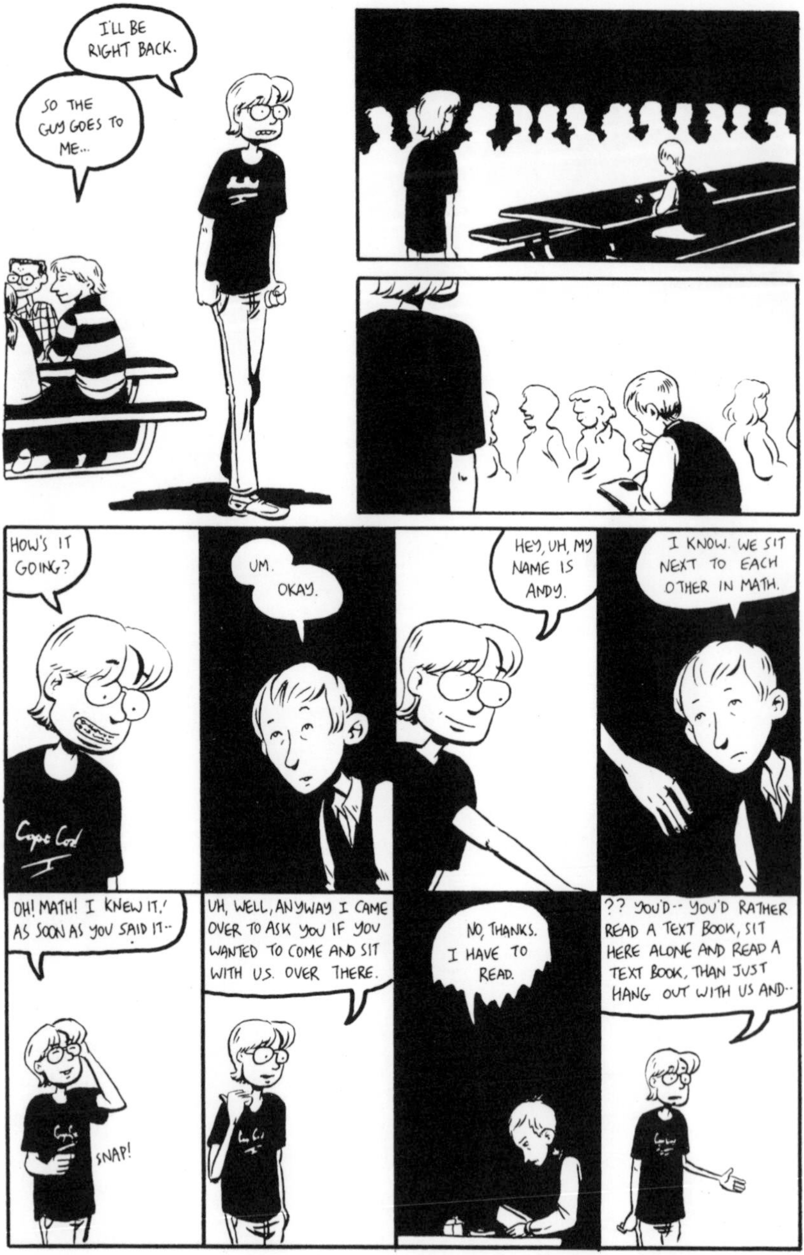
I'LL BE RIGHT BACK.
SO THE GUY GOES TO ME...
HOW'S IT GOING?
UM. OKAY.
HEY, UH, MY NAME IS ANDY.
I KNOW. WE SIT NEXT TO EACH OTHER IN MATH.
OH! MATH! I KNEW IT.! AS SOON AS YOU SAID IT..
SNAP!
UH, WELL, ANYWAY I CAME OVER TO ASK YOU IF YOU WANTED TO COME AND SIT WITH US. OVER THERE.
NO, THANKS. I HAVE TO READ.
?? YOU'D-- YOU'D RATHER READ A TEXT BOOK, SIT HERE ALONE AND READ A TEXT BOOK, THAN JUST HANG OUT WITH US AND..

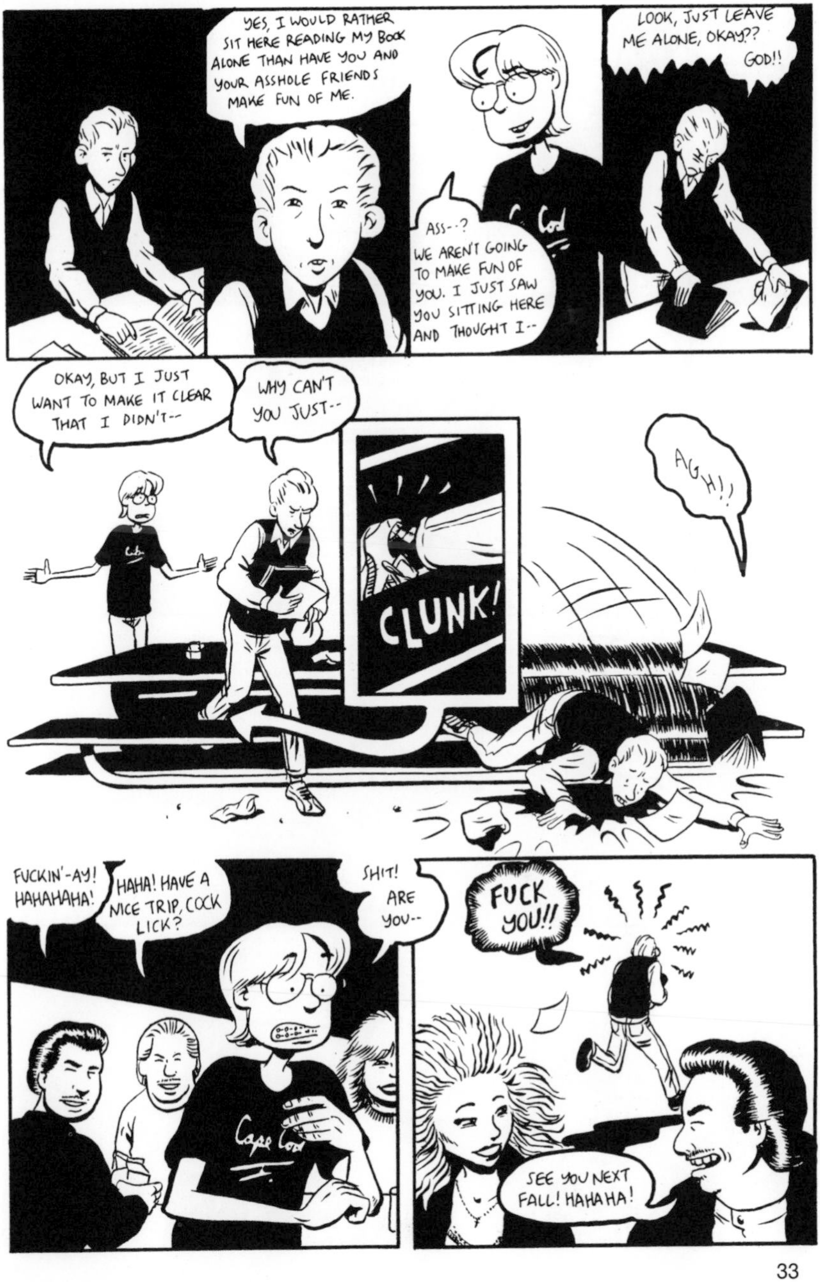
YES, I WOULD RATHER SIT HERE READING MY BOOK ALONE THAN HAVE YOU AND YOUR ASSHOLE FRIENDS MAKE FUN OF ME.
ASS--?
WE AREN'T GOING TO MAKE FUN OF YOU. I JUST SAW YOU SITTING HERE AND THOUGHT I--
LOOK, JUST LEAVE ME ALONE, OKAY?? GOD!!
OKAY, BUT I JUST WANT TO MAKE IT CLEAR THAT I DIDN'T--
WHY CAN'T YOU JUST--
CLUNK!
AGH!!
FUCKIN'-AY! HAHAHAHA!
HAHA! HAVE A NICE TRIP, COCK LICK?
SHIT! ARE YOU--
FUCK YOU!!
SEE YOU NEXT FALL! HAHAHA!

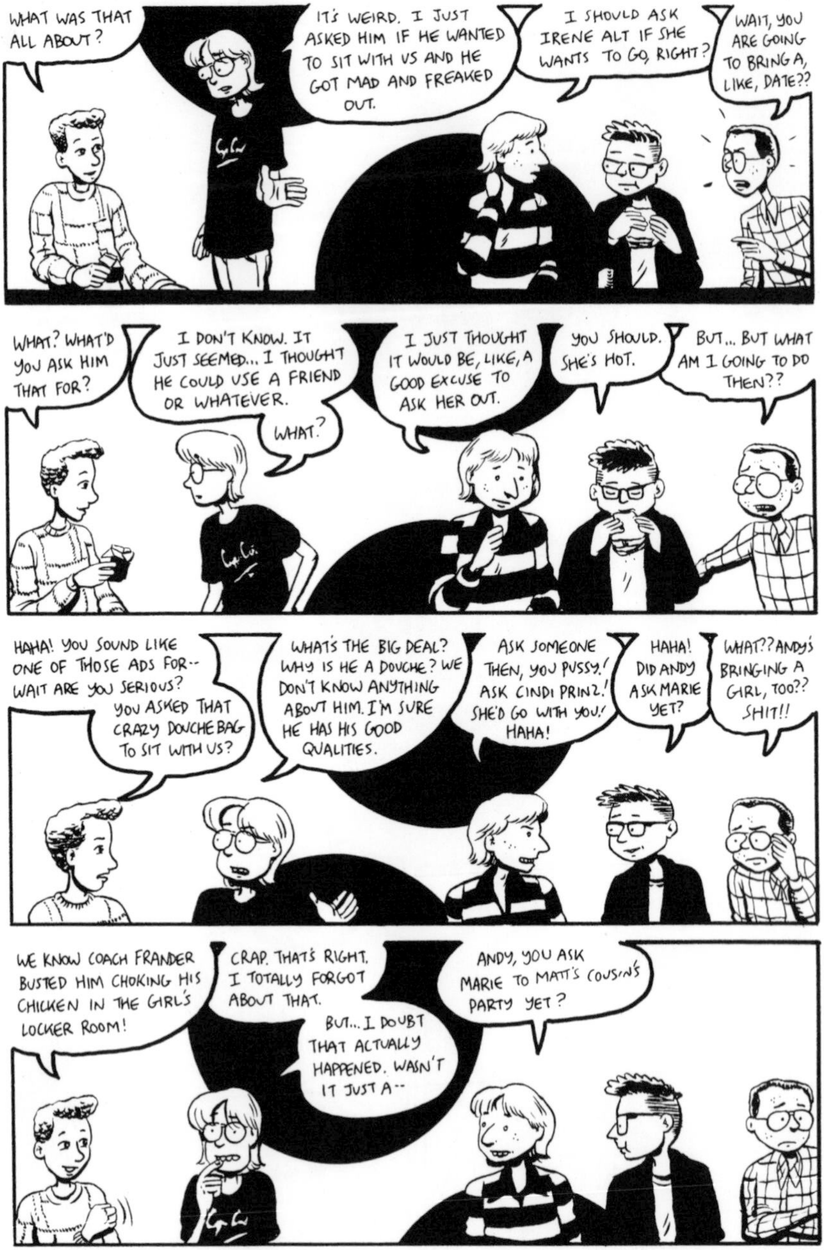
WHAT WAS THAT ALL ABOUT?
IT'S WEIRD. I JUST ASKED HIM IF HE WANTED TO SIT WITH US AND HE GOT MAD AND FREAKED OUT.
I SHOULD ASK IRENE ALT IF SHE WANTS TO GO, RIGHT?
WAIT, YOU ARE GOING TO BRING A, LIKE, DATE??
WHAT? WHAT'D YOU ASK HIM THAT FOR?
I DON'T KNOW. IT JUST SEEMED... I THOUGHT HE COULD USE A FRIEND OR WHATEVER.
WHAT?
I JUST THOUGHT IT WOULD BE, LIKE, A GOOD EXCUSE TO ASK HER OUT.
YOU SHOULD. SHE'S HOT.
BUT... BUT WHAT AM I GOING TO DO THEN??
HAHA! YOU SOUND LIKE ONE OF THOSE ADS FOR-- WAIT ARE YOU SERIOUS? YOU ASKED THAT CRAZY DOUCHE BAG TO SIT WITH US?
WHAT'S THE BIG DEAL? WHY IS HE A DOUCHE? WE DON'T KNOW ANYTHING ABOUT HIM. I'M SURE HE HAS HIS GOOD QUALITIES.
ASK SOMEONE THEN, YOU PUSSY! ASK CINDI PRINZ! SHE'D GO WITH YOU! HAHA!
HAHA! DID ANDY ASK MARIE YET?
WHAT?? ANDY'S BRINGING A GIRL, TOO?? SHIT!!
WE KNOW COACH FRANDER BUSTED HIM CHOKING HIS CHICKEN IN THE GIRL'S LOCKER ROOM!
CRAP. THAT'S RIGHT. I TOTALLY FORGOT ABOUT THAT.
BUT... I DOUBT THAT ACTUALLY HAPPENED. WASN'T IT JUST A--
ANDY, YOU ASK MARIE TO MATT'S COUSIN'S PARTY YET?

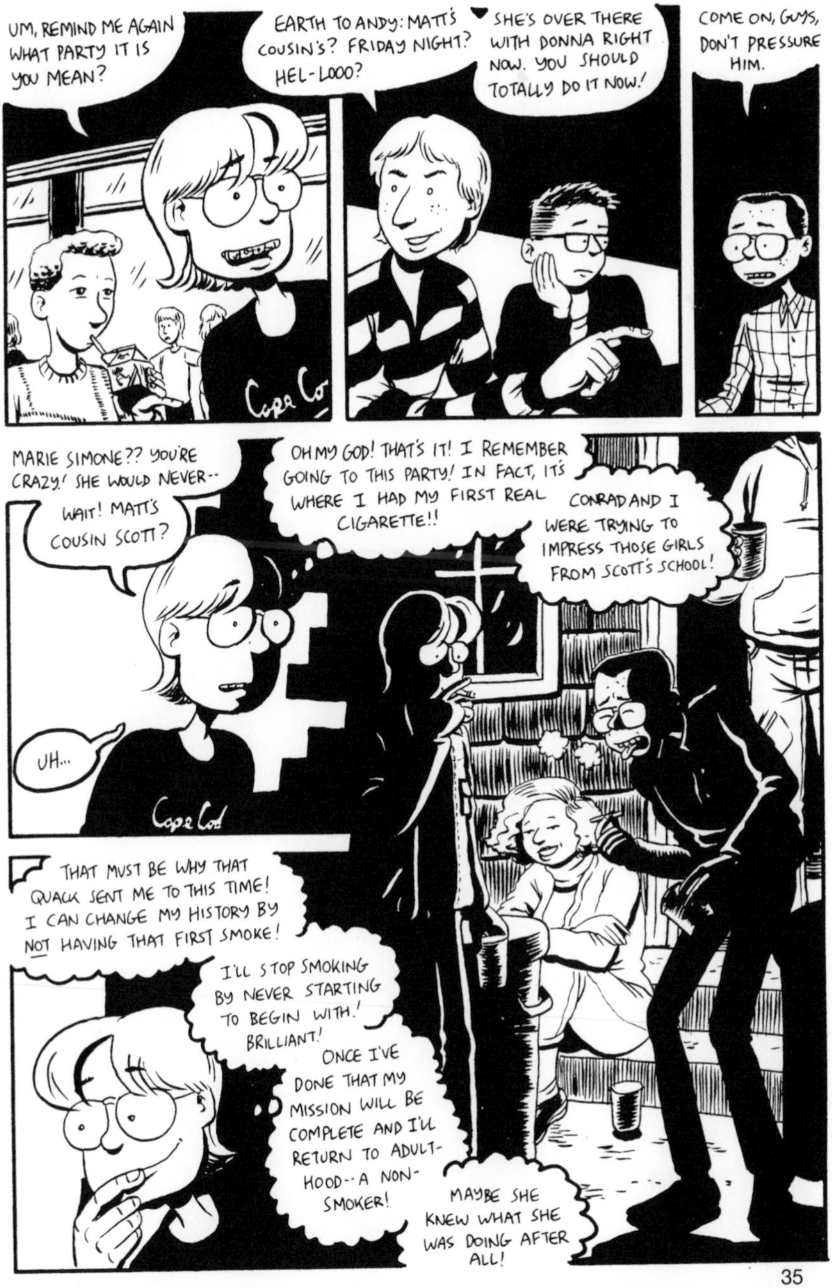

UM, REMIND ME AGAIN WHAT PARTY IT IS YOU MEAN?
EARTH TO ANDY: MATT'S COUSIN'S? FRIDAY NIGHT? HEL-LOOO?
SHE'S OVER THERE WITH DONNA RIGHT NOW. YOU SHOULD TOTALLY DO IT NOW!
COME ON, GUYS, DON'T PRESSURE HIM.
Cape Cod
MARIE SIMONE?? YOU'RE CRAZY! SHE WOULD NEVER--
WAIT! MATT'S COUSIN SCOTT?
OH MY GOD! THAT'S IT! I REMEMBER GOING TO THIS PARTY! IN FACT, IT'S WHERE I HAD MY FIRST REAL CIGARETTE!!
CONRAD AND I WERE TRYING TO IMPRESS THOSE GIRLS FROM SCOTT'S SCHOOL!
UH...
Cape Cod
THAT MUST BE WHY THAT QUACK SENT ME TO THIS TIME! I CAN CHANGE MY HISTORY BY NOT HAVING THAT FIRST SMOKE!
I'LL STOP SMOKING BY NEVER STARTING TO BEGIN WITH! BRILLIANT!
ONCE I'VE DONE THAT MY MISSION WILL BE COMPLETE AND I'LL RETURN TO ADULT-HOOD--A NON-SMOKER!
MAYBE SHE KNEW WHAT SHE WAS DOING AFTER ALL!

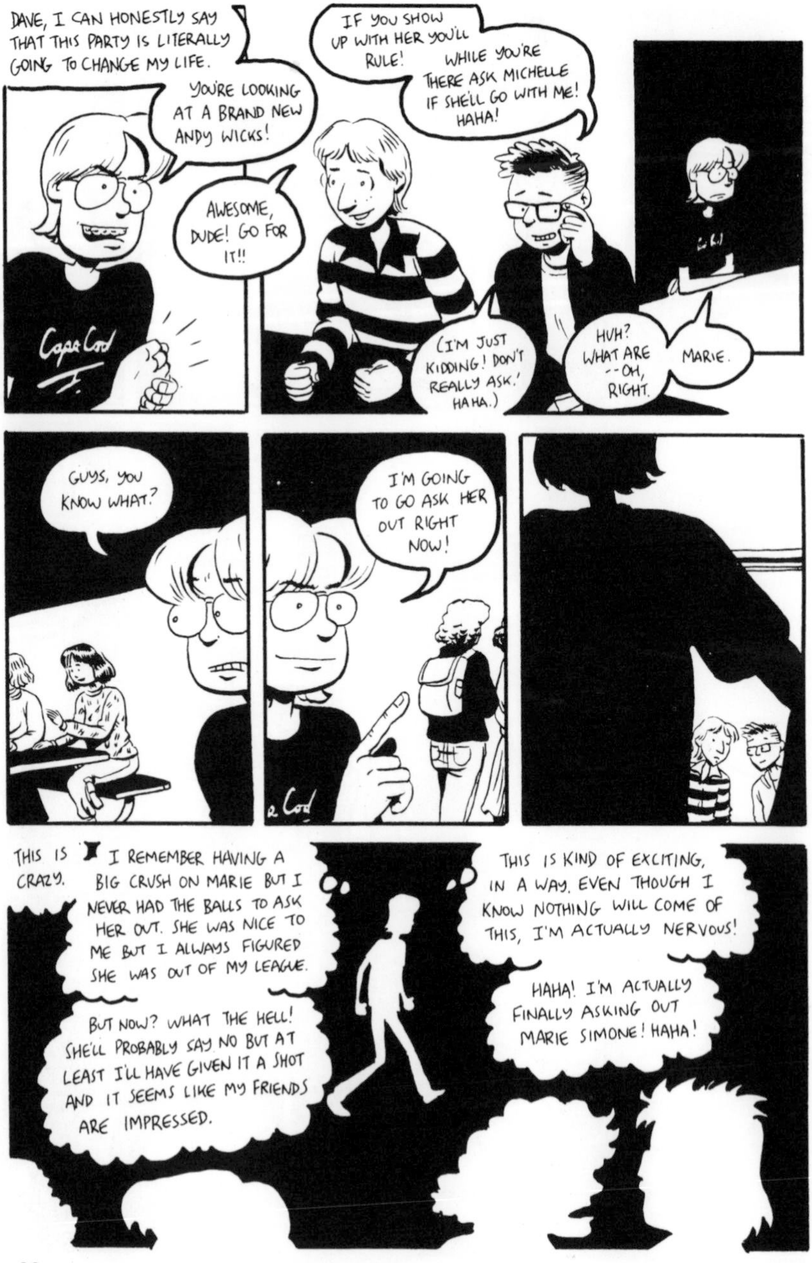
DAVE, I CAN HONESTLY SAY THAT THIS PARTY IS LITERALLY GOING TO CHANGE MY LIFE.
YOU'RE LOOKING AT A BRAND NEW ANDY WICKS!
AWESOME, DUDE! GO FOR IT!!
Cape Cod
IF YOU SHOW UP WITH HER YOU'LL RULE!
WHILE YOU'RE THERE ASK MICHELLE IF SHE'LL GO WITH ME! HAHA!
(I'M JUST KIDDING! DON'T REALLY ASK! HAHA.)
HUH? WHAT ARE --OH, RIGHT.
MARIE.
GUYS, YOU KNOW WHAT?
I'M GOING TO GO ASK HER OUT RIGHT NOW!
THIS IS CRAZY.
I REMEMBER HAVING A BIG CRUSH ON MARIE BUT I NEVER HAD THE BALLS TO ASK HER OUT. SHE WAS NICE TO ME BUT I ALWAYS FIGURED SHE WAS OUT OF MY LEAGUE.
BUT NOW? WHAT THE HELL! SHE'LL PROBABLY SAY NO BUT AT LEAST I'LL HAVE GIVEN IT A SHOT AND IT SEEMS LIKE MY FRIENDS ARE IMPRESSED.
THIS IS KIND OF EXCITING, IN A WAY. EVEN THOUGH I KNOW NOTHING WILL COME OF THIS, I'M ACTUALLY NERVOUS!
HAHA! I'M ACTUALLY FINALLY ASKING OUT MARIE SIMONE! HAHA!

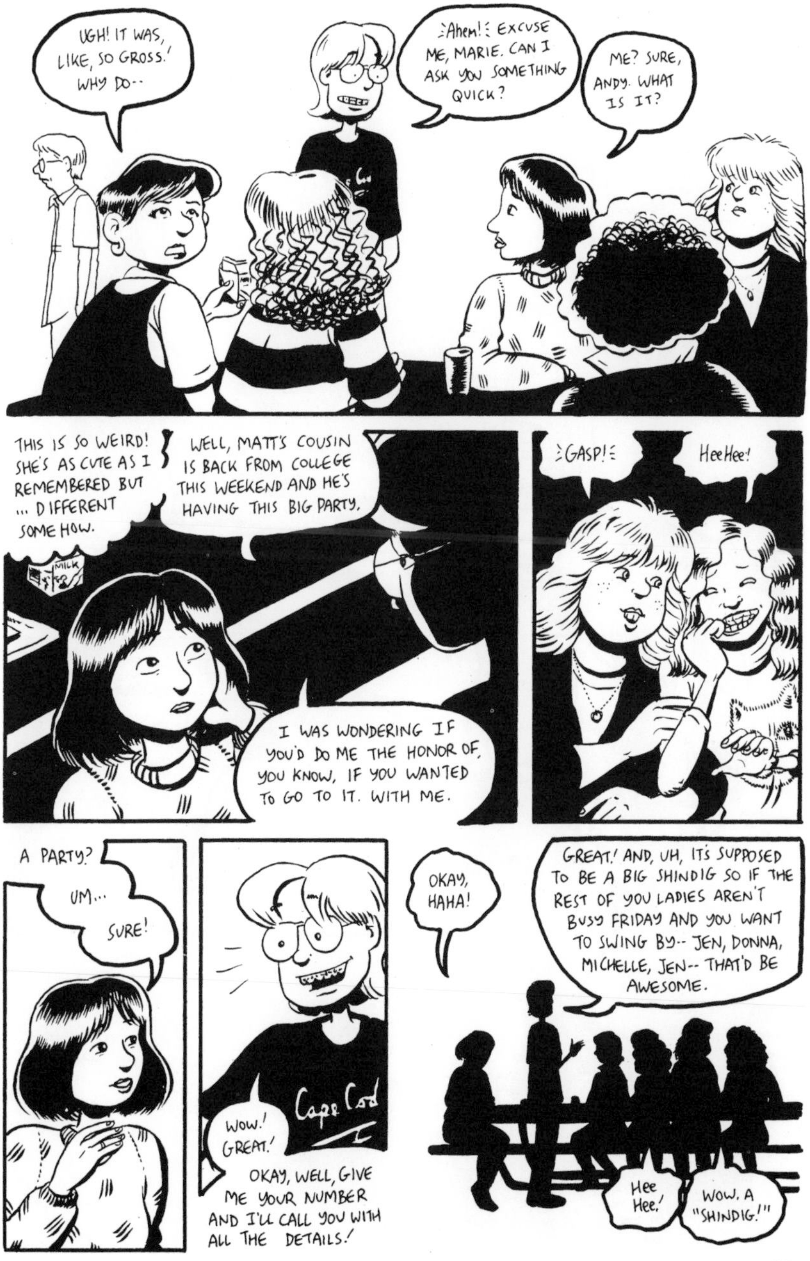
UGH! IT WAS, LIKE, SO GROSS! WHY DO--
:Ahem!: EXCUSE ME, MARIE. CAN I ASK YOU SOMETHING QUICK?
ME? SURE, ANDY. WHAT IS IT?
THIS IS SO WEIRD! SHE'S AS CUTE AS I REMEMBERED BUT ... DIFFERENT SOME HOW.
WELL, MATT'S COUSIN IS BACK FROM COLLEGE THIS WEEKEND AND HE'S HAVING THIS BIG PARTY.
MILK
I WAS WONDERING IF YOU'D DO ME THE HONOR OF, YOU KNOW, IF YOU WANTED TO GO TO IT. WITH ME.
:GASP!:
HeeHee!
A PARTY?
UM...
SURE!
Cape Cod
WOW! GREAT!
OKAY, WELL, GIVE ME YOUR NUMBER AND I'LL CALL YOU WITH ALL THE DETAILS!
OKAY, HAHA!
GREAT! AND, UH, IT'S SUPPOSED TO BE A BIG SHINDIG SO IF THE REST OF YOU LADIES AREN'T BUSY FRIDAY AND YOU WANT TO SWING BY-- JEN, DONNA, MICHELLE, JEN-- THAT'D BE AWESOME.
Hee Hee!
WOW. A "SHINDIG!"

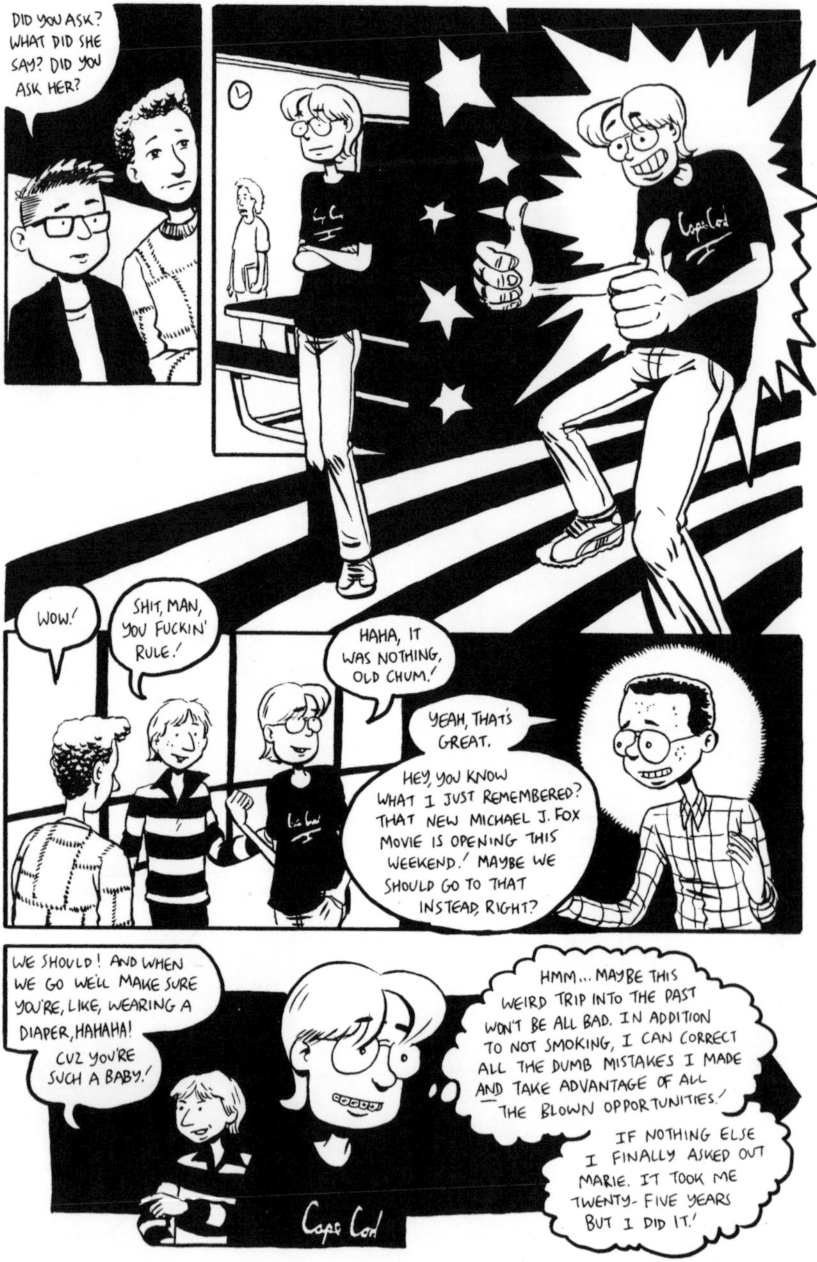
DID YOU ASK? WHAT DID SHE SAY? DID YOU ASK HER?
Cape Cod
WOW!
SHIT, MAN, YOU FUCKIN' RULE!
HAHA, IT WAS NOTHING, OLD CHUM!
YEAH, THAT'S GREAT.
HEY, YOU KNOW WHAT I JUST REMEMBERED? THAT NEW MICHAEL J. FOX MOVIE IS OPENING THIS WEEKEND! MAYBE WE SHOULD GO TO THAT INSTEAD, RIGHT?
WE SHOULD! AND WHEN WE GO WE'LL MAKE SURE YOU'RE, LIKE, WEARING A DIAPER, HAHAHA!
CUZ YOU'RE SUCH A BABY!
HMM... MAYBE THIS WEIRD TRIP INTO THE PAST WON'T BE ALL BAD. IN ADDITION TO NOT SMOKING, I CAN CORRECT ALL THE DUMB MISTAKES I MADE AND TAKE ADVANTAGE OF ALL THE BLOWN OPPORTUNITIES!
IF NOTHING ELSE I FINALLY ASKED OUT MARIE. IT TOOK ME TWENTY-FIVE YEARS BUT I DID IT!
Cape Cod

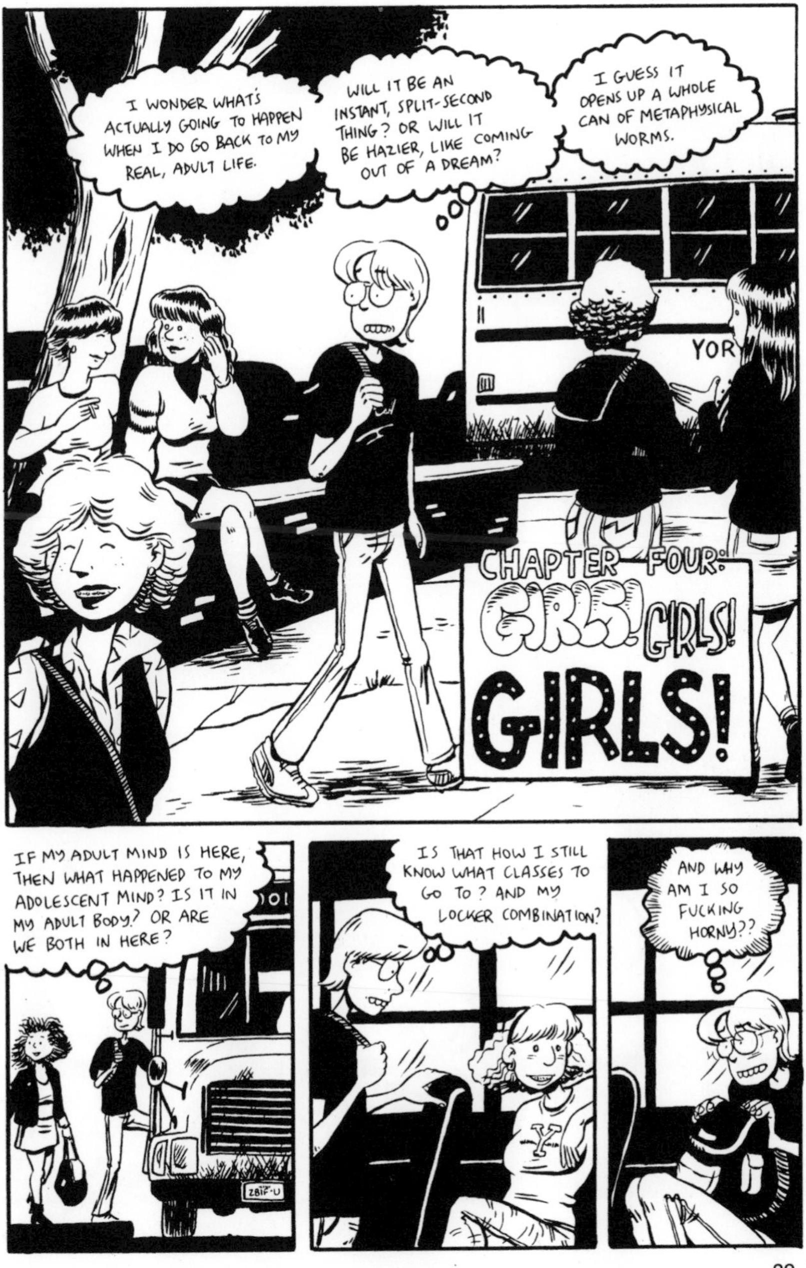
I WONDER WHAT'S ACTUALLY GOING TO HAPPEN WHEN I DO GO BACK TO MY REAL, ADULT LIFE.
WILL IT BE AN INSTANT, SPLIT-SECOND THING? OR WILL IT BE HAZIER, LIKE COMING OUT OF A DREAM?
I GUESS IT OPENS UP A WHOLE CAN OF METAPHYSICAL WORMS.
YOR
CHAPTER FOUR: GIRLS! GIRLS! GIRLS!
IF MY ADULT MIND IS HERE, THEN WHAT HAPPENED TO MY ADOLESCENT MIND? IS IT IN MY ADULT BODY? OR ARE WE BOTH IN HERE?
ZBIF-U
IS THAT HOW I STILL KNOW WHAT CLASSES TO GO TO? AND MY LOCKER COMBINATION?
AND WHY AM I SO FUCKING HORNY??

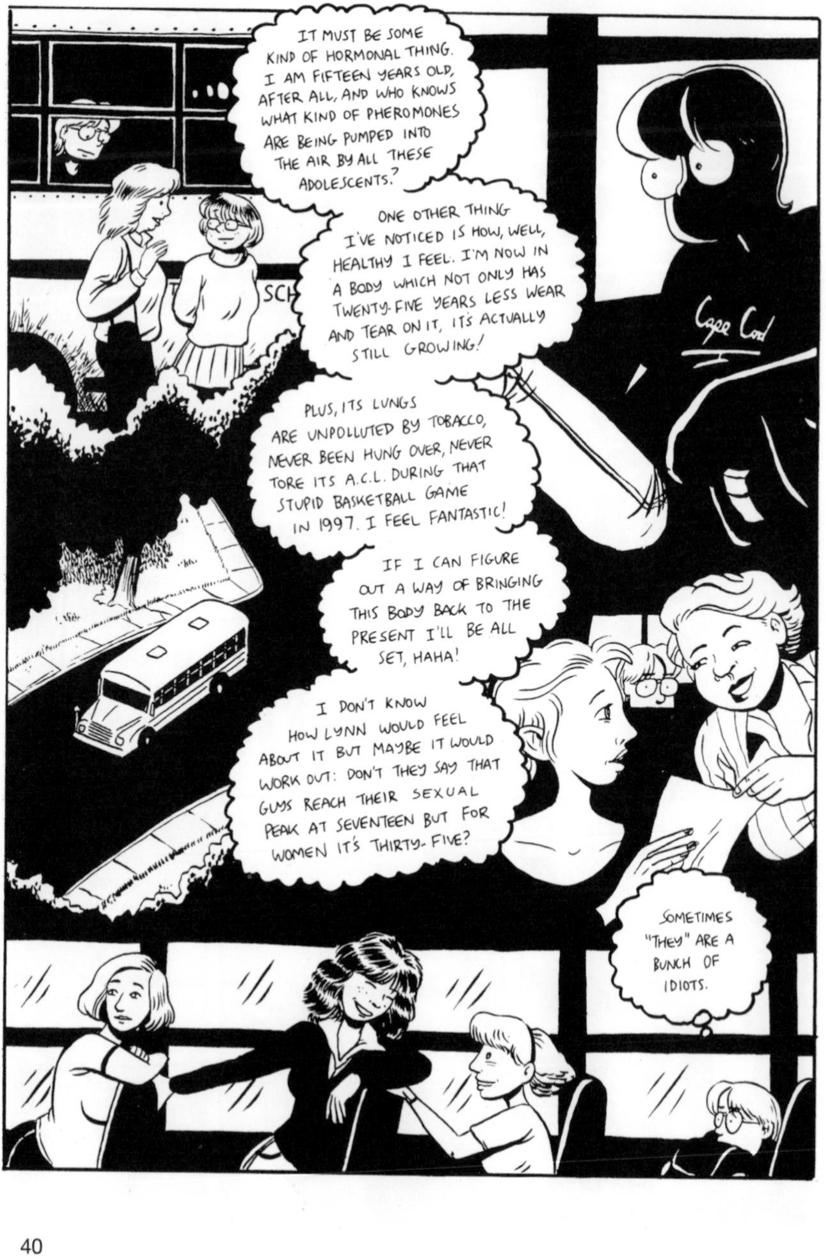
IT MUST BE SOME KIND OF HORMONAL THING. I AM FIFTEEN YEARS OLD, AFTER ALL, AND WHO KNOWS WHAT KIND OF PHEROMONES ARE BEING PUMPED INTO THE AIR BY ALL THESE ADOLESCENTS?
ONE OTHER THING I'VE NOTICED IS HOW, WELL, HEALTHY I FEEL. I'M NOW IN A BODY WHICH NOT ONLY HAS TWENTY-FIVE YEARS LESS WEAR AND TEAR ON IT, IT'S ACTUALLY STILL GROWING!
PLUS, ITS LUNGS ARE UNPOLLUTED BY TOBACCO, NEVER BEEN HUNG OVER, NEVER TORE ITS A.C.L. DURING THAT STUPID BASKETBALL GAME IN 1997. I FEEL FANTASTIC!
IF I CAN FIGURE OUT A WAY OF BRINGING THIS BODY BACK TO THE PRESENT I'LL BE ALL SET, HAHA!
I DON'T KNOW HOW LYNN WOULD FEEL ABOUT IT BUT MAYBE IT WOULD WORK OUT: DON'T THEY SAY THAT GUYS REACH THEIR SEXUAL PEAK AT SEVENTEEN BUT FOR WOMEN IT'S THIRTY-FIVE?
SOMETIMES "THEY" ARE A BUNCH OF IDIOTS.
SCH
Cape Cod

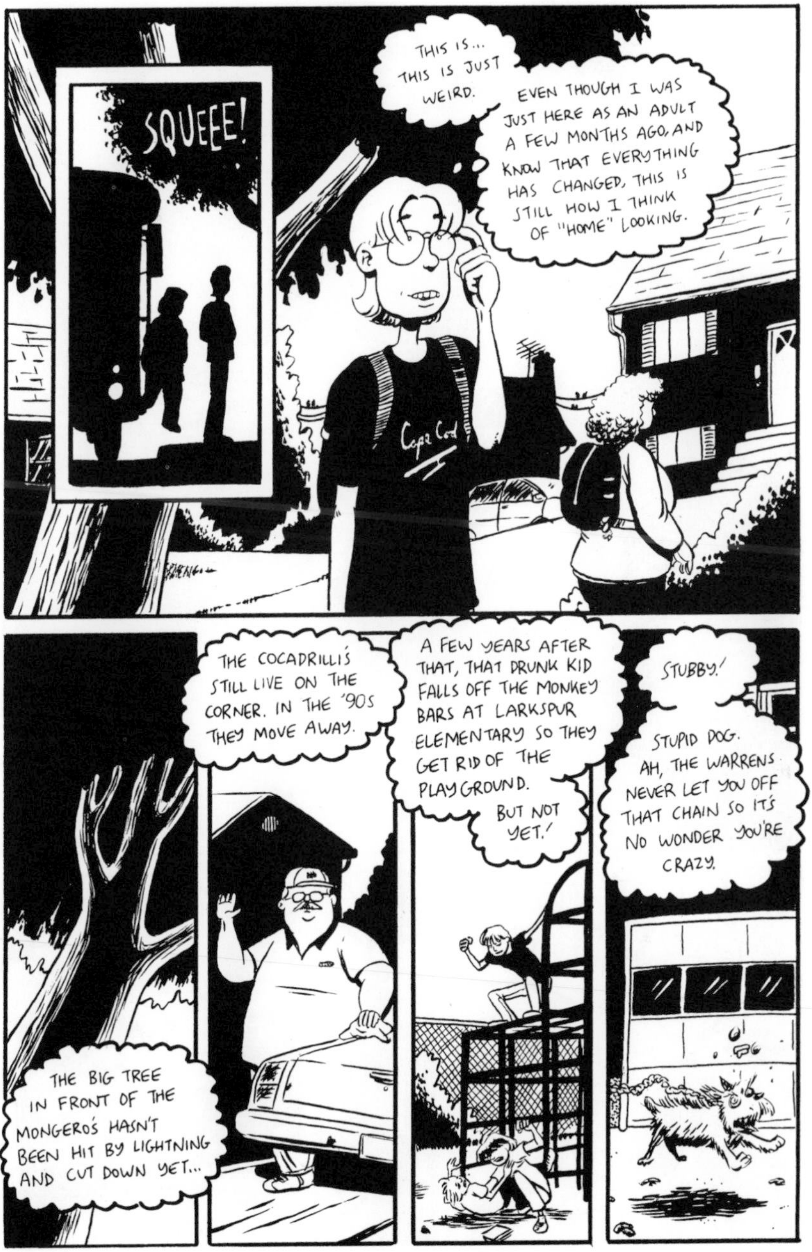
SQUEEE!
THIS IS... THIS IS JUST WEIRD.
EVEN THOUGH I WAS JUST HERE AS AN ADULT A FEW MONTHS AGO, AND KNOW THAT EVERYTHING HAS CHANGED, THIS IS STILL HOW I THINK OF "HOME" LOOKING.
Cape Cod
THE BIG TREE IN FRONT OF THE MONGERO'S HASN'T BEEN HIT BY LIGHTNING AND CUT DOWN YET...
THE COCADRILLI'S STILL LIVE ON THE CORNER. IN THE '90S THEY MOVE AWAY.
A FEW YEARS AFTER THAT, THAT DRUNK KID FALLS OFF THE MONKEY BARS AT LARKSPUR ELEMENTARY SO THEY GET RID OF THE PLAYGROUND.
BUT NOT YET!
STUBBY!
STUPID DOG. AH, THE WARRENS NEVER LET YOU OFF THAT CHAIN SO IT'S NO WONDER YOU'RE CRAZY.

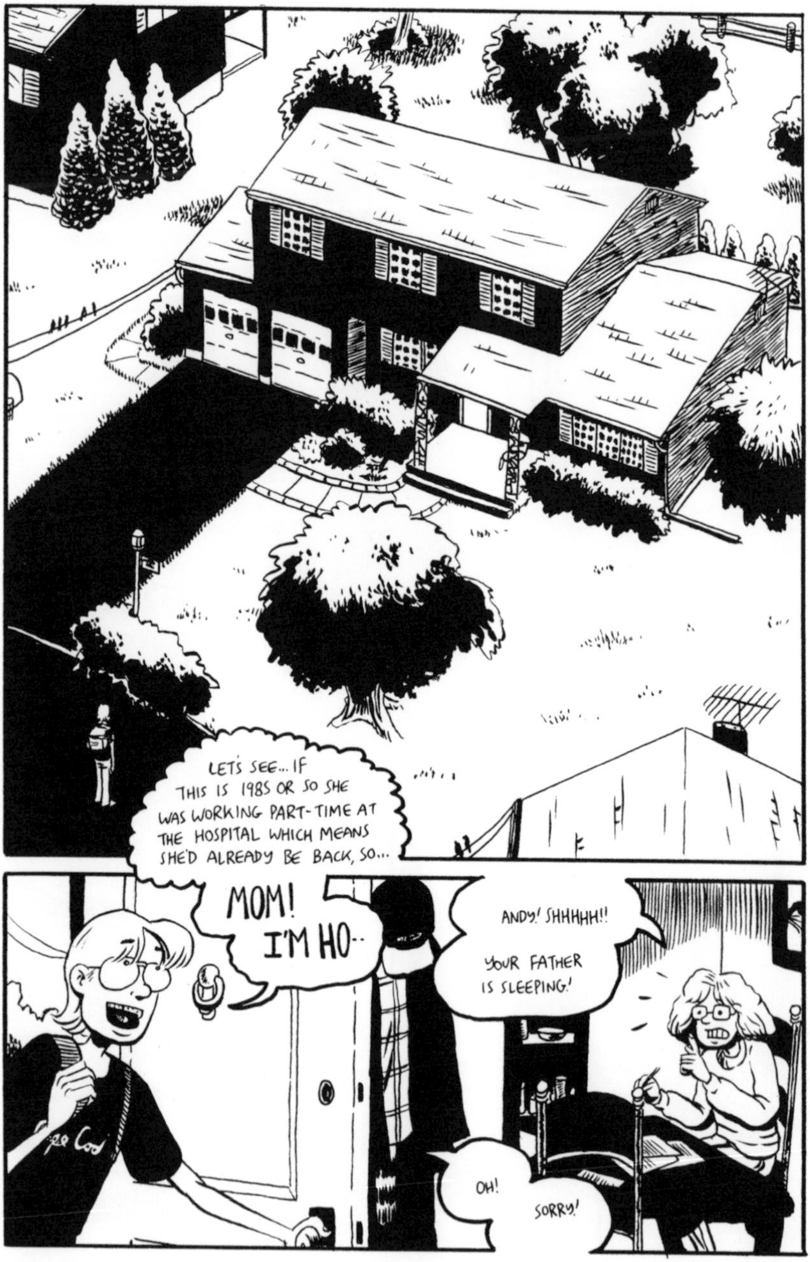

LET'S SEE... IF THIS IS 1985 OR SO SHE WAS WORKING PART-TIME AT THE HOSPITAL WHICH MEANS SHE'D ALREADY BE BACK, SO...
MOM! I'M HO--
ANDY! SHHHHH!!
YOUR FATHER IS SLEEPING!
OH!
SORRY!

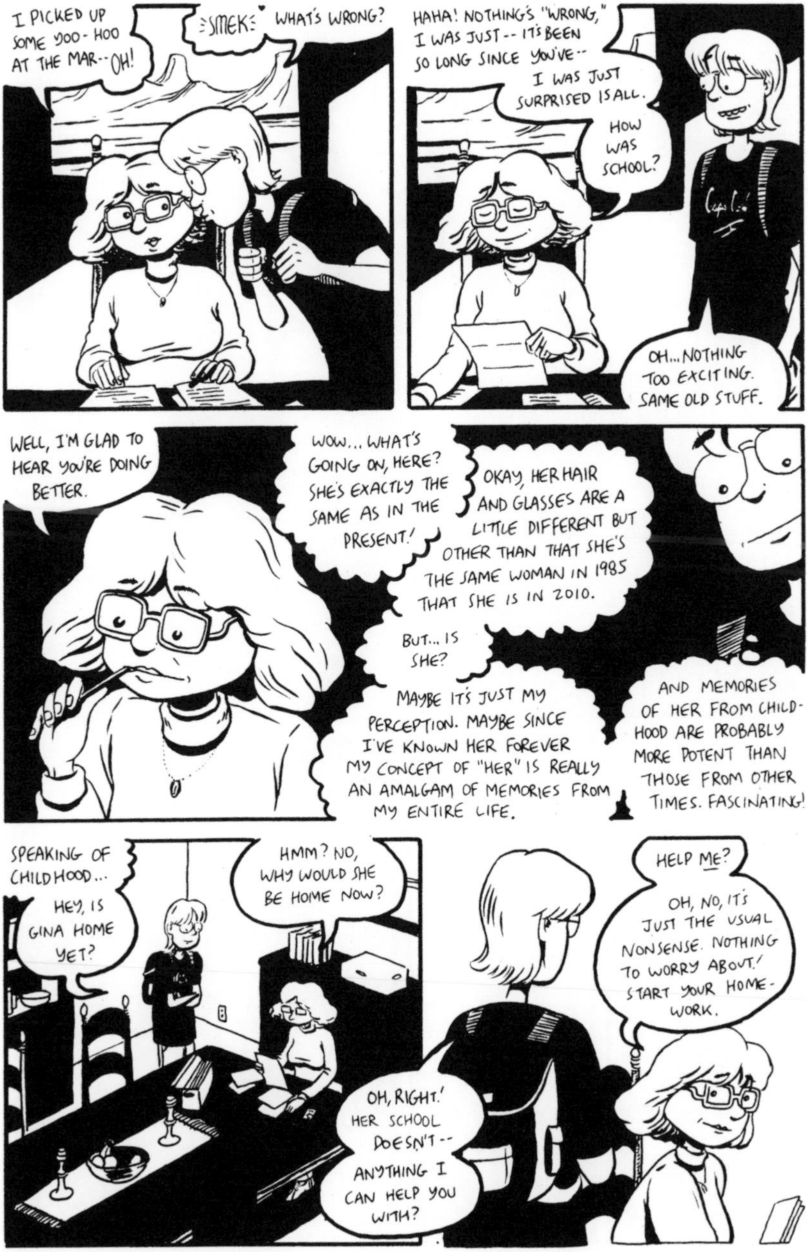
I PICKED UP SOME YOO-HOO AT THE MAR-- OH!
SMEK
WHAT'S WRONG?
HAHA! NOTHING'S "WRONG," I WAS JUST -- IT'S BEEN SO LONG SINCE YOU'VE --
I WAS JUST SURPRISED IS ALL.
HOW WAS SCHOOL?
OH... NOTHING TOO EXCITING. SAME OLD STUFF.
WELL, I'M GLAD TO HEAR YOU'RE DOING BETTER.
WOW... WHAT'S GOING ON, HERE? SHE'S EXACTLY THE SAME AS IN THE PRESENT!
OKAY, HER HAIR AND GLASSES ARE A LITTLE DIFFERENT BUT OTHER THAN THAT SHE'S THE SAME WOMAN IN 1985 THAT SHE IS IN 2010.
BUT... IS SHE?
MAYBE IT'S JUST MY PERCEPTION. MAYBE SINCE I'VE KNOWN HER FOREVER MY CONCEPT OF "HER" IS REALLY AN AMALGAM OF MEMORIES FROM MY ENTIRE LIFE.
AND MEMORIES OF HER FROM CHILDHOOD ARE PROBABLY MORE POTENT THAN THOSE FROM OTHER TIMES. FASCINATING!
SPEAKING OF CHILDHOOD...
HEY, IS GINA HOME YET?
HMM? NO, WHY WOULD SHE BE HOME NOW?
OH, RIGHT! HER SCHOOL DOESN'T --
ANYTHING I CAN HELP YOU WITH?
HELP ME?
OH, NO, IT'S JUST THE USUAL NONSENSE. NOTHING TO WORRY ABOUT! START YOUR HOMEWORK.

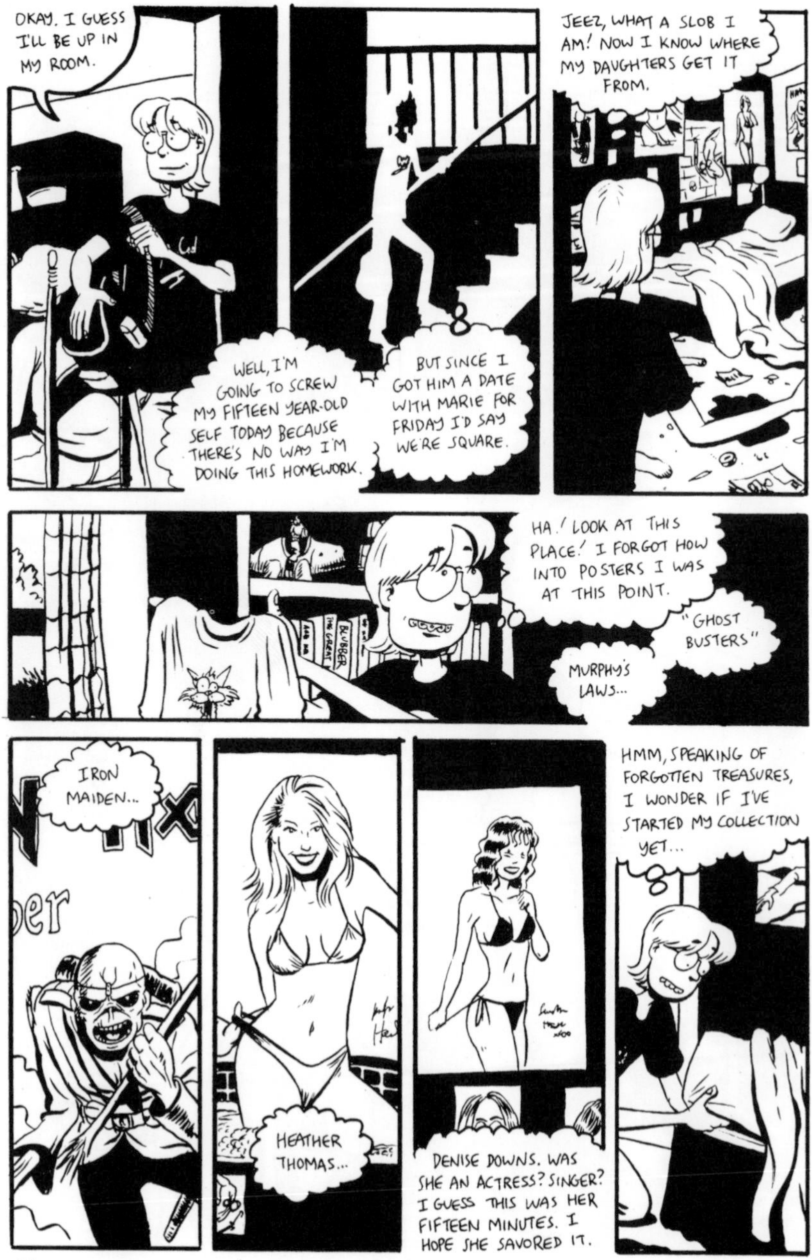
OKAY. I GUESS I'LL BE UP IN MY ROOM.
WELL, I'M GOING TO SCREW MY FIFTEEN YEAR-OLD SELF TODAY BECAUSE THERE'S NO WAY I'M DOING THIS HOMEWORK.
BUT SINCE I GOT HIM A DATE WITH MARIE FOR FRIDAY I'D SAY WE'RE SQUARE.
JEEZ, WHAT A SLOB I AM! NOW I KNOW WHERE MY DAUGHTERS GET IT FROM.
HA! LOOK AT THIS PLACE! I FORGOT HOW INTO POSTERS I WAS AT THIS POINT.
"GHOST BUSTERS"
MURPHY'S LAWS...
IRON MAIDEN...
HEATHER THOMAS...
DENISE DOWNS. WAS SHE AN ACTRESS? SINGER? I GUESS THIS WAS HER FIFTEEN MINUTES. I HOPE SHE SAVORED IT.
HMM, SPEAKING OF FORGOTTEN TREASURES, I WONDER IF I'VE STARTED MY COLLECTION YET...

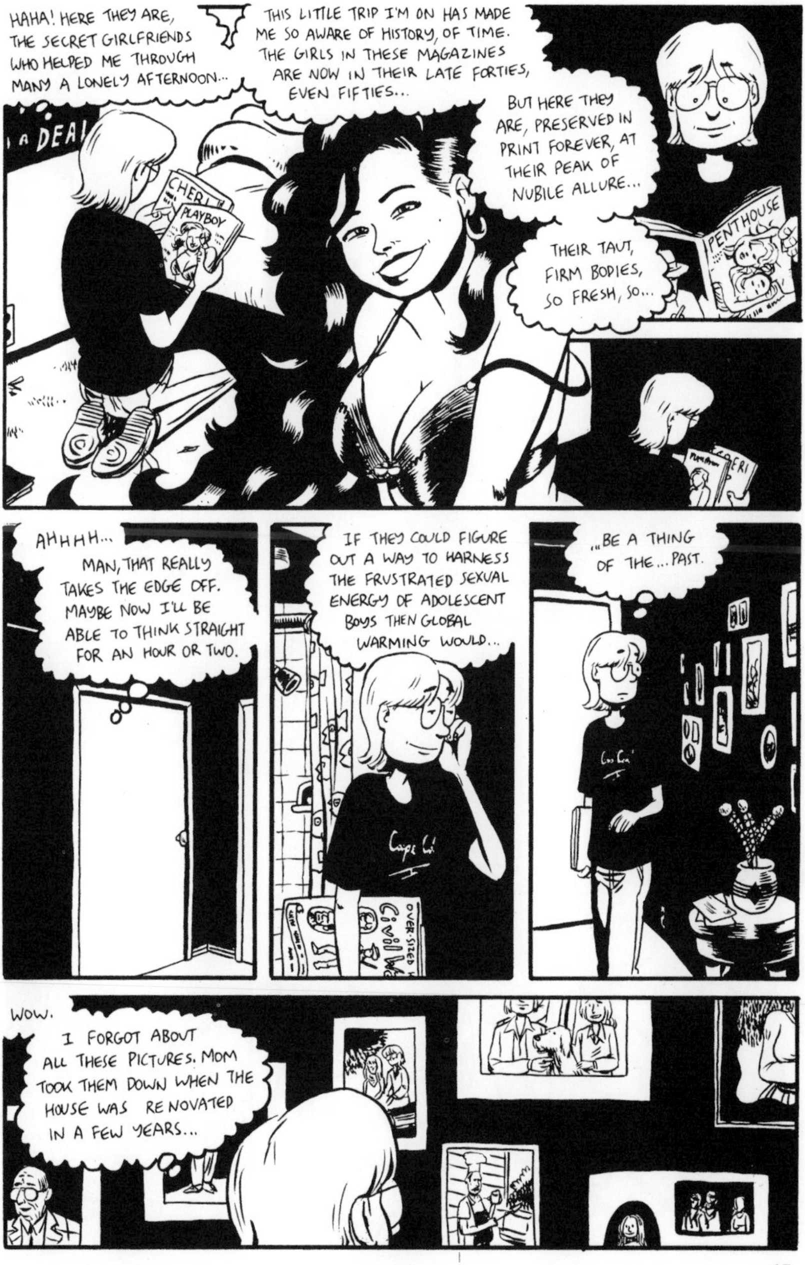
HAHA! HERE THEY ARE, THE SECRET GIRLFRIENDS WHO HELPED ME THROUGH MANY A LONELY AFTERNOON...
THIS LITTLE TRIP I'M ON HAS MADE ME SO AWARE OF HISTORY, OF TIME. THE GIRLS IN THESE MAGAZINES ARE NOW IN THEIR LATE FORTIES, EVEN FIFTIES...
BUT HERE THEY ARE, PRESERVED IN PRINT FOREVER, AT THEIR PEAK OF NUBILE ALLURE...
THEIR TAUT, FIRM BODIES, SO FRESH, SO...
CHERI
PLAYBOY
PENTHOUSE
AHHHH... MAN, THAT REALLY TAKES THE EDGE OFF. MAYBE NOW I'LL BE ABLE TO THINK STRAIGHT FOR AN HOUR OR TWO.
IF THEY COULD FIGURE OUT A WAY TO HARNESS THE FRUSTRATED SEXUAL ENERGY OF ADOLESCENT BOYS THEN GLOBAL WARMING WOULD...
...BE A THING OF THE... PAST.
WOW. I FORGOT ABOUT ALL THESE PICTURES. MOM TOOK THEM DOWN WHEN THE HOUSE WAS RENOVATED IN A FEW YEARS...

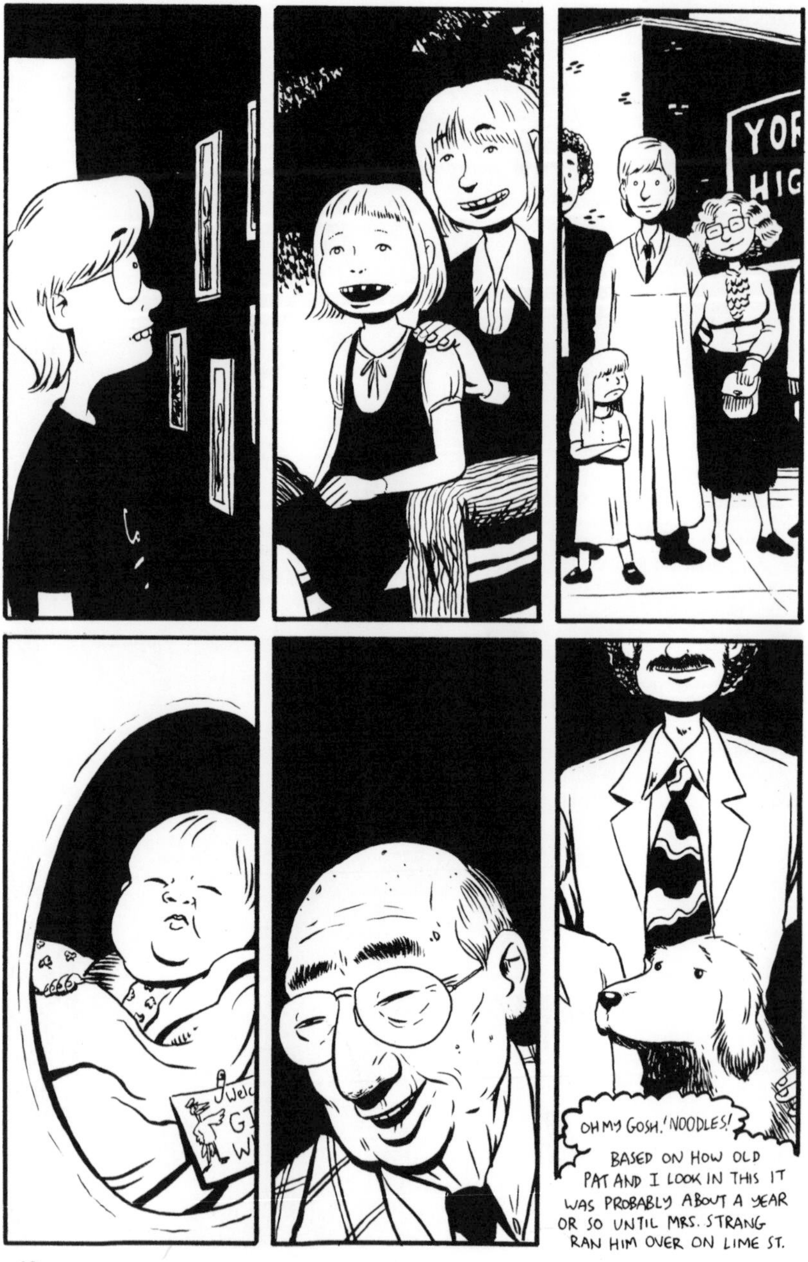
YOR
HIG
OH MY GOSH! NOODLES!
BASED ON HOW OLD PAT AND I LOOK IN THIS IT WAS PROBABLY ABOUT A YEAR OR SO UNTIL MRS. STRANG RAN HIM OVER ON LIME ST.

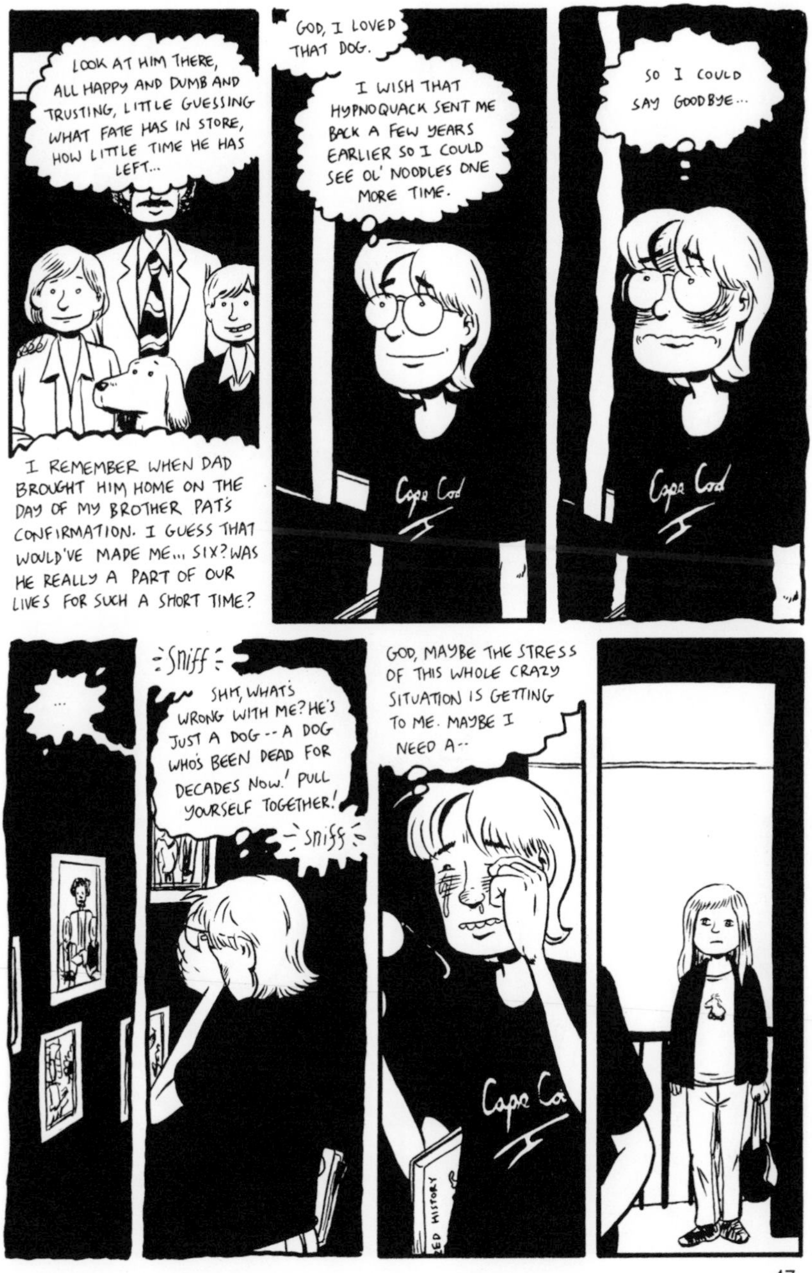
LOOK AT HIM THERE, ALL HAPPY AND DUMB AND TRUSTING, LITTLE GUESSING WHAT FATE HAS IN STORE, HOW LITTLE TIME HE HAS LEFT...
I REMEMBER WHEN DAD BROUGHT HIM HOME ON THE DAY OF MY BROTHER PAT'S CONFIRMATION. I GUESS THAT WOULD'VE MADE ME... SIX? WAS HE REALLY A PART OF OUR LIVES FOR SUCH A SHORT TIME?
GOD, I LOVED THAT DOG.
I WISH THAT HYPNOQUACK SENT ME BACK A FEW YEARS EARLIER SO I COULD SEE OL' NOODLES ONE MORE TIME.
Cape Cod
SO I COULD SAY GOODBYE...
Cape Cod
...
SNIFF
SHIT, WHAT'S WRONG WITH ME? HE'S JUST A DOG -- A DOG WHO'S BEEN DEAD FOR DECADES NOW! PULL YOURSELF TOGETHER!
SNIFF
GOD, MAYBE THE STRESS OF THIS WHOLE CRAZY SITUATION IS GETTING TO ME. MAYBE I NEED A--
Cape Co
ED HISTORY

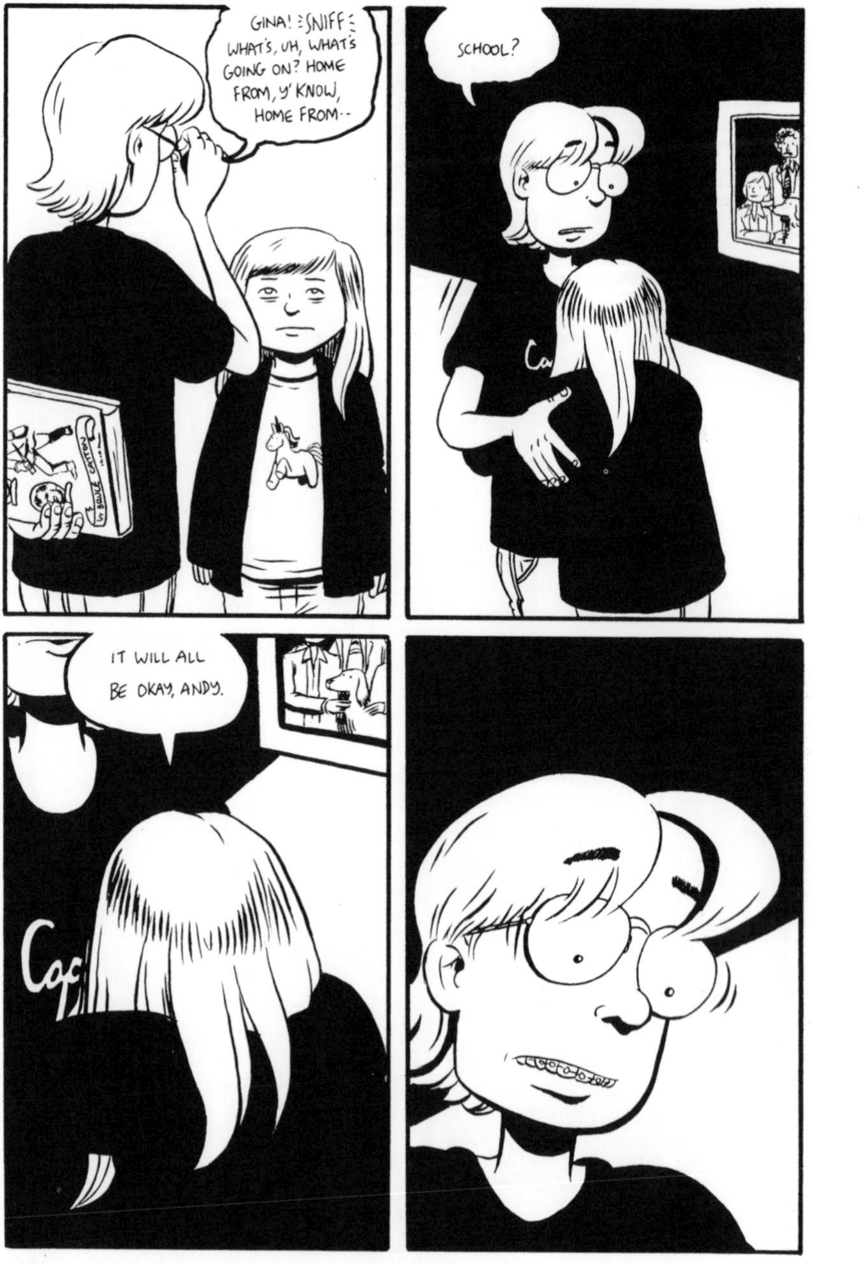
GINA! SNIFF WHAT'S, UH, WHAT'S GOING ON? HOME FROM, Y' KNOW, HOME FROM--
SCHOOL?
IT WILL ALL BE OKAY, ANDY.

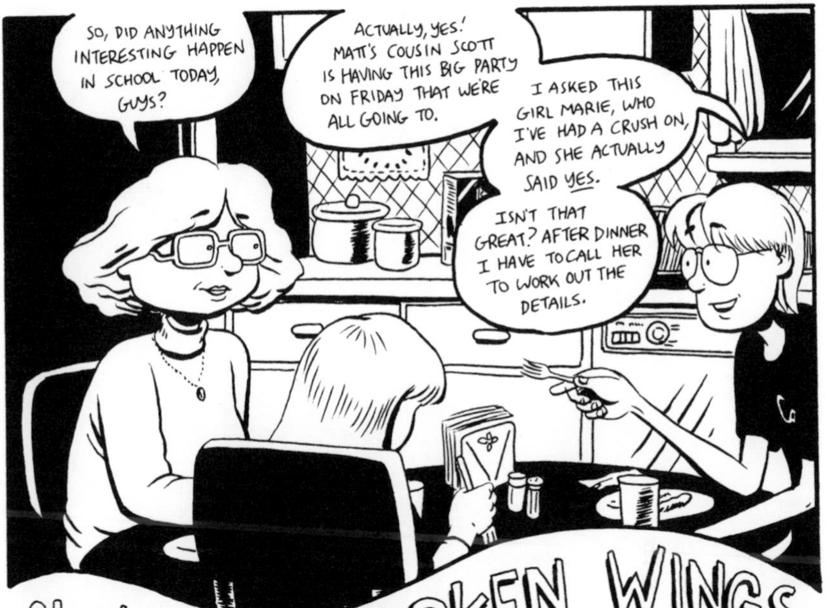
SO, DID ANYTHING INTERESTING HAPPEN IN SCHOOL TODAY, GUYS?
ACTUALLY, YES! MATT'S COUSIN SCOTT IS HAVING THIS BIG PARTY ON FRIDAY THAT WE'RE ALL GOING TO.
I ASKED THIS GIRL MARIE, WHO I'VE HAD A CRUSH ON, AND SHE ACTUALLY SAID YES.
ISN'T THAT GREAT? AFTER DINNER I HAVE TO CALL HER TO WORK OUT THE DETAILS.

Chapter Five: BROKEN WINGS

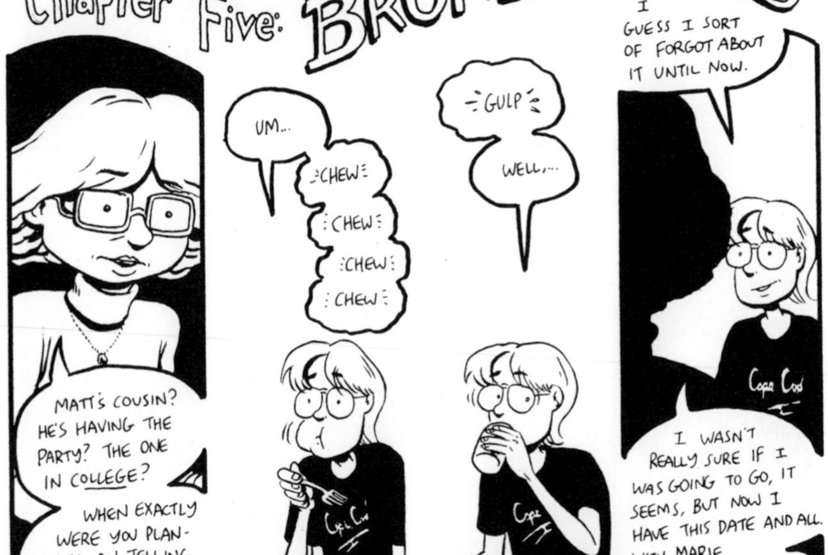
MATT'S COUSIN? HE'S HAVING THE PARTY? THE ONE IN COLLEGE?
WHEN EXACTLY WERE YOU PLANNING ON TELLING ME ABOUT ALL OF THIS?
UM...
CHEW
CHEW
CHEW
CHEW
GULP
WELL,...
I GUESS I SORT OF FORGOT ABOUT IT UNTIL NOW.
I WASN'T REALLY SURE IF I WAS GOING TO GO, IT SEEMS, BUT NOW I HAVE THIS DATE AND ALL. WITH MARIE.
AREN'T YOU HAPPY I HAVE A DATE?

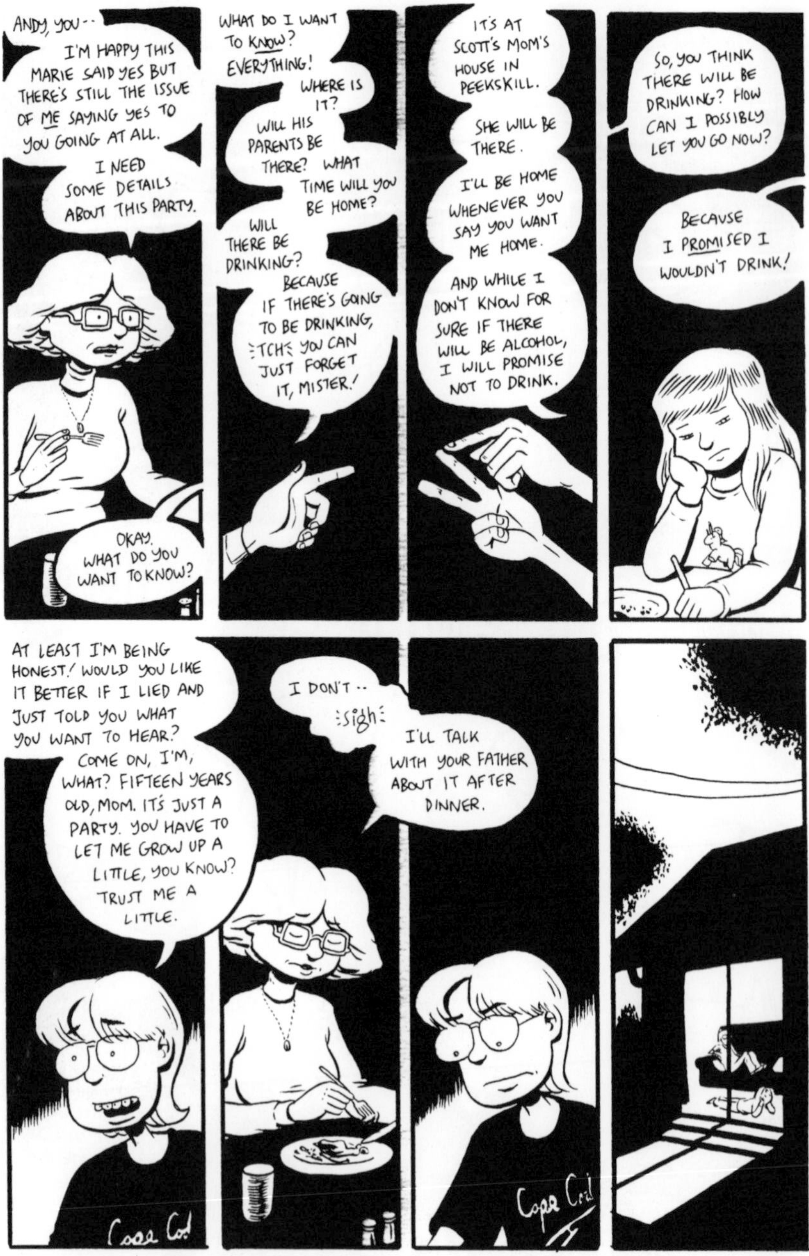
ANDY, YOU--
I'M HAPPY THIS MARIE SAID YES BUT THERE'S STILL THE ISSUE OF ME SAYING YES TO YOU GOING AT ALL.
I NEED SOME DETAILS ABOUT THIS PARTY.
OKAY. WHAT DO YOU WANT TO KNOW?
WHAT DO I WANT TO KNOW? EVERYTHING!
WHERE IS IT?
WILL HIS PARENTS BE THERE? WHAT TIME WILL YOU BE HOME?
WILL THERE BE DRINKING?
BECAUSE IF THERE'S GOING TO BE DRINKING, TCH YOU CAN JUST FORGET IT, MISTER!
IT'S AT SCOTT'S MOM'S HOUSE IN PEEKSKILL.
SHE WILL BE THERE.
I'LL BE HOME WHENEVER YOU SAY YOU WANT ME HOME.
AND WHILE I DON'T KNOW FOR SURE IF THERE WILL BE ALCOHOL, I WILL PROMISE NOT TO DRINK.
SO, YOU THINK THERE WILL BE DRINKING? HOW CAN I POSSIBLY LET YOU GO NOW?
BECAUSE I PROMISED I WOULDN'T DRINK!
AT LEAST I'M BEING HONEST! WOULD YOU LIKE IT BETTER IF I LIED AND JUST TOLD YOU WHAT YOU WANT TO HEAR?
COME ON, I'M, WHAT? FIFTEEN YEARS OLD, MOM. IT'S JUST A PARTY. YOU HAVE TO LET ME GROW UP A LITTLE, YOU KNOW? TRUST ME A LITTLE.
I DON'T--
sigh
I'LL TALK WITH YOUR FATHER ABOUT IT AFTER DINNER.

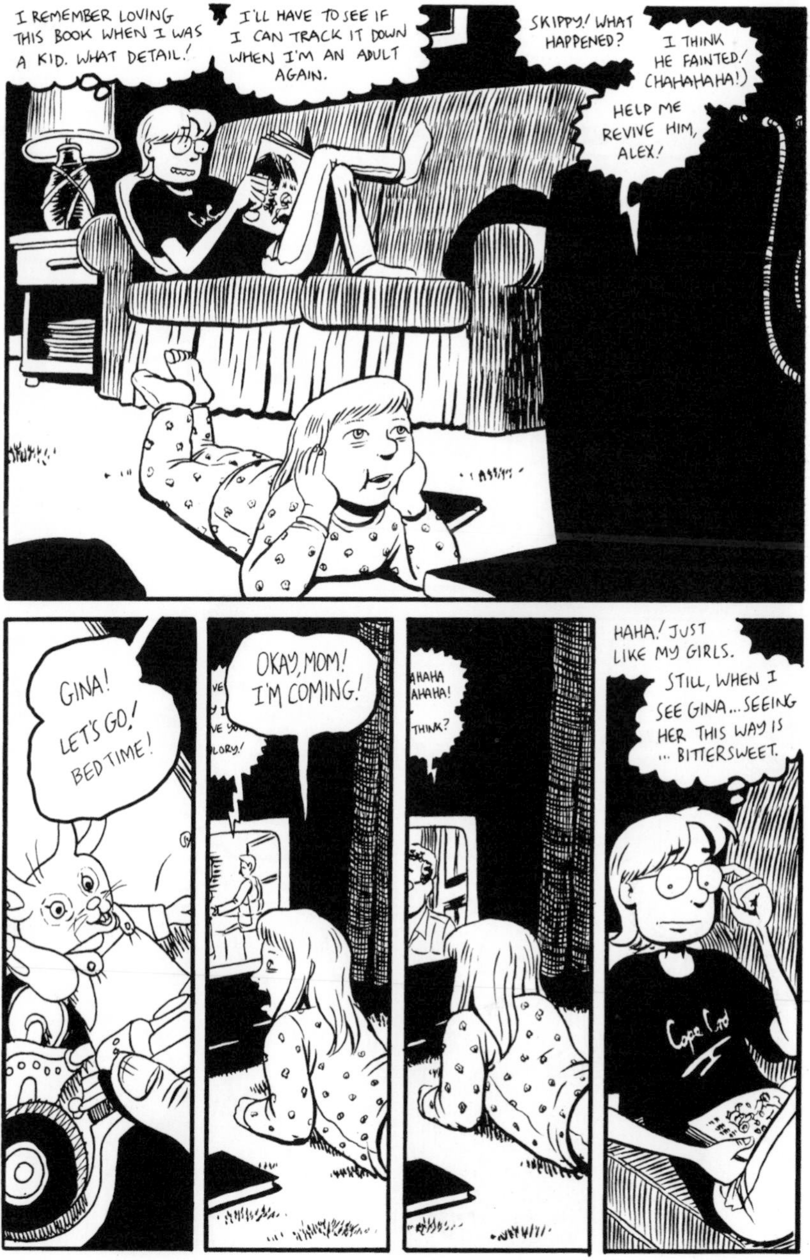
I REMEMBER LOVING THIS BOOK WHEN I WAS A KID. WHAT DETAIL!
I'LL HAVE TO SEE IF I CAN TRACK IT DOWN WHEN I'M AN ADULT AGAIN.
SKIPPY! WHAT HAPPENED?
I THINK HE FAINTED! (HAHAHAHA!)
HELP ME REVIVE HIM, ALEX!
GINA! LET'S GO! BED TIME!
OKAY, MOM! I'M COMING!
HAHA! JUST LIKE MY GIRLS.
STILL, WHEN I SEE GINA... SEEING HER THIS WAY IS ... BITTERSWEET.

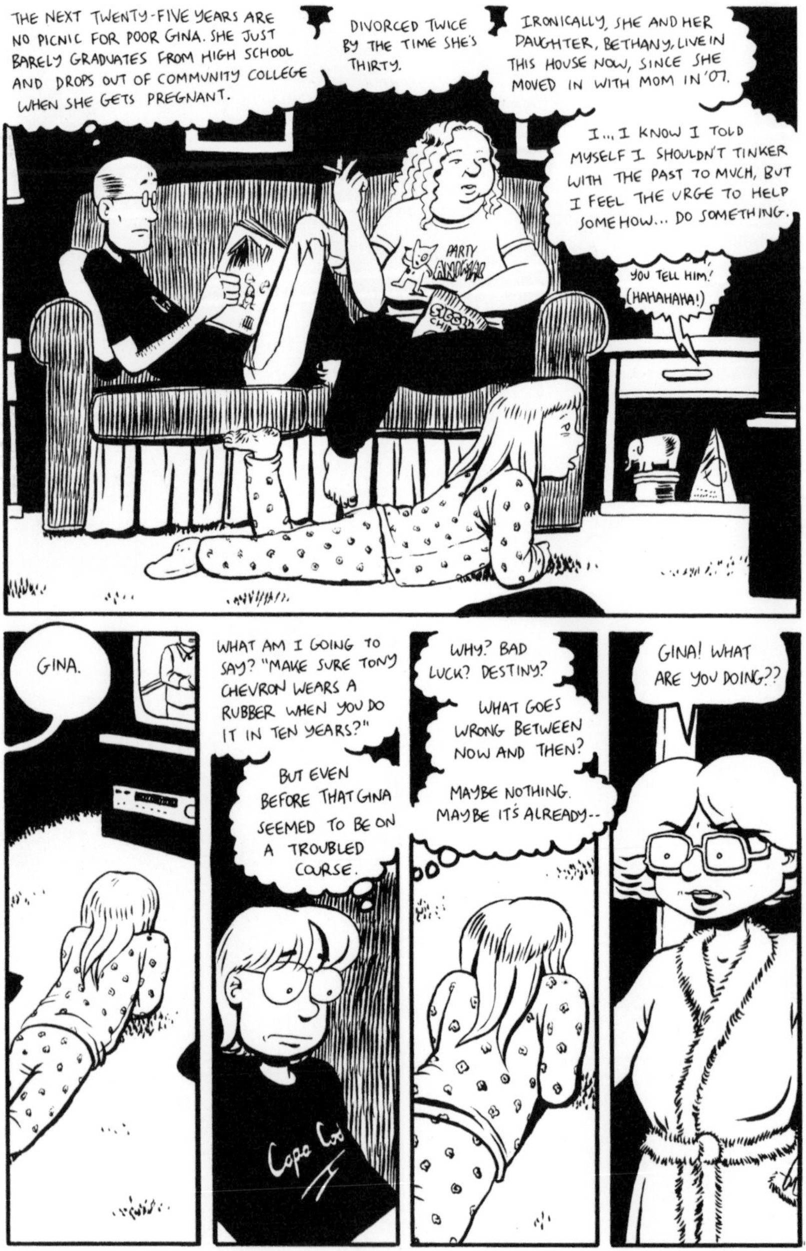
THE NEXT TWENTY-FIVE YEARS ARE NO PICNIC FOR POOR GINA. SHE JUST BARELY GRADUATES FROM HIGH SCHOOL AND DROPS OUT OF COMMUNITY COLLEGE WHEN SHE GETS PREGNANT.
DIVORCED TWICE BY THE TIME SHE'S THIRTY.
IRONICALLY, SHE AND HER DAUGHTER, BETHANY, LIVE IN THIS HOUSE NOW, SINCE SHE MOVED IN WITH MOM IN '07.
I... I KNOW I TOLD MYSELF I SHOULDN'T TINKER WITH THE PAST TO MUCH, BUT I FEEL THE URGE TO HELP SOMEHOW... DO SOMETHING.
PARTY ANIMAL
YOU TELL HIM! (HAHAHAHA!)
GINA.
WHAT AM I GOING TO SAY? "MAKE SURE TONY CHEVRON WEARS A RUBBER WHEN YOU DO IT IN TEN YEARS?"
BUT EVEN BEFORE THAT GINA SEEMED TO BE ON A TROUBLED COURSE.
Cape Cod
WHY? BAD LUCK? DESTINY?
WHAT GOES WRONG BETWEEN NOW AND THEN?
MAYBE NOTHING. MAYBE IT'S ALREADY--
GINA! WHAT ARE YOU DOING??

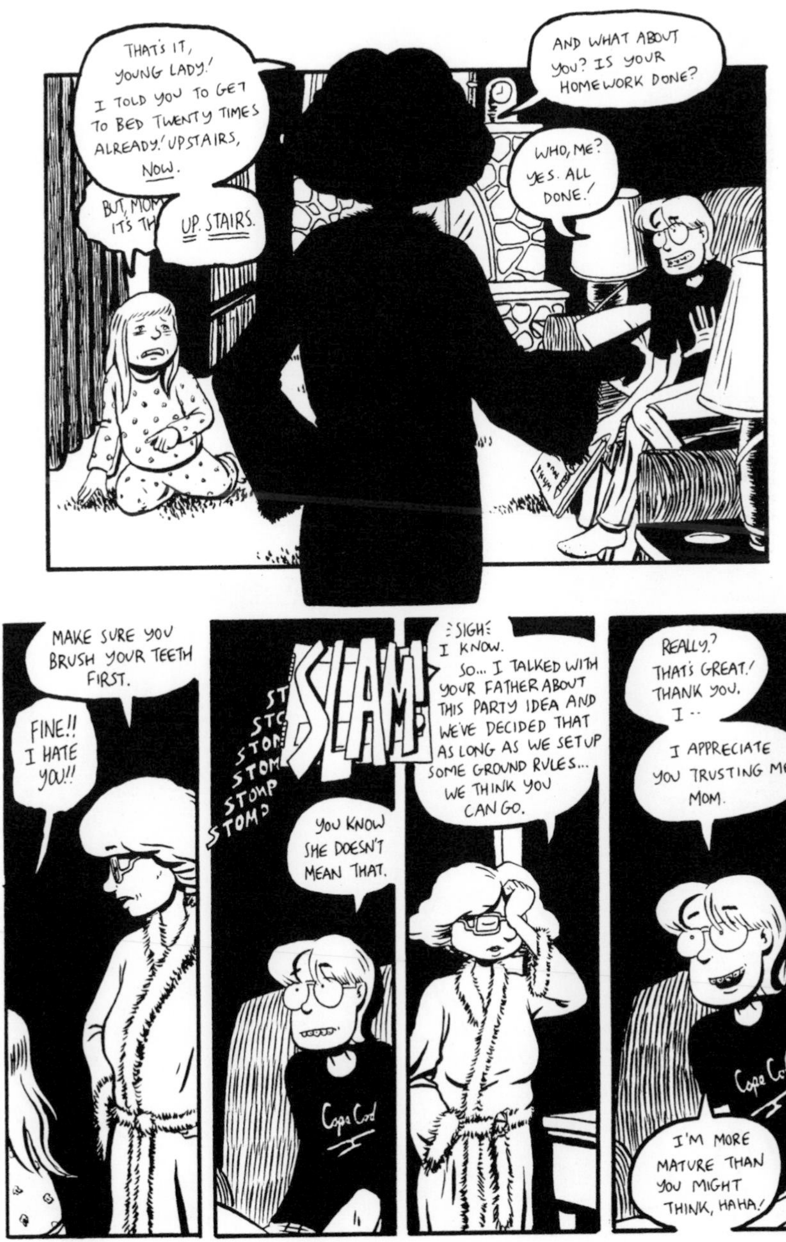
THAT'S IT, YOUNG LADY! I TOLD YOU TO GET TO BED TWENTY TIMES ALREADY! UPSTAIRS, NOW.
AND WHAT ABOUT YOU? IS YOUR HOMEWORK DONE?
WHO, ME? YES. ALL DONE!
UP. STAIRS.
MAKE SURE YOU BRUSH YOUR TEETH FIRST.
FINE!! I HATE YOU!!
SLAM!
STOMP STOMP STOMP
YOU KNOW SHE DOESN'T MEAN THAT.
SIGH I KNOW.
SO... I TALKED WITH YOUR FATHER ABOUT THIS PARTY IDEA AND WE'VE DECIDED THAT AS LONG AS WE SET UP SOME GROUND RULES... WE THINK YOU CAN GO.
REALLY? THAT'S GREAT! THANK YOU. I --
I APPRECIATE YOU TRUSTING ME, MOM.
Cape Cod
I'M MORE MATURE THAN YOU MIGHT THINK, HAHA!

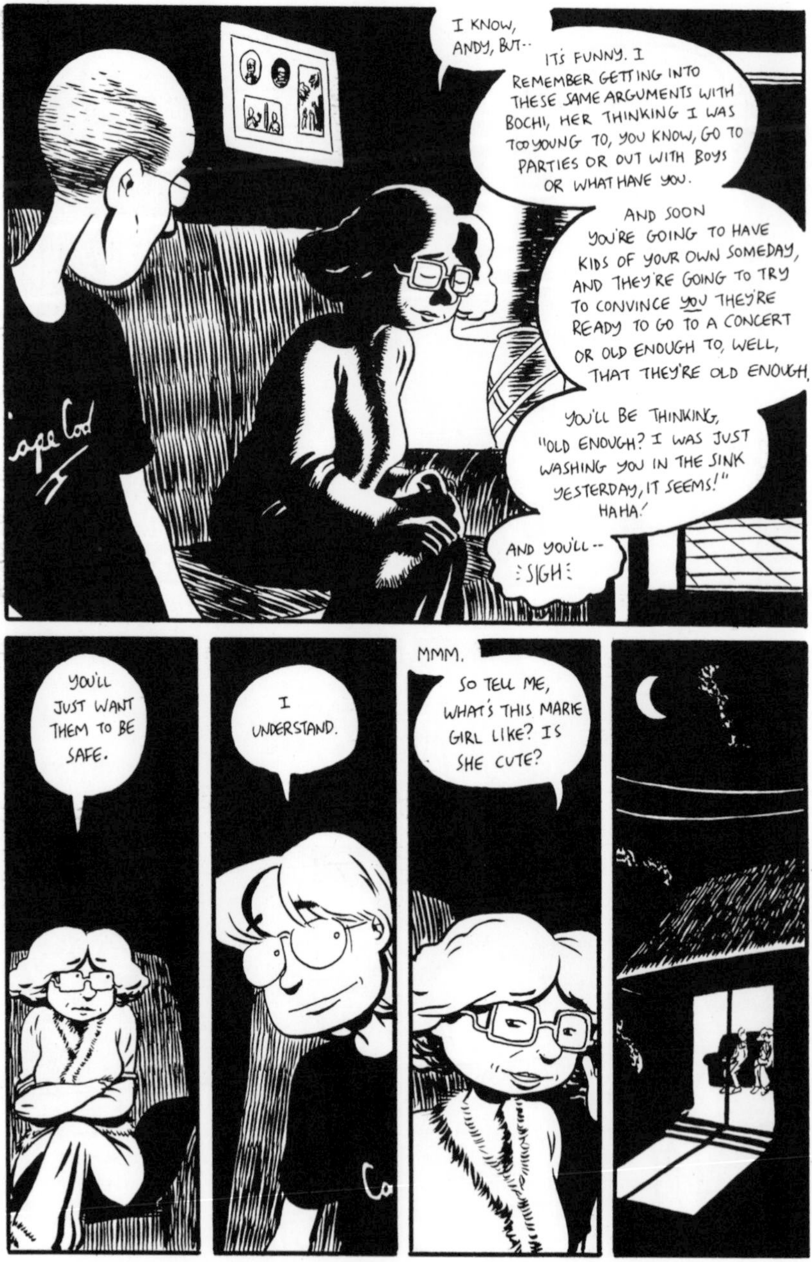

I KNOW, ANDY, BUT..
IT'S FUNNY. I REMEMBER GETTING INTO THESE SAME ARGUMENTS WITH BOCHI, HER THINKING I WAS TOO YOUNG TO, YOU KNOW, GO TO PARTIES OR OUT WITH BOYS OR WHAT HAVE YOU.
AND SOON YOU'RE GOING TO HAVE KIDS OF YOUR OWN SOMEDAY, AND THEY'RE GOING TO TRY TO CONVINCE YOU THEY'RE READY TO GO TO A CONCERT OR OLD ENOUGH TO, WELL, THAT THEY'RE OLD ENOUGH.
YOU'LL BE THINKING, "OLD ENOUGH? I WAS JUST WASHING YOU IN THE SINK YESTERDAY, IT SEEMS!" HAHA!
AND YOU'LL --
SIGH
YOU'LL JUST WANT THEM TO BE SAFE.
I UNDERSTAND.
MMM.
SO TELL ME, WHAT'S THIS MARIE GIRL LIKE? IS SHE CUTE?

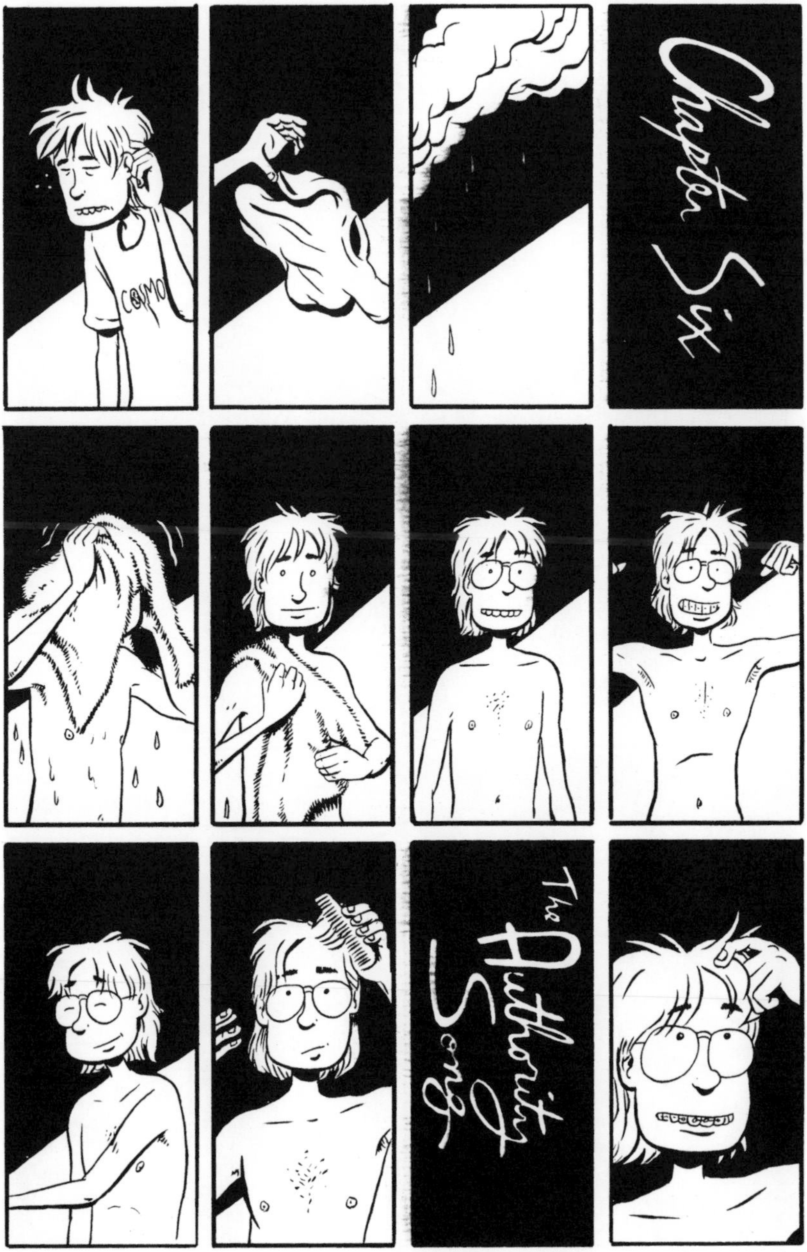
COSMO
Chapter Six
The Authority Song

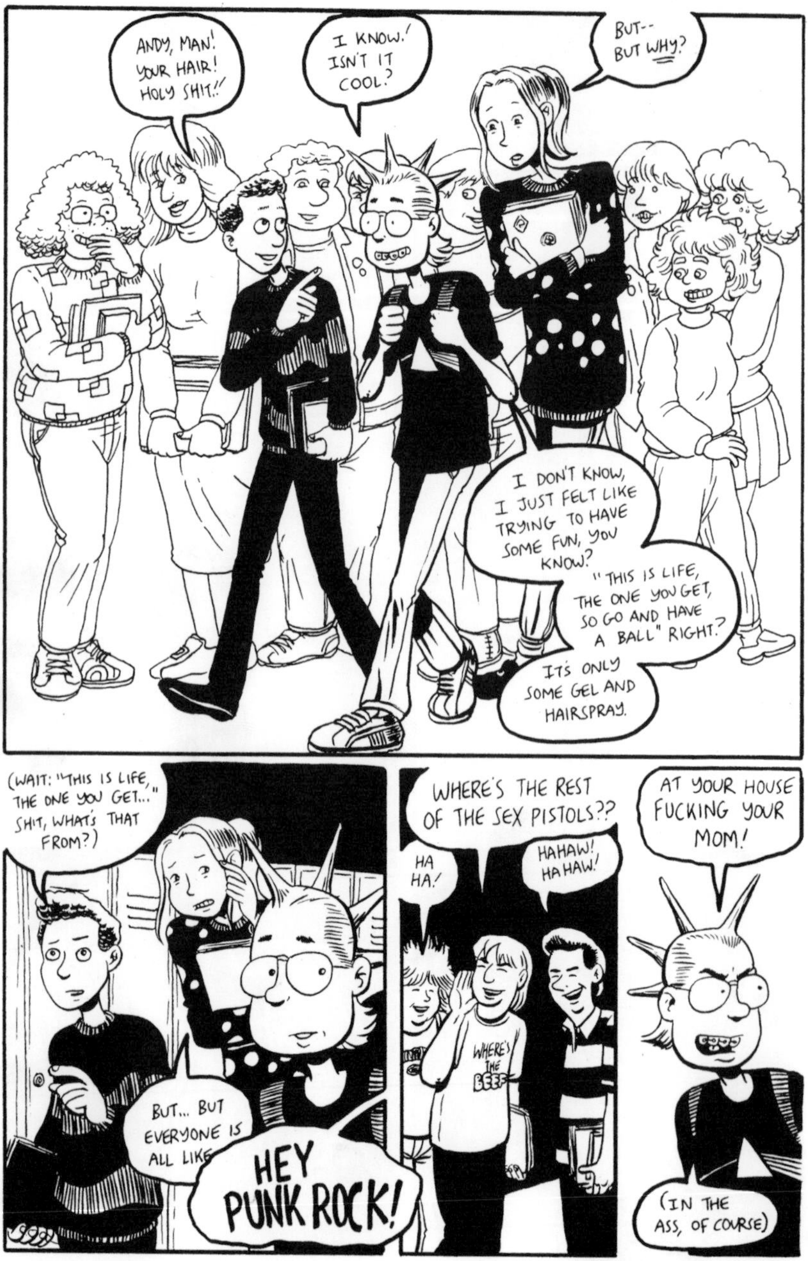
ANDY, MAN! YOUR HAIR! HOLY SHIT!!
I KNOW! ISN'T IT COOL?
BUT-- BUT WHY?
I DON'T KNOW, I JUST FELT LIKE TRYING TO HAVE SOME FUN, YOU KNOW?
"THIS IS LIFE, THE ONE YOU GET, SO GO AND HAVE A BALL" RIGHT?
IT'S ONLY SOME GEL AND HAIRSPRAY.
(WAIT: "THIS IS LIFE, THE ONE YOU GET..." SHIT, WHAT'S THAT FROM?)
BUT... BUT EVERYONE IS ALL LIKE
HEY PUNK ROCK!
WHERE'S THE REST OF THE SEX PISTOLS??
HA HA!
HAHAW! HAHAW!
WHERE'S THE BEEF
AT YOUR HOUSE FUCKING YOUR MOM!
(IN THE ASS, OF COURSE)

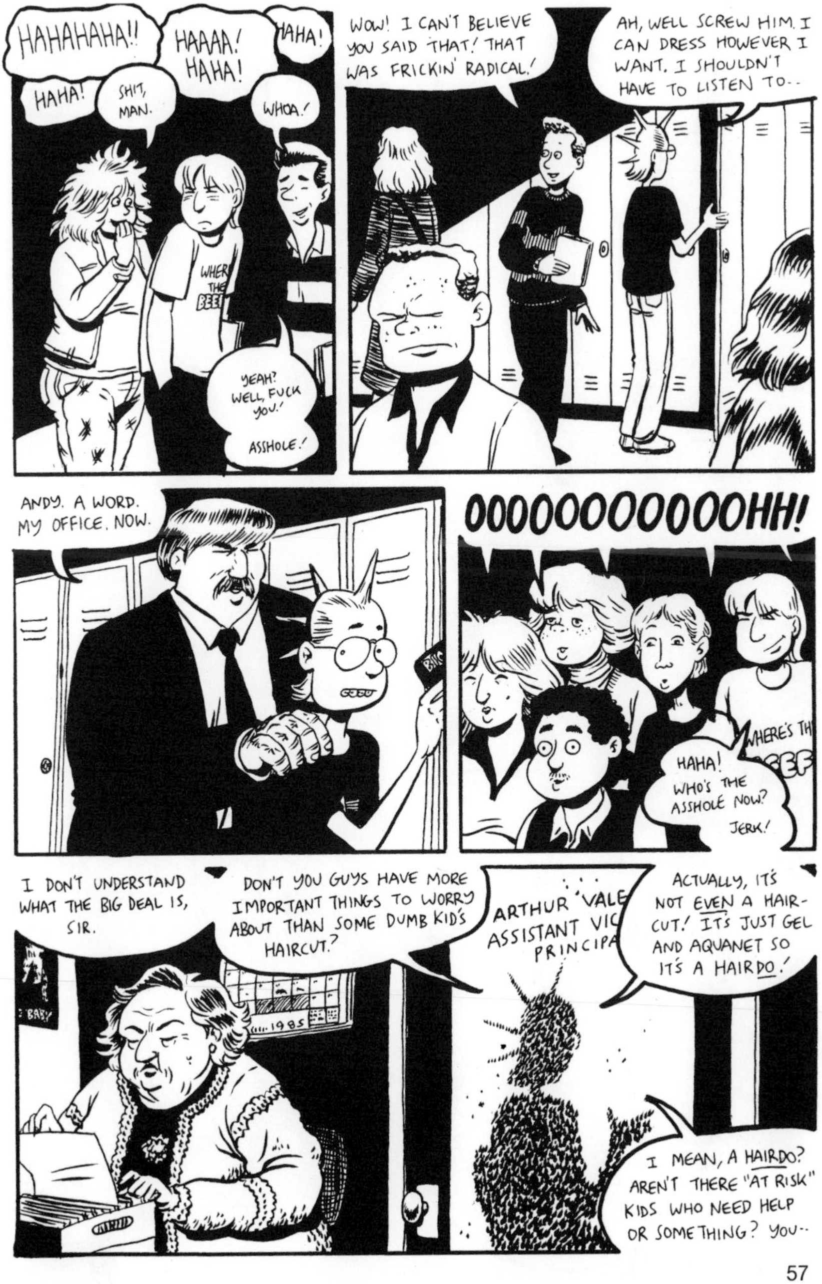
HAHAHAHA!!
HAHA!
SHIT, MAN.
HAAAA! HAHA!
HAHA!
WHOA!
WHERE'S THE BEEF
YEAH? WELL, FUCK YOU! ASSHOLE!
WOW! I CAN'T BELIEVE YOU SAID THAT! THAT WAS FRICKIN' RADICAL!
AH, WELL SCREW HIM. I CAN DRESS HOWEVER I WANT. I SHOULDN'T HAVE TO LISTEN TO..
ANDY. A WORD. MY OFFICE. NOW.
OOOOOOOOOOOOHH!
WHERE'S TH
HAHA! WHO'S THE ASSHOLE NOW? JERK!
I DON'T UNDERSTAND WHAT THE BIG DEAL IS, SIR.
DON'T YOU GUYS HAVE MORE IMPORTANT THINGS TO WORRY ABOUT THAN SOME DUMB KID'S HAIRCUT?
1985
ARTHUR VALE ASSISTANT VIC PRINCIPA
ACTUALLY, IT'S NOT EVEN A HAIRCUT! IT'S JUST GEL AND AQUANET SO IT'S A HAIRDO!
I MEAN, A HAIRDO? AREN'T THERE "AT RISK" KIDS WHO NEED HELP OR SOMETHING? YOU..

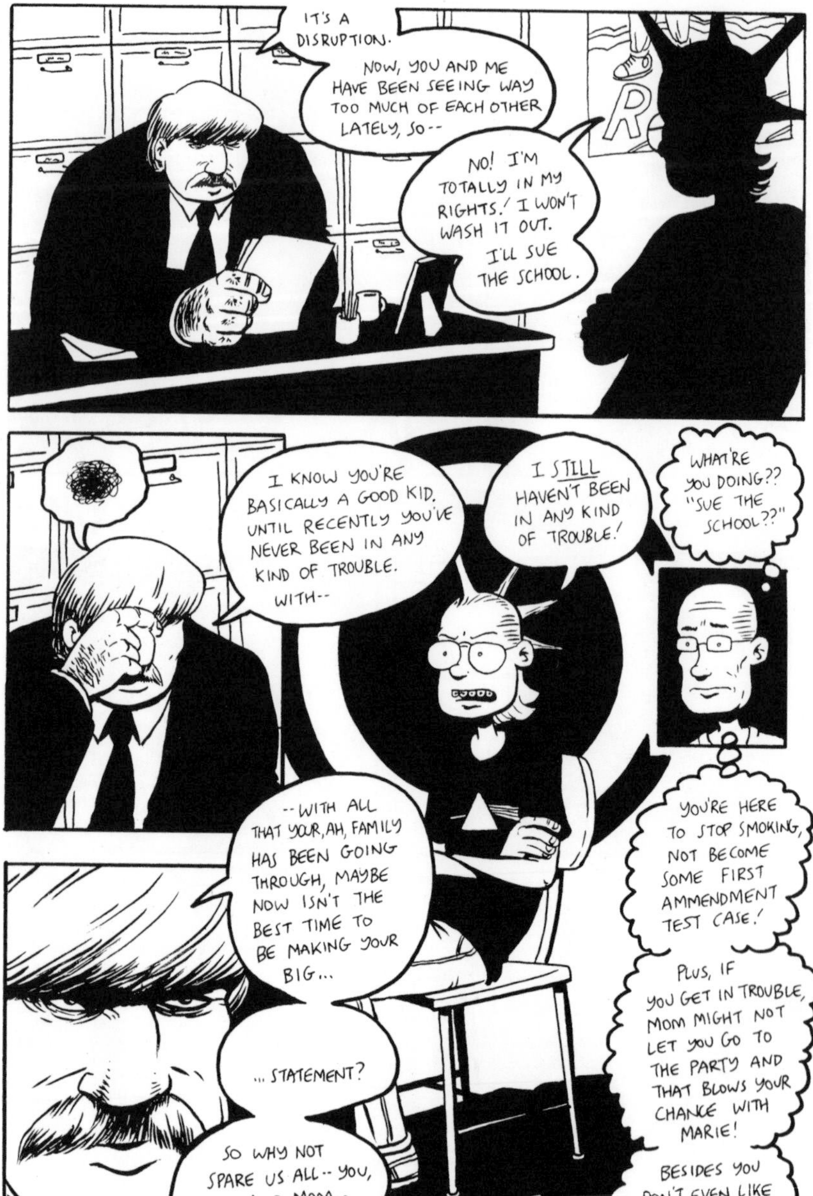
IT'S A DISRUPTION.
NOW, YOU AND ME HAVE BEEN SEEING WAY TOO MUCH OF EACH OTHER LATELY, SO--
NO! I'M TOTALLY IN MY RIGHTS! I WON'T WASH IT OUT. I'LL SUE THE SCHOOL.
I KNOW YOU'RE BASICALLY A GOOD KID. UNTIL RECENTLY YOU'VE NEVER BEEN IN ANY KIND OF TROUBLE. WITH--
I STILL HAVEN'T BEEN IN ANY KIND OF TROUBLE!
WHAT'RE YOU DOING?? "SUE THE SCHOOL??"
--WITH ALL THAT YOUR, AH, FAMILY HAS BEEN GOING THROUGH, MAYBE NOW ISN'T THE BEST TIME TO BE MAKING YOUR BIG...
...STATEMENT?
SO WHY NOT SPARE US ALL-- YOU, ME, YOUR MOM-- ANY MORE, AH, HEARTACHE?
YOU'RE HERE TO STOP SMOKING, NOT BECOME SOME FIRST AMMENDMENT TEST CASE!
PLUS, IF YOU GET IN TROUBLE, MOM MIGHT NOT LET YOU GO TO THE PARTY AND THAT BLOWS YOUR CHANCE WITH MARIE!
BESIDES YOU DON'T EVEN LIKE PUNK ROCK!

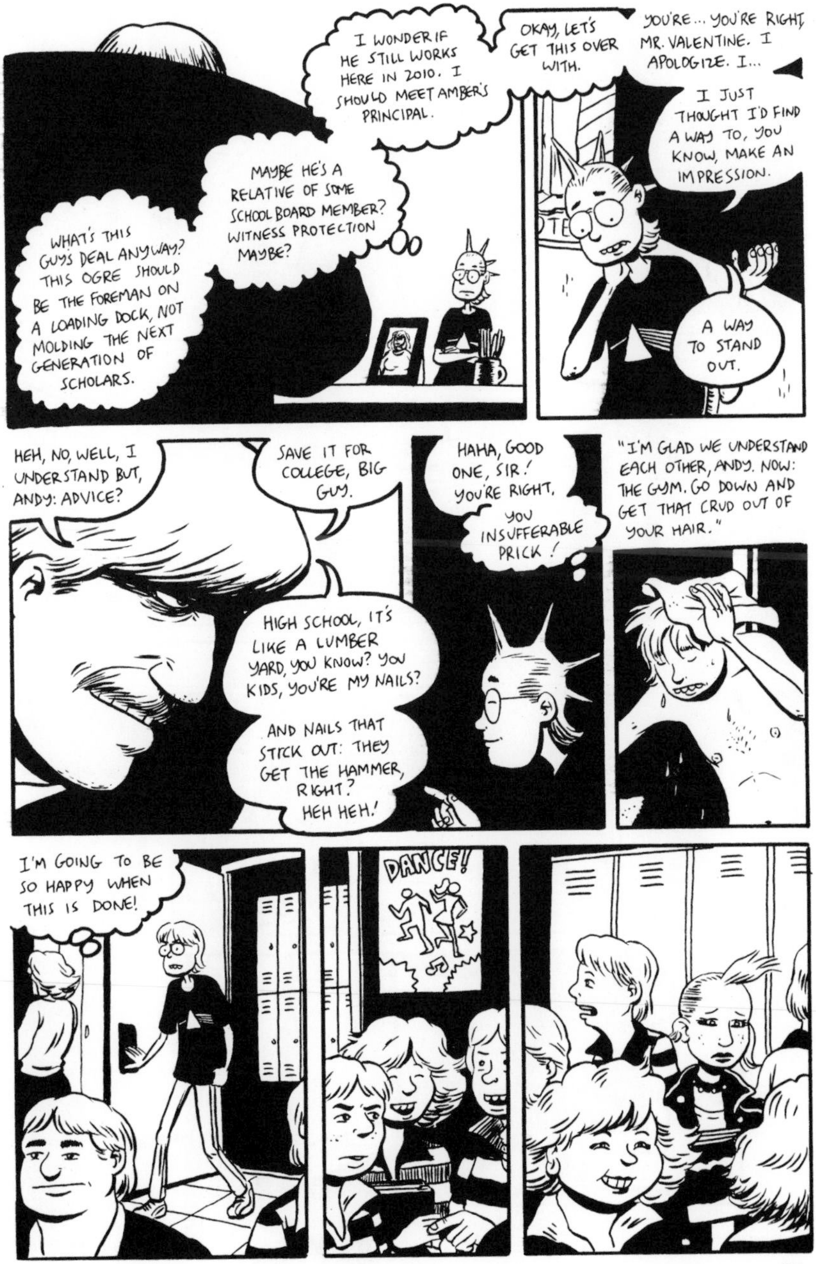
WHAT'S THIS GUY'S DEAL ANYWAY? THIS OGRE SHOULD BE THE FOREMAN ON A LOADING DOCK, NOT MOLDING THE NEXT GENERATION OF SCHOLARS.
MAYBE HE'S A RELATIVE OF SOME SCHOOL BOARD MEMBER? WITNESS PROTECTION MAYBE?
I WONDER IF HE STILL WORKS HERE IN 2010. I SHOULD MEET AMBER'S PRINCIPAL.
OKAY, LET'S GET THIS OVER WITH.
YOU'RE... YOU'RE RIGHT, MR. VALENTINE. I APOLOGIZE. I...
I JUST THOUGHT I'D FIND A WAY TO, YOU KNOW, MAKE AN IMPRESSION.
A WAY TO STAND OUT.
HEH, NO, WELL, I UNDERSTAND BUT, ANDY: ADVICE?
SAVE IT FOR COLLEGE, BIG GUY.
HIGH SCHOOL, IT'S LIKE A LUMBER YARD, YOU KNOW? YOU KIDS, YOU'RE MY NAILS?
AND NAILS THAT STICK OUT: THEY GET THE HAMMER, RIGHT? HEH HEH!
HAHA, GOOD ONE, SIR! YOU'RE RIGHT,
YOU INSUFFERABLE PRICK!
"I'M GLAD WE UNDERSTAND EACH OTHER, ANDY. NOW: THE GYM. GO DOWN AND GET THAT CRUD OUT OF YOUR HAIR."
I'M GOING TO BE SO HAPPY WHEN THIS IS DONE!
DANCE!

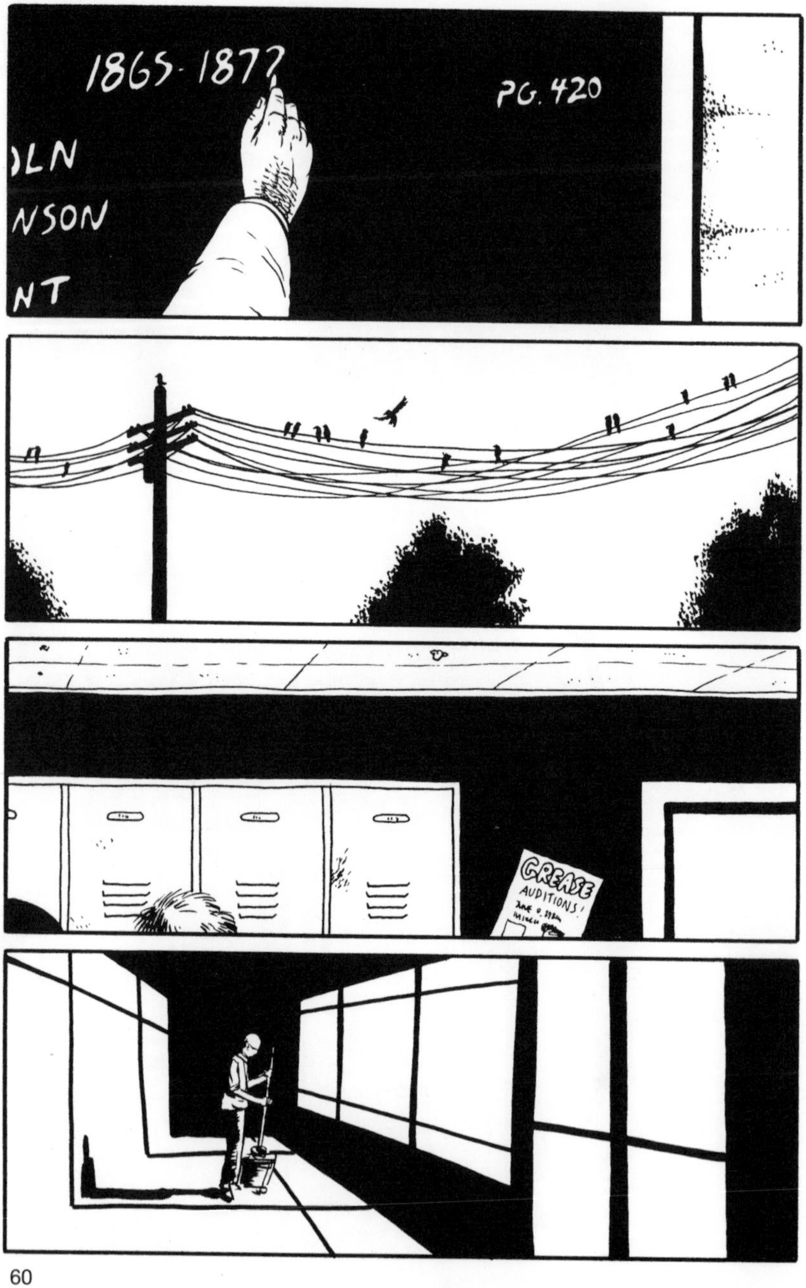
1865-1877
PG. 420
OLN
NSON
NT
GREASE
AUDITIONS!

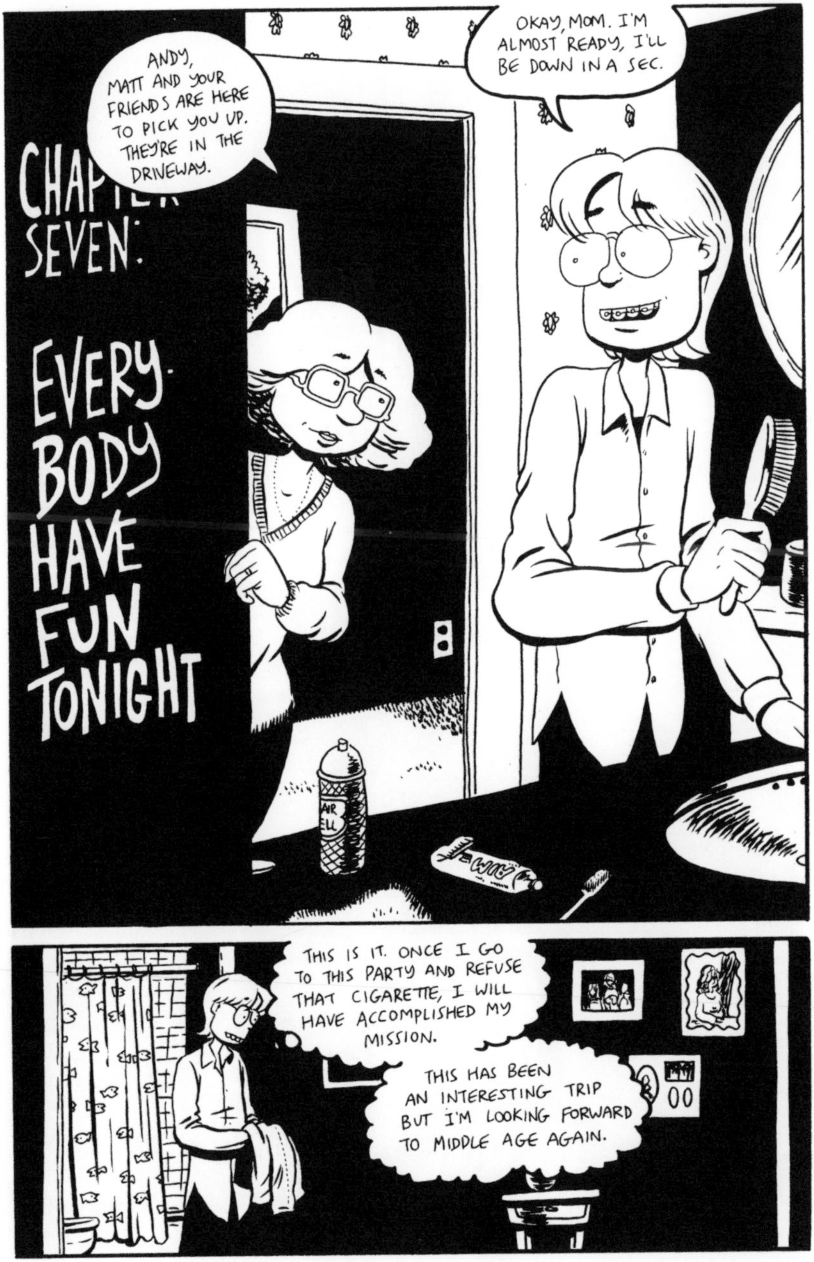
CHAPTER SEVEN:
EVERY-BODY HAVE FUN TONIGHT
ANDY, MATT AND YOUR FRIENDS ARE HERE TO PICK YOU UP. THEY'RE IN THE DRIVEWAY.
OKAY, MOM. I'M ALMOST READY, I'LL BE DOWN IN A SEC.
THIS IS IT. ONCE I GO TO THIS PARTY AND REFUSE THAT CIGARETTE, I WILL HAVE ACCOMPLISHED MY MISSION.
THIS HAS BEEN AN INTERESTING TRIP BUT I'M LOOKING FORWARD TO MIDDLE AGE AGAIN.

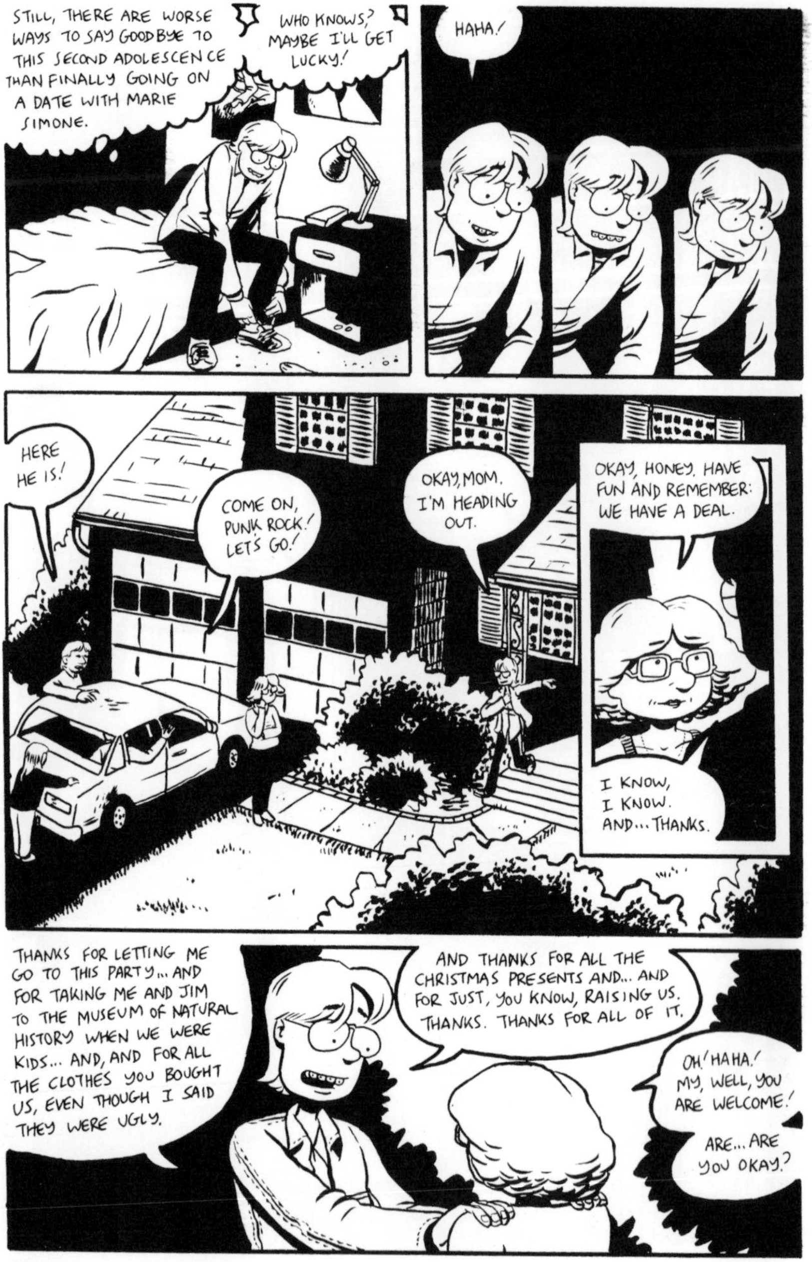

STILL, THERE ARE WORSE WAYS TO SAY GOODBYE TO THIS SECOND ADOLESCENCE THAN FINALLY GOING ON A DATE WITH MARIE SIMONE.
WHO KNOWS? MAYBE I'LL GET LUCKY!
HAHA!
HERE HE IS!
COME ON, PUNK ROCK! LET'S GO!
OKAY, MOM. I'M HEADING OUT.
OKAY, HONEY. HAVE FUN AND REMEMBER: WE HAVE A DEAL.
I KNOW, I KNOW. AND... THANKS.
THANKS FOR LETTING ME GO TO THIS PARTY... AND FOR TAKING ME AND JIM TO THE MUSEUM OF NATURAL HISTORY WHEN WE WERE KIDS... AND, AND FOR ALL THE CLOTHES YOU BOUGHT US, EVEN THOUGH I SAID THEY WERE UGLY.
AND THANKS FOR ALL THE CHRISTMAS PRESENTS AND... AND FOR JUST, YOU KNOW, RAISING US. THANKS. THANKS FOR ALL OF IT.
OH! HAHA! MY, WELL, YOU ARE WELCOME!
ARE... ARE YOU OKAY?

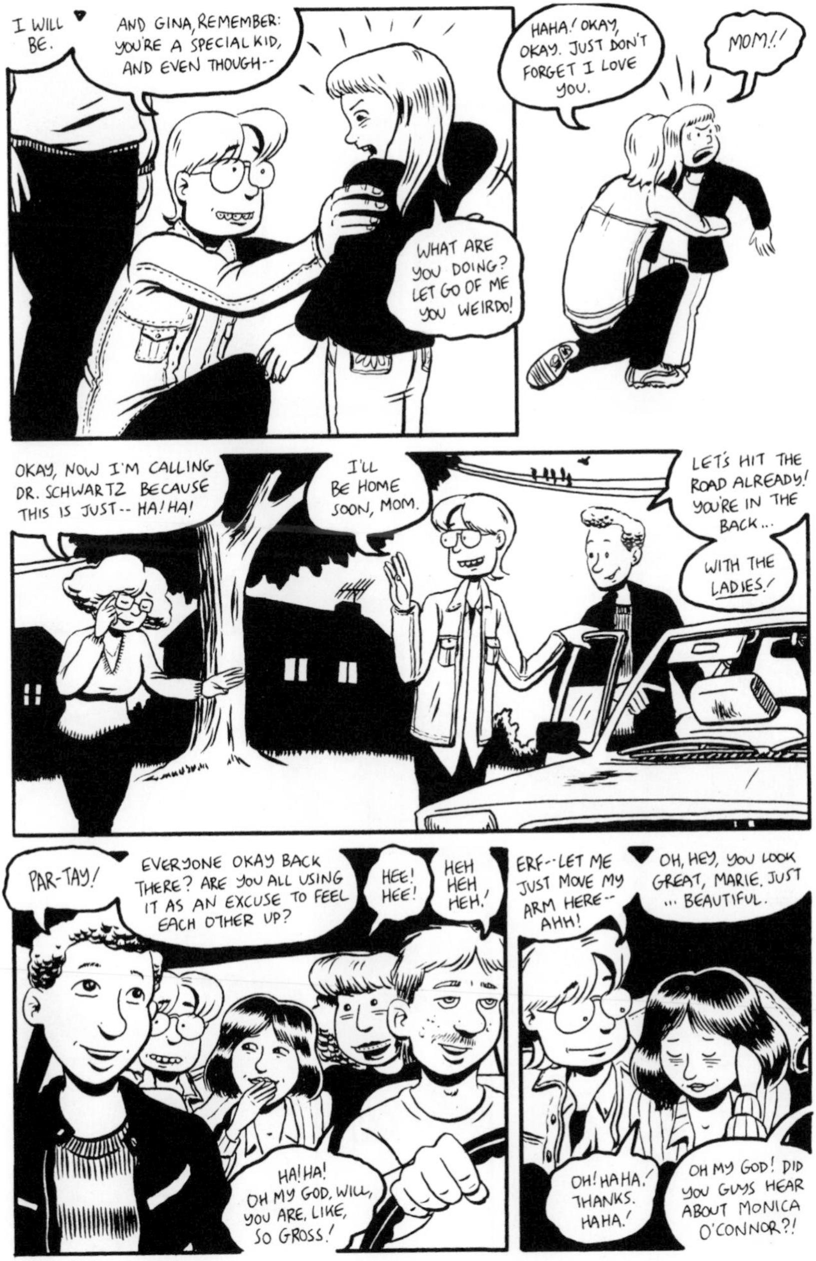
I WILL BE.
AND GINA, REMEMBER: YOU'RE A SPECIAL KID, AND EVEN THOUGH--
WHAT ARE YOU DOING? LET GO OF ME YOU WEIRDO!
HAHA! OKAY, OKAY. JUST DON'T FORGET I LOVE YOU.
MOM!!
OKAY, NOW I'M CALLING DR. SCHWARTZ BECAUSE THIS IS JUST-- HA! HA!
I'LL BE HOME SOON, MOM.
LET'S HIT THE ROAD ALREADY! YOU'RE IN THE BACK...
WITH THE LADIES!
PAR-TAY!
EVERYONE OKAY BACK THERE? ARE YOU ALL USING IT AS AN EXCUSE TO FEEL EACH OTHER UP?
HEE! HEE!
HEH HEH HEH!
HA! HA! OH MY GOD, WILL, YOU ARE, LIKE, SO GROSS!
ERF--LET ME JUST MOVE MY ARM HERE-- AHH!
OH, HEY, YOU LOOK GREAT, MARIE. JUST ... BEAUTIFUL.
OH! HAHA! THANKS. HAHA!
OH MY GOD! DID YOU GUYS HEAR ABOUT MONICA O'CONNOR?!

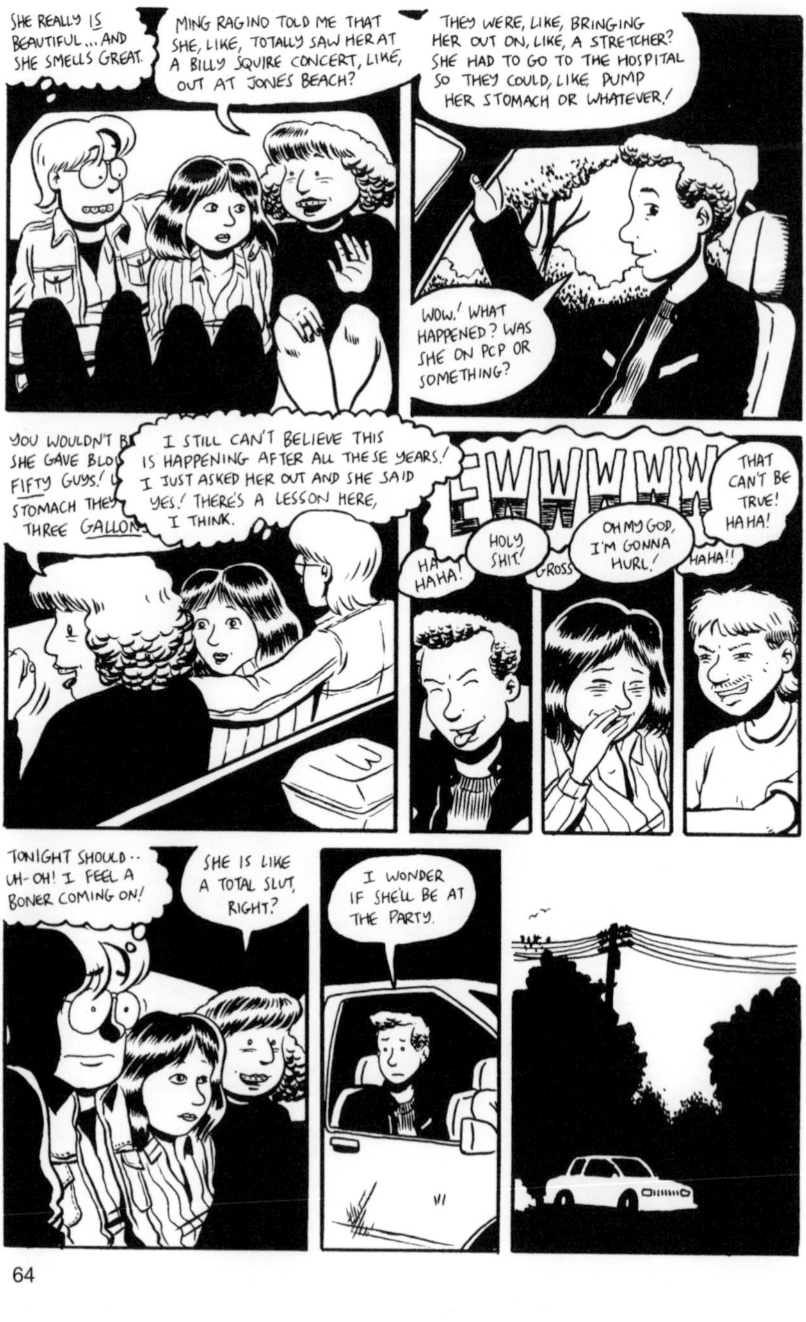
SHE REALLY IS BEAUTIFUL... AND SHE SMELLS GREAT.
MING RAGINO TOLD ME THAT SHE, LIKE, TOTALLY SAW HER AT A BILLY SQUIRE CONCERT, LIKE, OUT AT JONES BEACH?
THEY WERE, LIKE, BRINGING HER OUT ON, LIKE, A STRETCHER? SHE HAD TO GO TO THE HOSPITAL SO THEY COULD, LIKE, PUMP HER STOMACH OR WHATEVER!
WOW! WHAT HAPPENED? WAS SHE ON PCP OR SOMETHING?
YOU WOULDN'T
SHE GAVE
FIFTY GUYS!
STOMACH
THREE
I STILL CAN'T BELIEVE THIS IS HAPPENING AFTER ALL THESE YEARS! I JUST ASKED HER OUT AND SHE SAID YES! THERE'S A LESSON HERE, I THINK.
EWWWWW
THAT CAN'T BE TRUE! HAHA!
HA HAHA!
HOLY SHIT!
GROSS
OH MY GOD, I'M GONNA HURL!
HAHA!!
TONIGHT SHOULD.. UH-OH! I FEEL A BONER COMING ON!
SHE IS LIKE A TOTAL SLUT, RIGHT?
I WONDER IF SHE'LL BE AT THE PARTY.

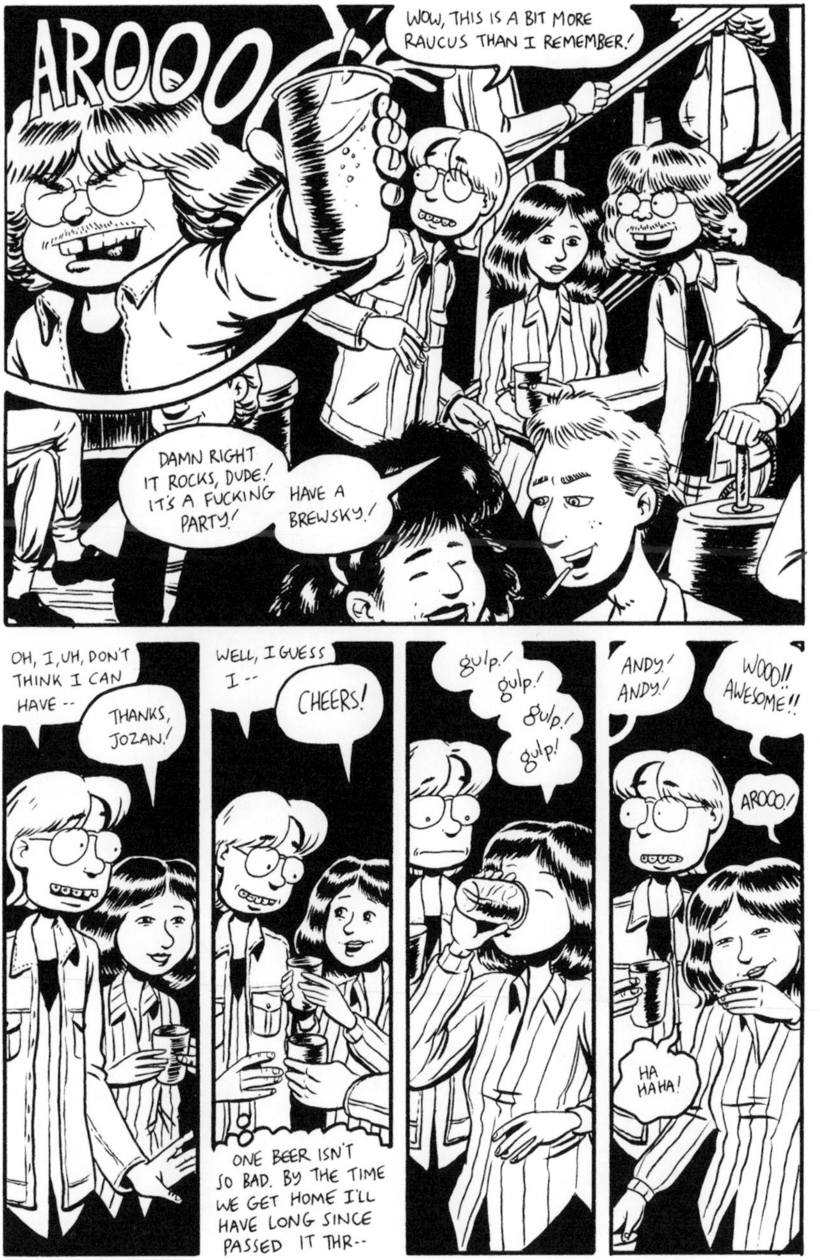
AROOO
WOW, THIS IS A BIT MORE RAUCUS THAN I REMEMBER!
DAMN RIGHT IT ROCKS, DUDE! IT'S A FUCKING PARTY!
HAVE A BREWSKY!
OH, I, UH, DON'T THINK I CAN HAVE --
THANKS, JOZAN!
WELL, I GUESS I --
CHEERS!
ONE BEER ISN'T SO BAD. BY THE TIME WE GET HOME I'LL HAVE LONG SINCE PASSED IT THR--
gulp! gulp! gulp! gulp!
ANDY! ANDY!
WOOO!! AWESOME!!
AROOO!
HA HAHA!

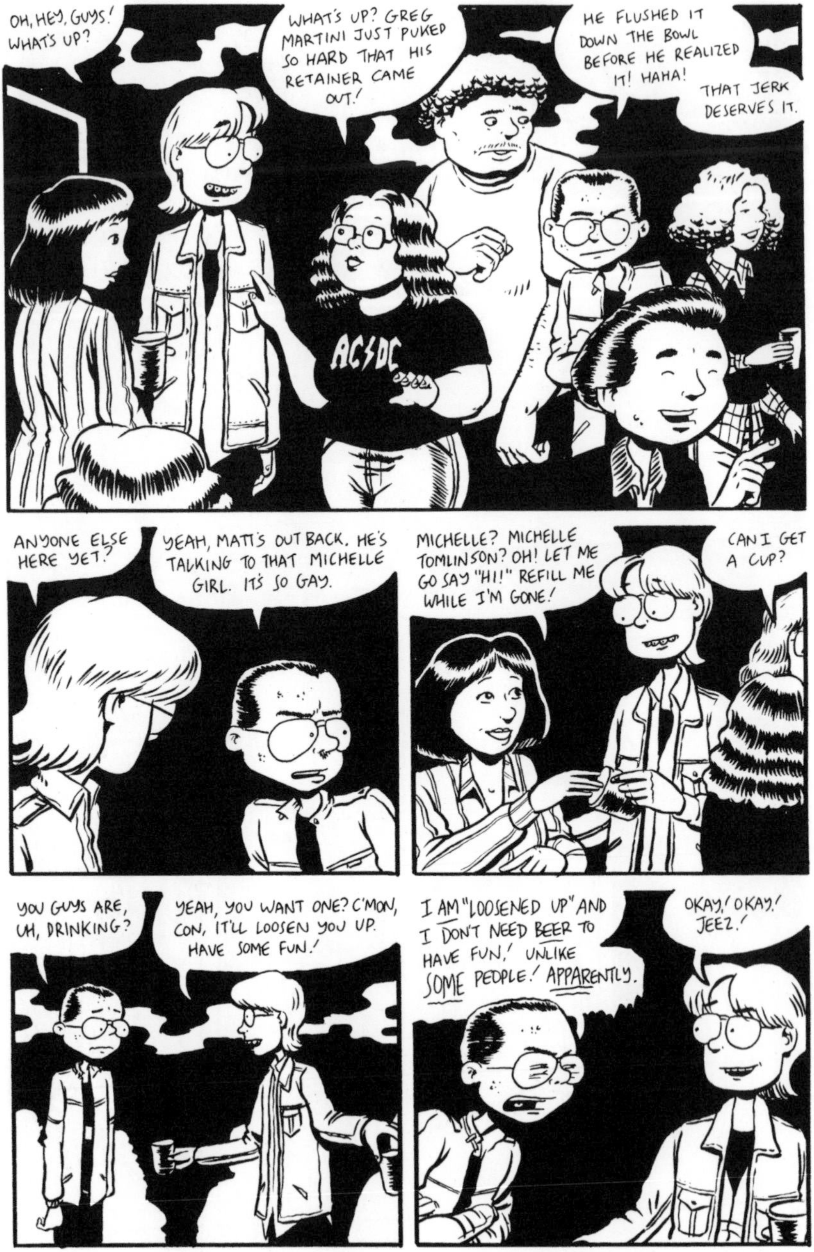
OH, HEY, GUYS! WHAT'S UP?
WHAT'S UP? GREG MARTINI JUST PUKED SO HARD THAT HIS RETAINER CAME OUT!
HE FLUSHED IT DOWN THE BOWL BEFORE HE REALIZED IT! HAHA!
THAT JERK DESERVES IT.
AC/DC
ANYONE ELSE HERE YET?
YEAH, MATT'S OUT BACK. HE'S TALKING TO THAT MICHELLE GIRL. IT'S SO GAY.
MICHELLE? MICHELLE TOMLINSON? OH! LET ME GO SAY "HI!" REFILL ME WHILE I'M GONE!
CAN I GET A CUP?
YOU GUYS ARE, UH, DRINKING?
YEAH, YOU WANT ONE? C'MON, CON, IT'LL LOOSEN YOU UP. HAVE SOME FUN!
I AM "LOOSENED UP" AND I DON'T NEED BEER TO HAVE FUN! UNLIKE SOME PEOPLE! APPARENTLY.
OKAY! OKAY! JEEZ!

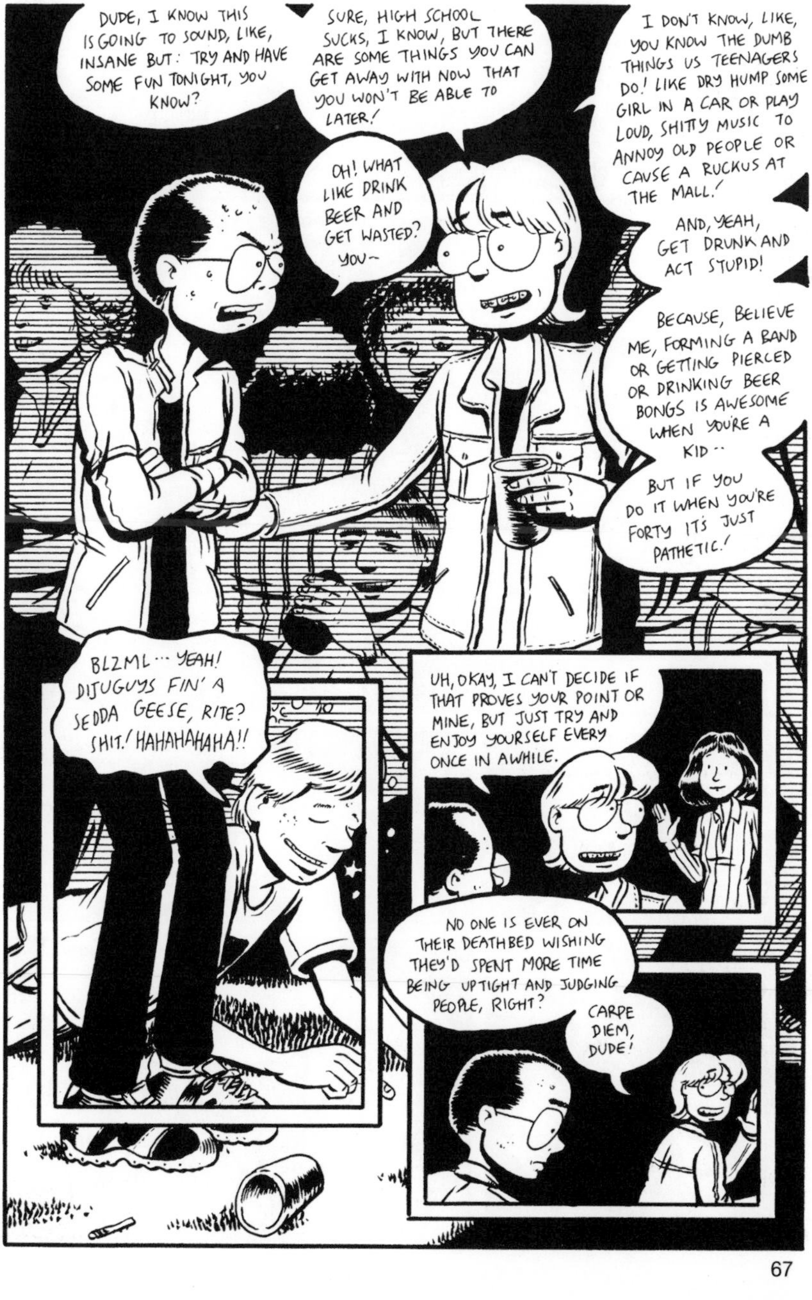
DUDE, I KNOW THIS IS GOING TO SOUND, LIKE, INSANE BUT: TRY AND HAVE SOME FUN TONIGHT, YOU KNOW?
SURE, HIGH SCHOOL SUCKS, I KNOW, BUT THERE ARE SOME THINGS YOU CAN GET AWAY WITH NOW THAT YOU WON'T BE ABLE TO LATER!
OH! WHAT LIKE DRINK BEER AND GET WASTED? YOU~
I DON'T KNOW, LIKE, YOU KNOW THE DUMB THINGS US TEENAGERS DO! LIKE DRY HUMP SOME GIRL IN A CAR OR PLAY LOUD, SHITTY MUSIC TO ANNOY OLD PEOPLE OR CAUSE A RUCKUS AT THE MALL!
AND, YEAH, GET DRUNK AND ACT STUPID!
BECAUSE, BELIEVE ME, FORMING A BAND OR GETTING PIERCED OR DRINKING BEER BONGS IS AWESOME WHEN YOU'RE A KID..
BUT IF YOU DO IT WHEN YOU'RE FORTY IT'S JUST PATHETIC!
BLZML... YEAH! DIJUGUYS FIN' A SEDDA GEESE, RITE? SHIT! HAHAHAHAHA!!
UH, OKAY, I CAN'T DECIDE IF THAT PROVES YOUR POINT OR MINE, BUT JUST TRY AND ENJOY YOURSELF EVERY ONCE IN AWHILE.
NO ONE IS EVER ON THEIR DEATHBED WISHING THEY'D SPENT MORE TIME BEING UPTIGHT AND JUDGING PEOPLE, RIGHT?
CARPE DIEM, DUDE!

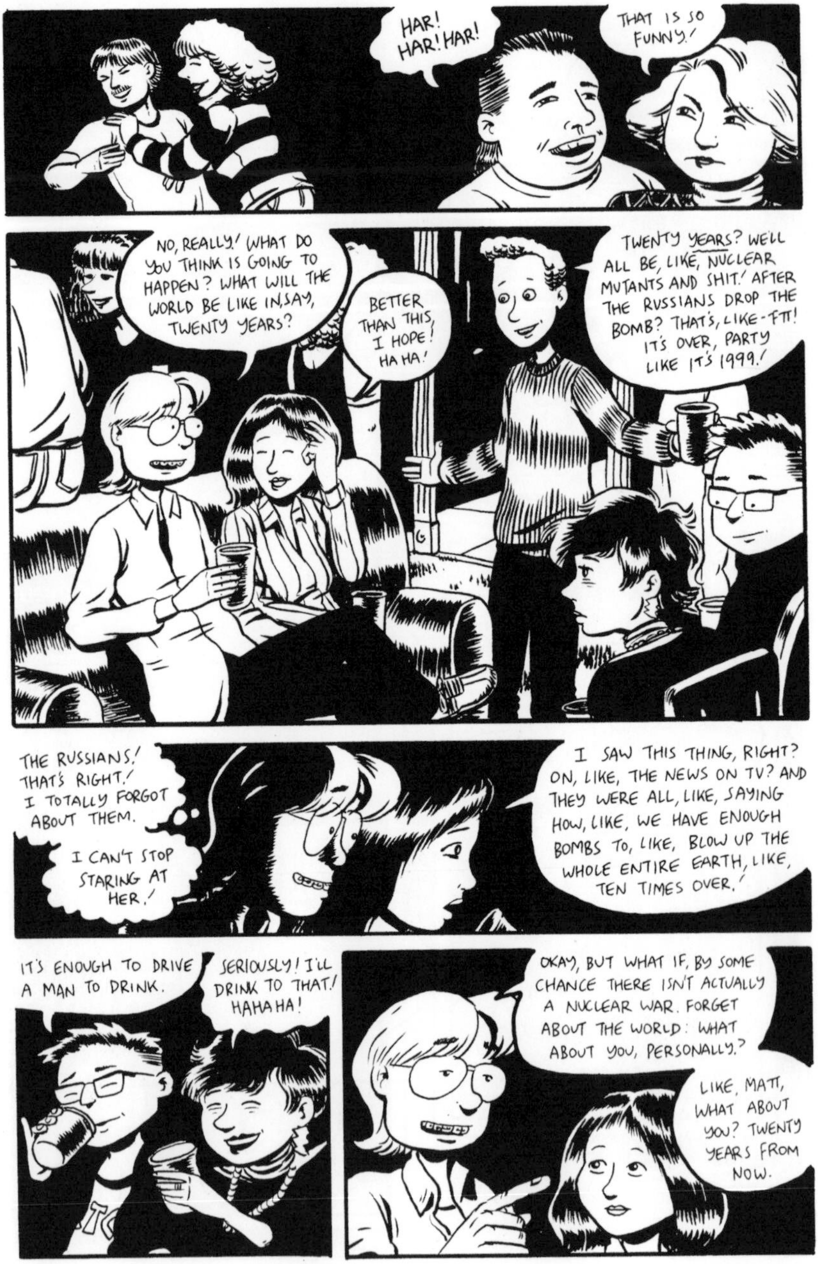
HAR! HAR! HAR!
THAT IS SO FUNNY!
NO, REALLY! WHAT DO YOU THINK IS GOING TO HAPPEN? WHAT WILL THE WORLD BE LIKE IN, SAY, TWENTY YEARS?
BETTER THAN THIS, I HOPE! HA HA!
TWENTY YEARS? WE'LL ALL BE, LIKE, NUCLEAR MUTANTS AND SHIT! AFTER THE RUSSIANS DROP THE BOMB? THAT'S, LIKE-FTT! IT'S OVER, PARTY LIKE IT'S 1999!
THE RUSSIANS! THAT'S RIGHT! I TOTALLY FORGOT ABOUT THEM.
I CAN'T STOP STARING AT HER!
I SAW THIS THING, RIGHT? ON, LIKE, THE NEWS ON TV? AND THEY WERE ALL, LIKE, SAYING HOW, LIKE, WE HAVE ENOUGH BOMBS TO, LIKE, BLOW UP THE WHOLE ENTIRE EARTH, LIKE, TEN TIMES OVER!
IT'S ENOUGH TO DRIVE A MAN TO DRINK.
SERIOUSLY! I'LL DRINK TO THAT! HAHAHA!
OKAY, BUT WHAT IF, BY SOME CHANCE THERE ISN'T ACTUALLY A NUCLEAR WAR. FORGET ABOUT THE WORLD: WHAT ABOUT YOU, PERSONALLY?
LIKE, MATT, WHAT ABOUT YOU? TWENTY YEARS FROM NOW.

TWENTY YEARS? GOD, I HAVE NO IDEA. I'D BE... THIRTY-SIX? SO I'LL PROBABLY BE ON MY THIRD WIFE AND SIXTH KID. (THAT I KNOW OF.)

THAT WOULD BE, LIKE, 2005! IT'S GONNA BE ALL, LIKE, THE JETSONS BY THEN, RIGHT?

OH, COME ON, MATTY, THAT'S TOTAL BULLSHIT! YOU KNOW THAT BY THEN YOU'LL BE A FAMOUS HOITY-TOITY BIG-SHOT WRITER.

THEY'LL PROBABLY BE FILMING THE SEQUEL TO THE "HIDDEN CAVERNS" MOVIE TWENTY YEARS FROM NOW.

(IF THEY EVEN MAKE MOVIES ANY MORE!)

"HIDDEN CAVERNS!" THAT WAS THE HUGE FANTASY EPIC MATT WAS WRITING ALL THROUGH SCHOOL! WE ALL COULDN'T WAIT TO READ THE NEXT CHAPTER!

JUST THIS THING. IT'S NOT A BIG DEAL.

YOU TOTALLY HAVE TO SHOW IT TO ME! OH MY GOD!

FROM WHAT I REMEMBER IT WAS PRETTY GOOD. I WONDER IF IT WOULD HOLD UP?

NOW THAT I THINK ABOUT IT, MATT WAS ALWAYS THE BRIGHTEST MEMBER OF OUR LITTLE NERD GANG. HE WAS ALWAYS AHEAD OF THE CURVE, DISCOVERING THE COOL...

HEY.

HUH? WHAT?

LET'S GO GET SOME MORE DRINKS.

⌐..ɔ̌ɔ AHEM!

OKAY!

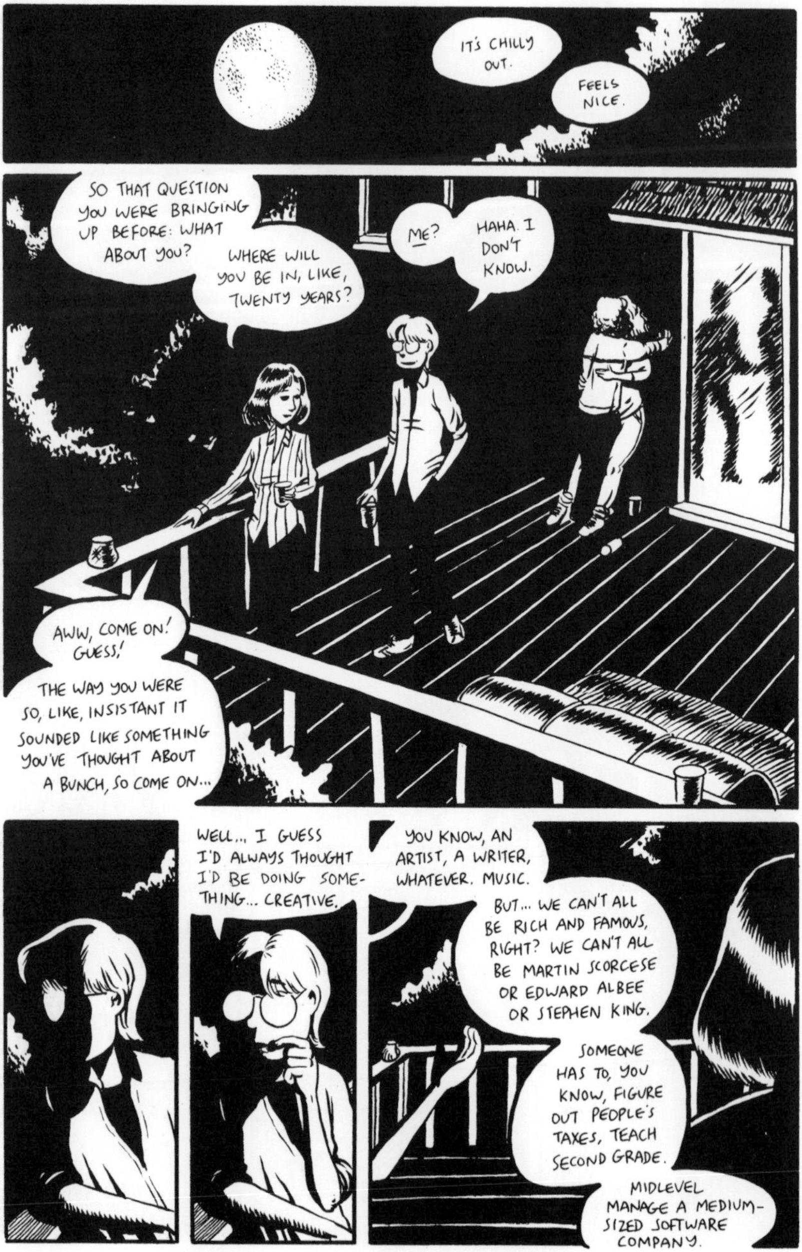
IT'S CHILLY OUT.
FEELS NICE.
SO THAT QUESTION YOU WERE BRINGING UP BEFORE: WHAT ABOUT YOU?
WHERE WILL YOU BE IN, LIKE, TWENTY YEARS?
ME?
HAHA. I DON'T KNOW.
AWW, COME ON! GUESS!
THE WAY YOU WERE SO, LIKE, INSISTANT IT SOUNDED LIKE SOMETHING YOU'VE THOUGHT ABOUT A BUNCH, SO COME ON...
WELL... I GUESS I'D ALWAYS THOUGHT I'D BE DOING SOMETHING... CREATIVE.
YOU KNOW, AN ARTIST, A WRITER, WHATEVER. MUSIC.
BUT... WE CAN'T ALL BE RICH AND FAMOUS, RIGHT? WE CAN'T ALL BE MARTIN SCORCESE OR EDWARD ALBEE OR STEPHEN KING.
SOMEONE HAS TO, YOU KNOW, FIGURE OUT PEOPLE'S TAXES, TEACH SECOND GRADE.
MIDLEVEL MANAGE A MEDIUM-SIZED SOFTWARE COMPANY.

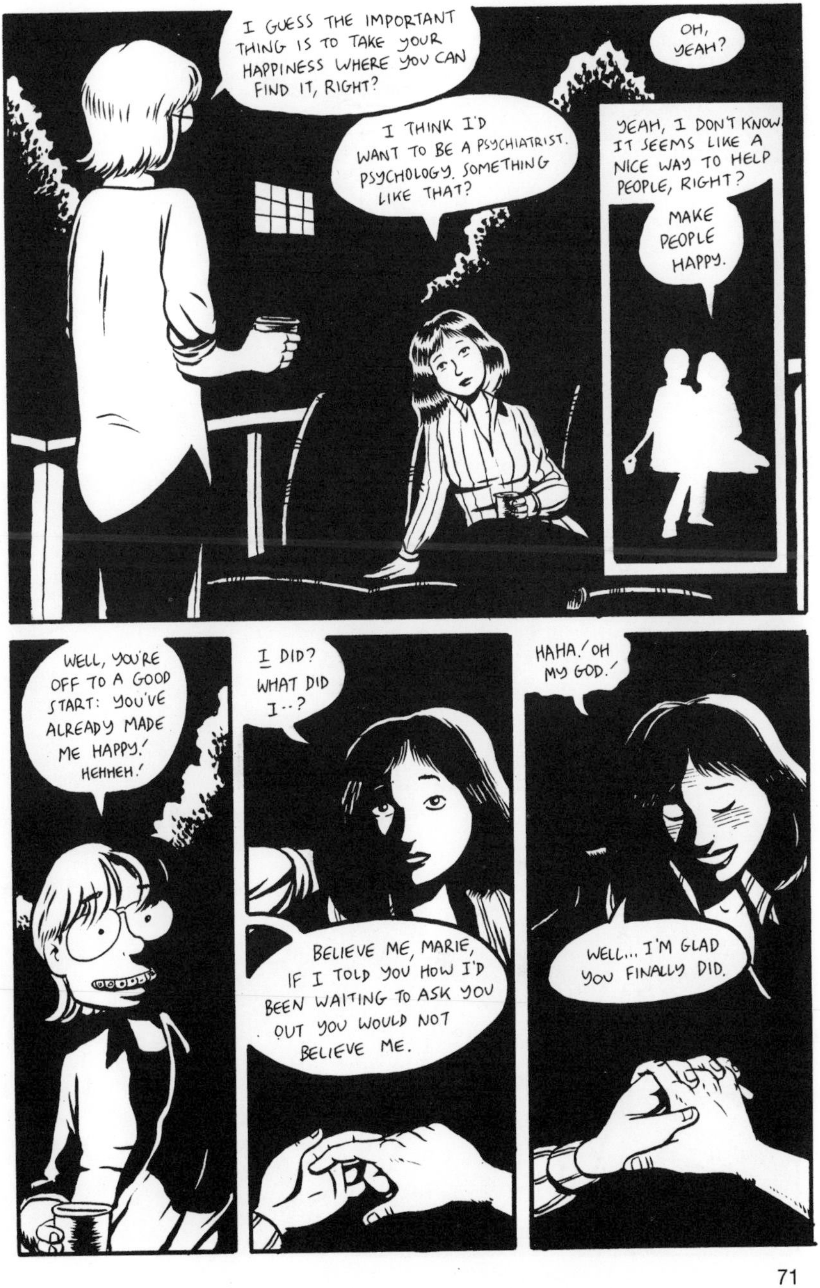
I GUESS THE IMPORTANT THING IS TO TAKE YOUR HAPPINESS WHERE YOU CAN FIND IT, RIGHT?
OH, YEAH?
I THINK I'D WANT TO BE A PSYCHIATRIST. PSYCHOLOGY. SOMETHING LIKE THAT?
YEAH, I DON'T KNOW. IT SEEMS LIKE A NICE WAY TO HELP PEOPLE, RIGHT?
MAKE PEOPLE HAPPY.
WELL, YOU'RE OFF TO A GOOD START: YOU'VE ALREADY MADE ME HAPPY! HEHHEH!
I DID? WHAT DID I--?
BELIEVE ME, MARIE, IF I TOLD YOU HOW I'D BEEN WAITING TO ASK YOU OUT YOU WOULD NOT BELIEVE ME.
HAHA! OH MY GOD!
WELL... I'M GLAD YOU FINALLY DID.

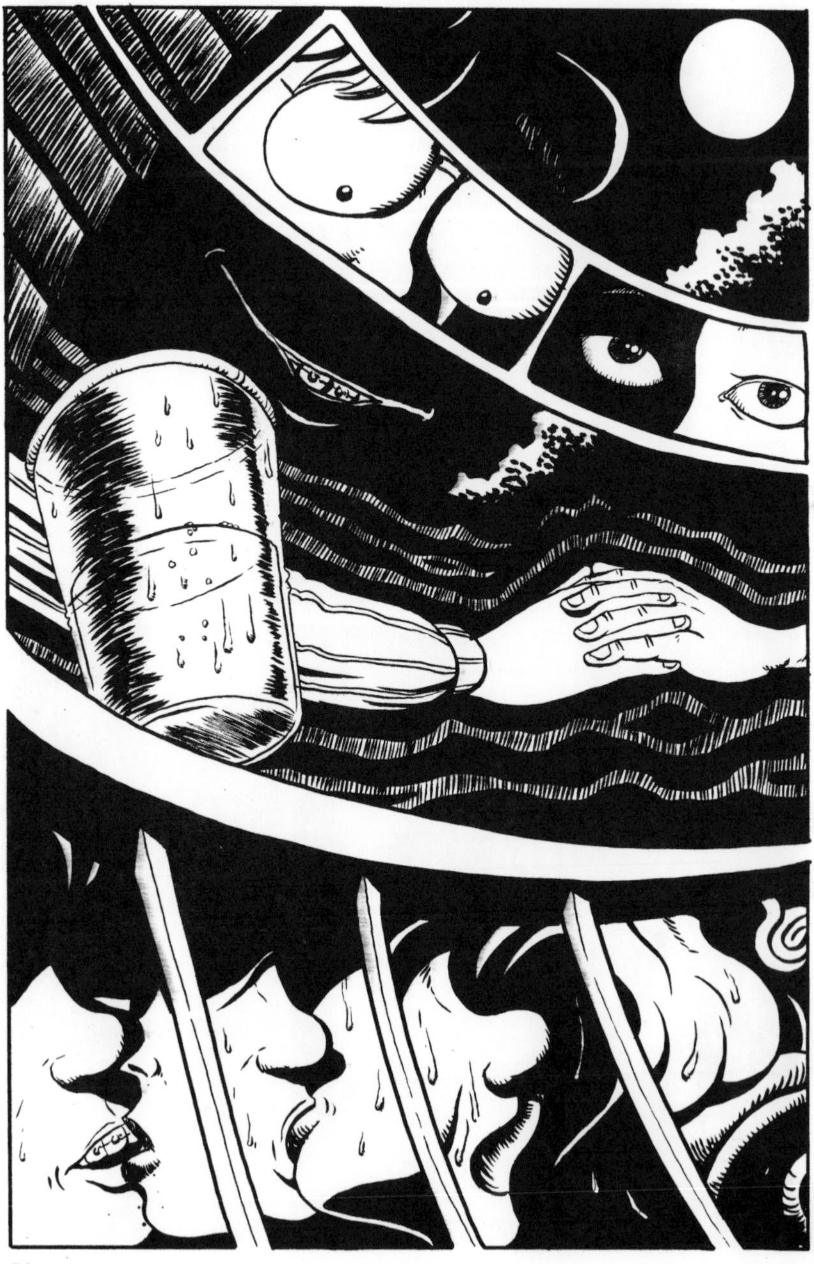

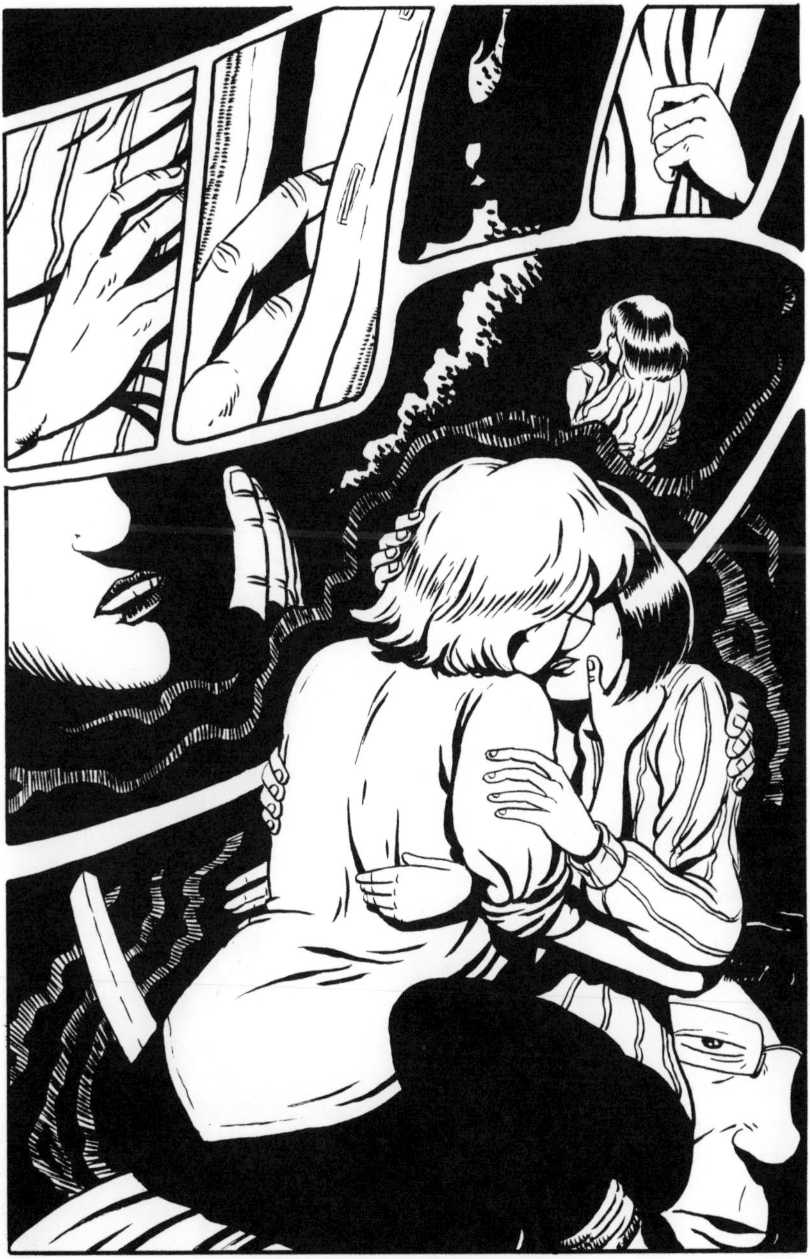

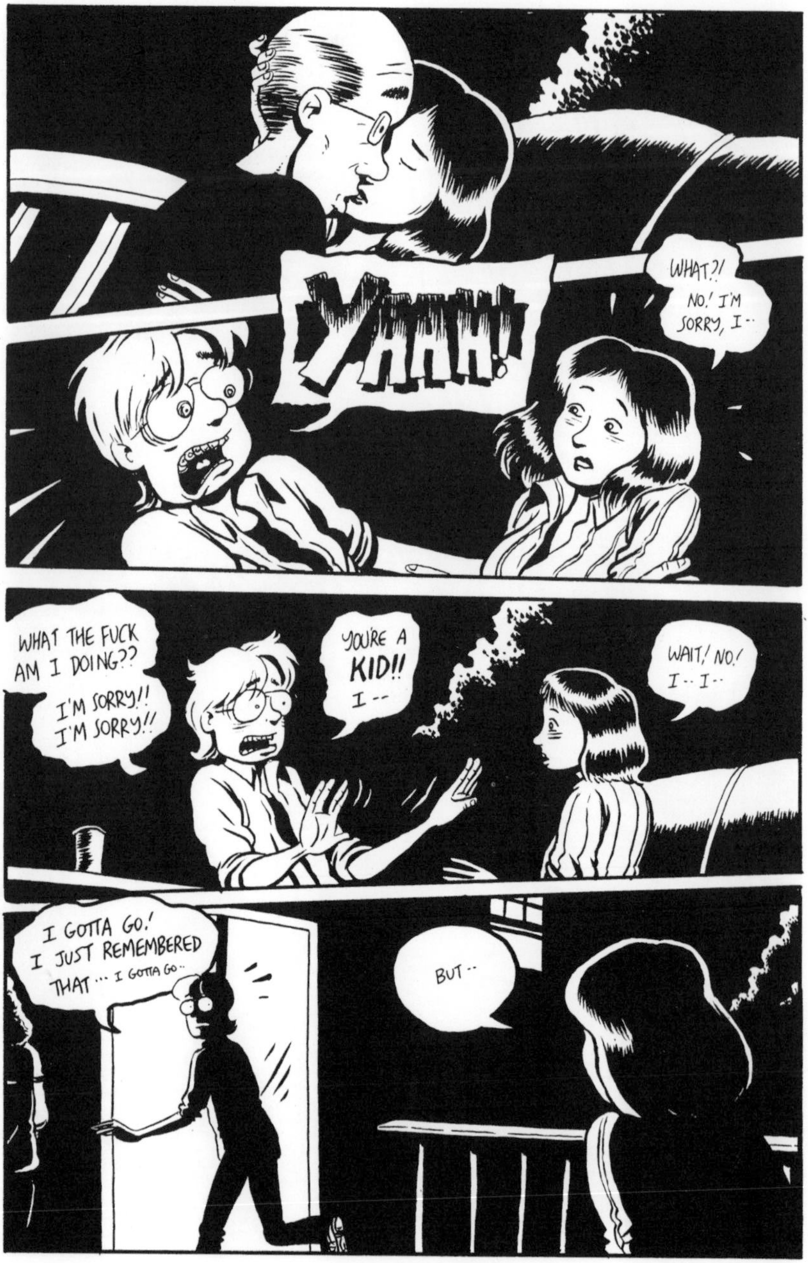
YAAH!!
WHAT?! NO! I'M SORRY, I--
WHAT THE FUCK AM I DOING?? I'M SORRY!! I'M SORRY!!
YOU'RE A KID!! I--
WAIT! NO! I-- I--
I GOTTA GO! I JUST REMEMBERED THAT... I GOTTA GO..
BUT--

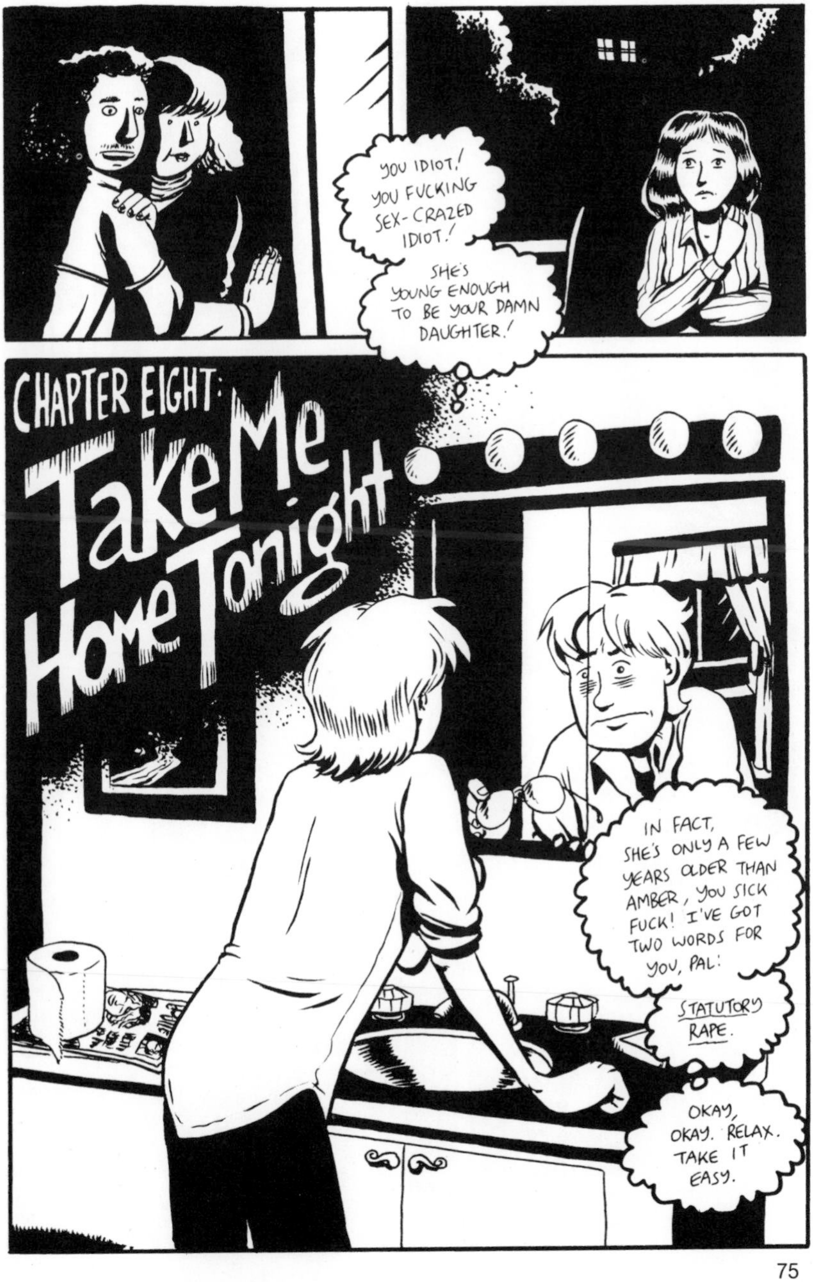
YOU IDIOT! YOU FUCKING SEX-CRAZED IDIOT!
SHE'S YOUNG ENOUGH TO BE YOUR DAMN DAUGHTER!
CHAPTER EIGHT:
Take Me Home Tonight
IN FACT, SHE'S ONLY A FEW YEARS OLDER THAN AMBER, YOU SICK FUCK! I'VE GOT TWO WORDS FOR YOU, PAL:
STATUTORY RAPE.
OKAY, OKAY. RELAX. TAKE IT EASY.

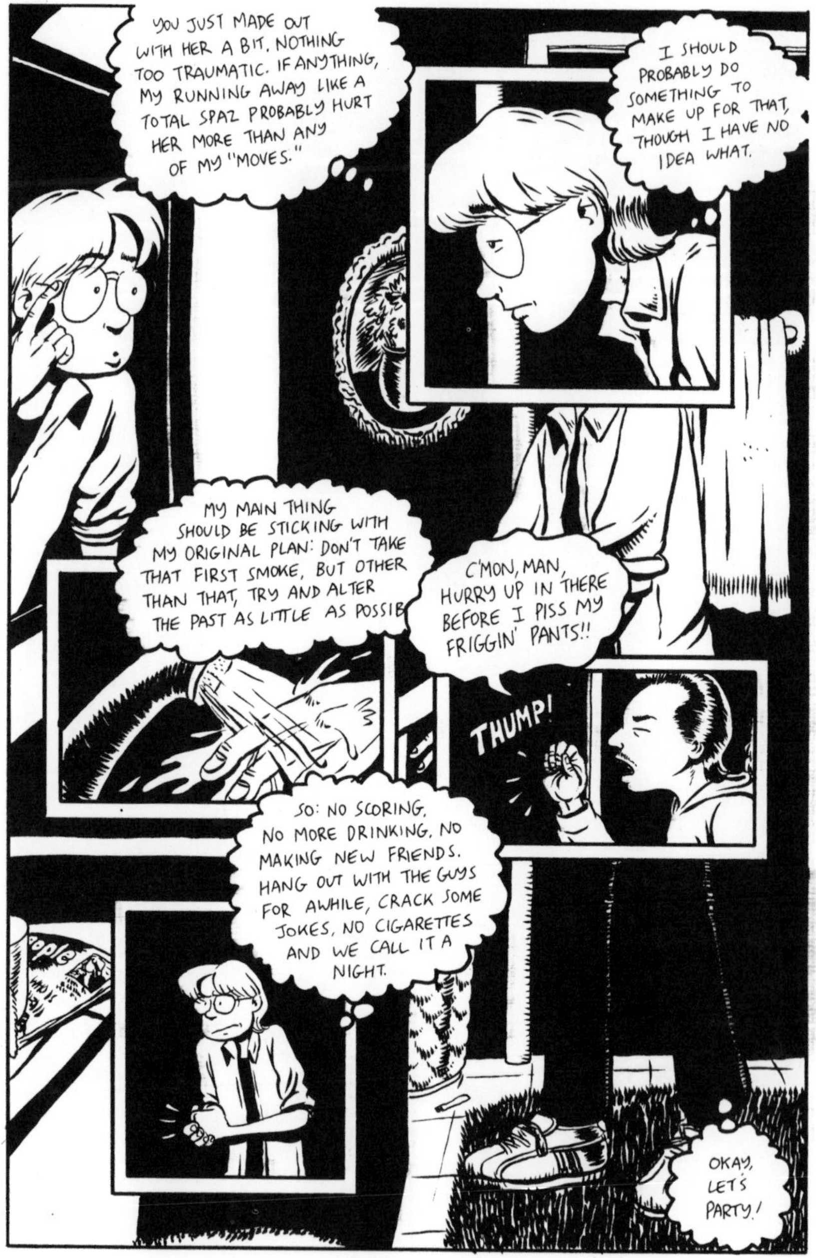
YOU JUST MADE OUT WITH HER A BIT. NOTHING TOO TRAUMATIC. IF ANYTHING, MY RUNNING AWAY LIKE A TOTAL SPAZ PROBABLY HURT HER MORE THAN ANY OF MY "MOVES."
I SHOULD PROBABLY DO SOMETHING TO MAKE UP FOR THAT, THOUGH I HAVE NO IDEA WHAT.
MY MAIN THING SHOULD BE STICKING WITH MY ORIGINAL PLAN: DON'T TAKE THAT FIRST SMOKE, BUT OTHER THAN THAT, TRY AND ALTER THE PAST AS LITTLE AS POSSIB
C'MON, MAN, HURRY UP IN THERE BEFORE I PISS MY FRIGGIN' PANTS!!
THUMP!
SO: NO SCORING, NO MORE DRINKING, NO MAKING NEW FRIENDS. HANG OUT WITH THE GUYS FOR AWHILE, CRACK SOME JOKES, NO CIGARETTES AND WE CALL IT A NIGHT.
OKAY, LET'S PARTY!

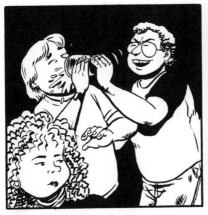

IT WILL BE NICE TO BE HOME AND HAVE SOME NORMAL ADULT CONVERSATION AGAIN. EVEN THE MOST SOPHISTICATED TEENAGER IS STILL A TEENAGER.

T.V. AND MOVIES CAN MAKE YOU FORGET HOW AWKWARD AND... UNFORMED THEY ARE. MAYBE A REALISTIC PORTRAYAL WOULD BE TOO BORING... OR TOO PAINFUL.

HAS THE SONG "PARENTS JUST DON'T UNDERSTAND" COME OUT YET? I THINK WE ACTUALLY DO UNDERSTAND BUT WILLFULLY BLOCK IT OUT. MAYBE WE UNCONSCIOUSLY REPLACE IT ALL WITH MEMORIES FROM "FAMILY TIES" OR "HAPPY DAYS."

IF NOTHING ELSE, MAYBE THIS WHOLE TRIP WILL HELP ME COPE WHEN AMBER AND SOPH ENTER THEIR OWN YEARS OF DRAMA AND ANGST.

HEY! SPEAKING OF WHICH, WHAT'S UP, CON?

NOTHING. I CALLED MY MOM. SHE'S PICKING ME UP IN HALF AN HOUR.

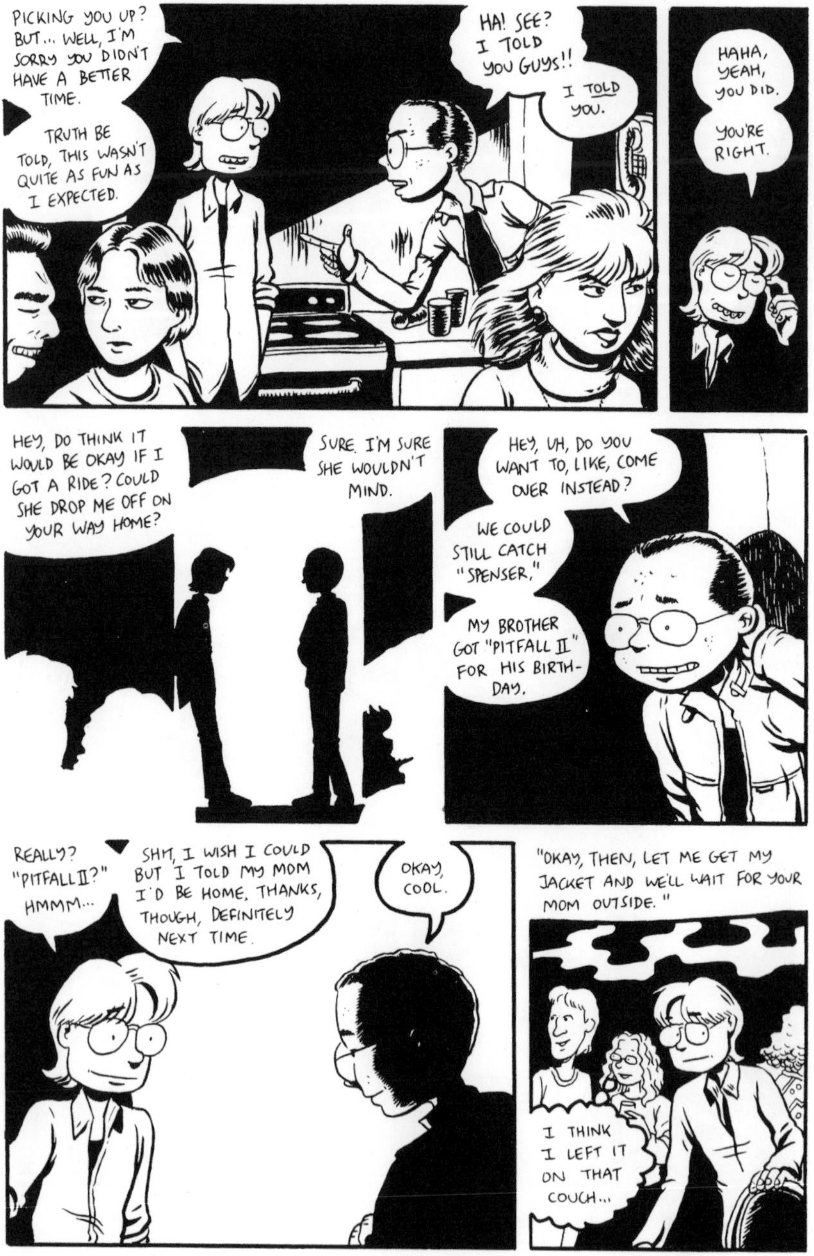
PICKING YOU UP? BUT... WELL, I'M SORRY YOU DIDN'T HAVE A BETTER TIME.
TRUTH BE TOLD, THIS WASN'T QUITE AS FUN AS I EXPECTED.
HA! SEE? I TOLD YOU GUYS!!
I TOLD YOU.
HAHA, YEAH, YOU DID.
YOU'RE RIGHT.
HEY, DO THINK IT WOULD BE OKAY IF I GOT A RIDE? COULD SHE DROP ME OFF ON YOUR WAY HOME?
SURE. I'M SURE SHE WOULDN'T MIND.
HEY, UH, DO YOU WANT TO, LIKE, COME OVER INSTEAD?
WE COULD STILL CATCH "SPENSER."
MY BROTHER GOT "PITFALL II" FOR HIS BIRTHDAY.
REALLY? "PITFALL II?" HMMM...
SHIT, I WISH I COULD BUT I TOLD MY MOM I'D BE HOME. THANKS, THOUGH, DEFINITELY NEXT TIME.
OKAY, COOL.
"OKAY, THEN, LET ME GET MY JACKET AND WE'LL WAIT FOR YOUR MOM OUTSIDE."
I THINK I LEFT IT ON THAT COUCH...

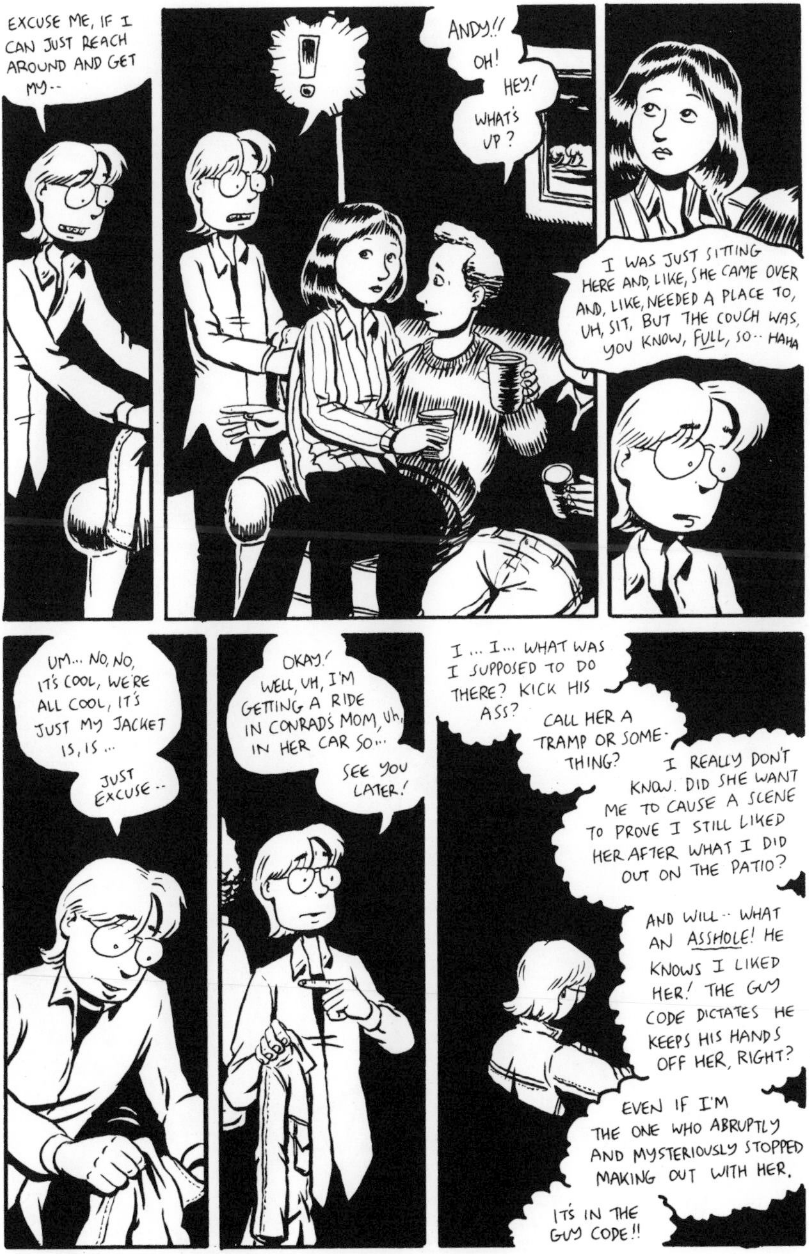
EXCUSE ME, IF I CAN JUST REACH AROUND AND GET MY--
!
ANDY!!
OH!
HEY!
WHAT'S UP?
I WAS JUST SITTING HERE AND, LIKE, SHE CAME OVER AND, LIKE, NEEDED A PLACE TO, UH, SIT, BUT THE COUCH WAS, YOU KNOW, FULL, SO-- HAHA
UM... NO, NO, IT'S COOL, WE'RE ALL COOL, IT'S JUST MY JACKET IS, IS...
JUST EXCUSE--
OKAY! WELL, UH, I'M GETTING A RIDE IN CONRAD'S MOM, UH, IN HER CAR SO...
SEE YOU LATER!
I... I... WHAT WAS I SUPPOSED TO DO THERE? KICK HIS ASS?
CALL HER A TRAMP OR SOMETHING?
I REALLY DON'T KNOW. DID SHE WANT ME TO CAUSE A SCENE TO PROVE I STILL LIKED HER AFTER WHAT I DID OUT ON THE PATIO?
AND WILL-- WHAT AN ASSHOLE! HE KNOWS I LIKED HER! THE GUY CODE DICTATES HE KEEPS HIS HANDS OFF HER, RIGHT?
EVEN IF I'M THE ONE WHO ABRUPTLY AND MYSTERIOUSLY STOPPED MAKING OUT WITH HER.
IT'S IN THE GUY CODE!!

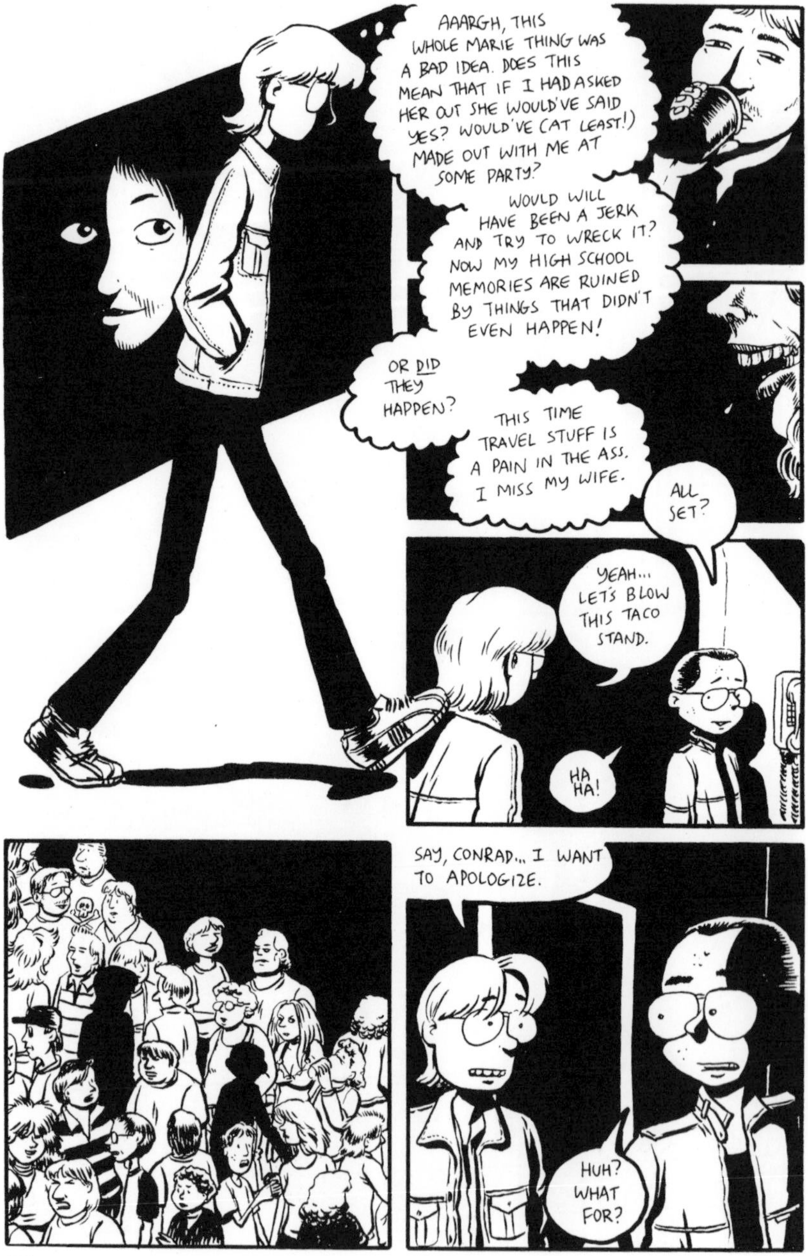
AAARGH, THIS WHOLE MARIE THING WAS A BAD IDEA. DOES THIS MEAN THAT IF I HAD ASKED HER OUT SHE WOULD'VE SAID YES? WOULD'VE (AT LEAST!) MADE OUT WITH ME AT SOME PARTY?
WOULD WILL HAVE BEEN A JERK AND TRY TO WRECK IT? NOW MY HIGH SCHOOL MEMORIES ARE RUINED BY THINGS THAT DIDN'T EVEN HAPPEN!
OR DID THEY HAPPEN?
THIS TIME TRAVEL STUFF IS A PAIN IN THE ASS. I MISS MY WIFE.
ALL SET?
YEAH... LET'S BLOW THIS TACO STAND.
HA HA!
SAY, CONRAD... I WANT TO APOLOGIZE.
HUH? WHAT FOR?

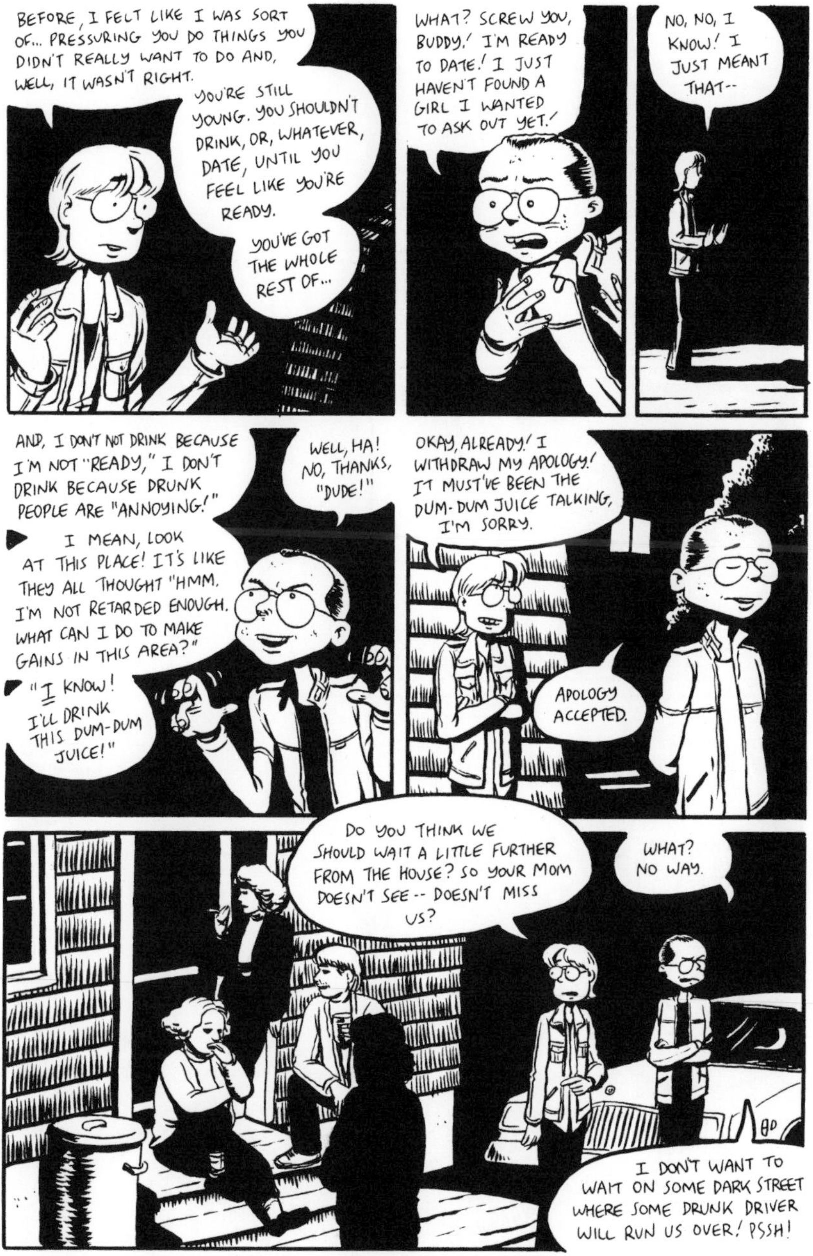
BEFORE, I FELT LIKE I WAS SORT OF... PRESSURING YOU DO THINGS YOU DIDN'T REALLY WANT TO DO AND, WELL, IT WASN'T RIGHT.
YOU'RE STILL YOUNG. YOU SHOULDN'T DRINK, OR, WHATEVER, DATE, UNTIL YOU FEEL LIKE YOU'RE READY.
YOU'VE GOT THE WHOLE REST OF...
WHAT? SCREW YOU, BUDDY! I'M READY TO DATE! I JUST HAVEN'T FOUND A GIRL I WANTED TO ASK OUT YET!
NO, NO, I KNOW! I JUST MEANT THAT--
AND, I DON'T NOT DRINK BECAUSE I'M NOT "READY," I DON'T DRINK BECAUSE DRUNK PEOPLE ARE "ANNOYING!"
I MEAN, LOOK AT THIS PLACE! IT'S LIKE THEY ALL THOUGHT "HMM. I'M NOT RETARDED ENOUGH. WHAT CAN I DO TO MAKE GAINS IN THIS AREA?"
"I KNOW! I'LL DRINK THIS DUM-DUM JUICE!"
WELL, HA! NO, THANKS, "DUDE!"
OKAY, ALREADY! I WITHDRAW MY APOLOGY! IT MUST'VE BEEN THE DUM-DUM JUICE TALKING, I'M SORRY.
APOLOGY ACCEPTED.
DO YOU THINK WE SHOULD WAIT A LITTLE FURTHER FROM THE HOUSE? SO YOUR MOM DOESN'T SEE -- DOESN'T MISS US?
WHAT? NO WAY.
I DON'T WANT TO WAIT ON SOME DARK STREET WHERE SOME DRUNK DRIVER WILL RUN US OVER! PSSH!

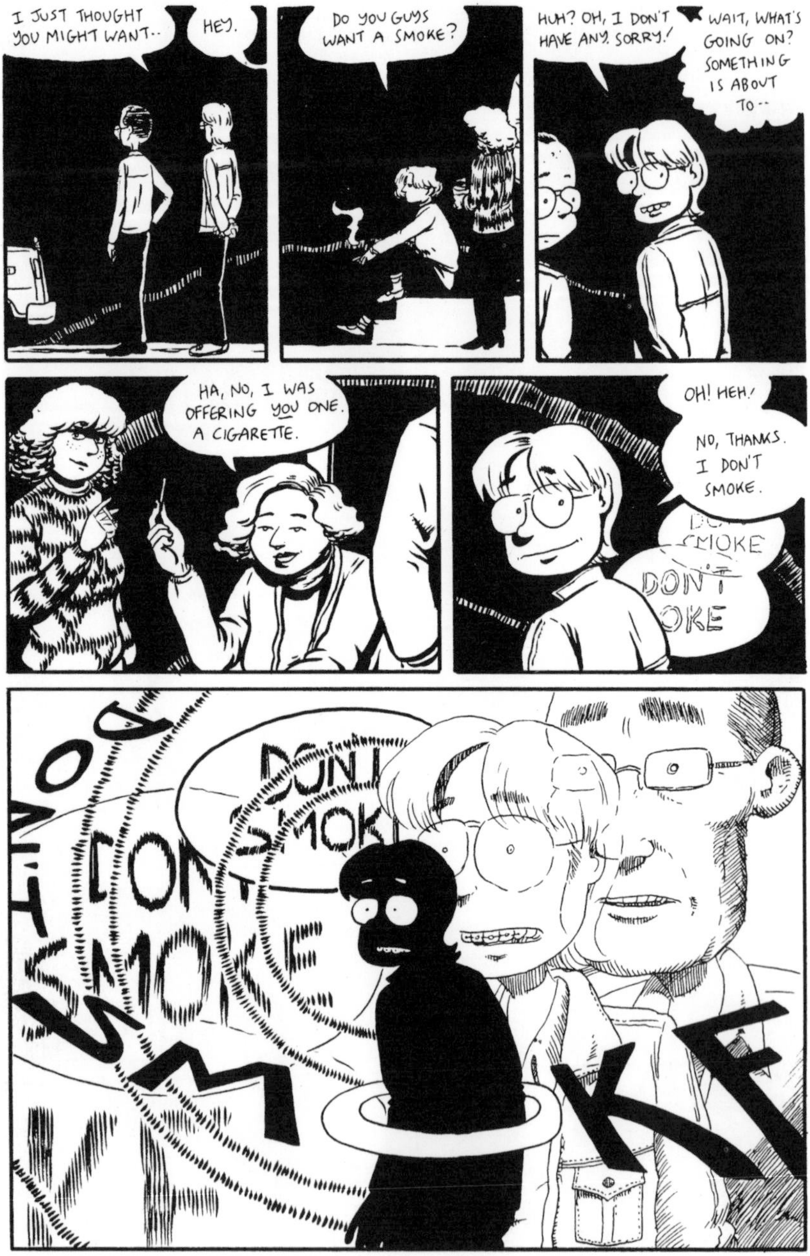
I JUST THOUGHT YOU MIGHT WANT..
HEY.
DO YOU GUYS WANT A SMOKE?
HUH? OH, I DON'T HAVE ANY. SORRY.
WAIT, WHAT'S GOING ON? SOMETHING IS ABOUT TO--
HA, NO, I WAS OFFERING YOU ONE. A CIGARETTE.
OH! HEH.
NO, THANKS. I DON'T SMOKE.
DON'T SMOKE
DON'T SMOKE

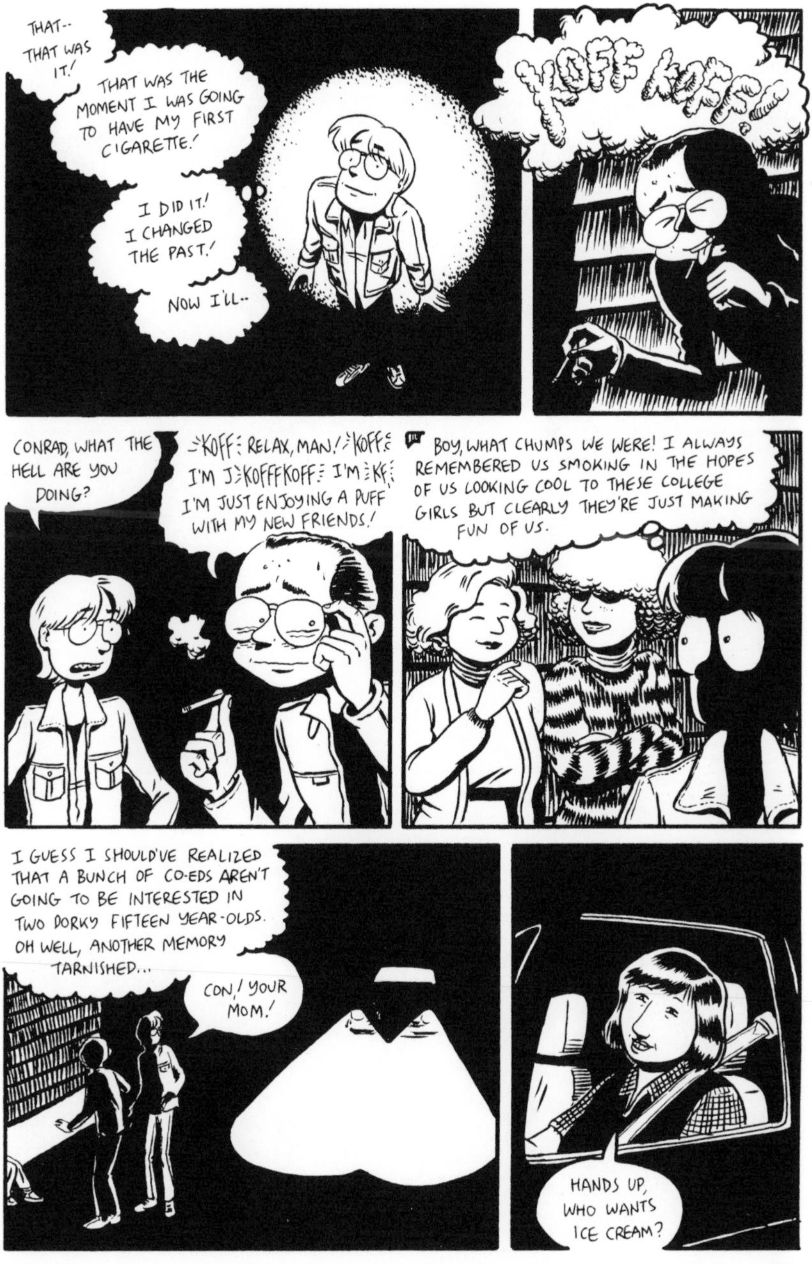
THAT-- THAT WAS IT!
THAT WAS THE MOMENT I WAS GOING TO HAVE MY FIRST CIGARETTE!
I DID IT! I CHANGED THE PAST!
NOW I'LL..
KOFF KOFF!
CONRAD, WHAT THE HELL ARE YOU DOING?
KOFF RELAX, MAN! KOFF I'M J KOFFFKOFF I'M KF I'M JUST ENJOYING A PUFF WITH MY NEW FRIENDS!
BOY, WHAT CHUMPS WE WERE! I ALWAYS REMEMBERED US SMOKING IN THE HOPES OF US LOOKING COOL TO THESE COLLEGE GIRLS BUT CLEARLY THEY'RE JUST MAKING FUN OF US.
I GUESS I SHOULD'VE REALIZED THAT A BUNCH OF CO-EDS AREN'T GOING TO BE INTERESTED IN TWO DORKY FIFTEEN YEAR-OLDS. OH WELL, ANOTHER MEMORY TARNISHED...
CON! YOUR MOM!
HANDS UP, WHO WANTS ICE CREAM?

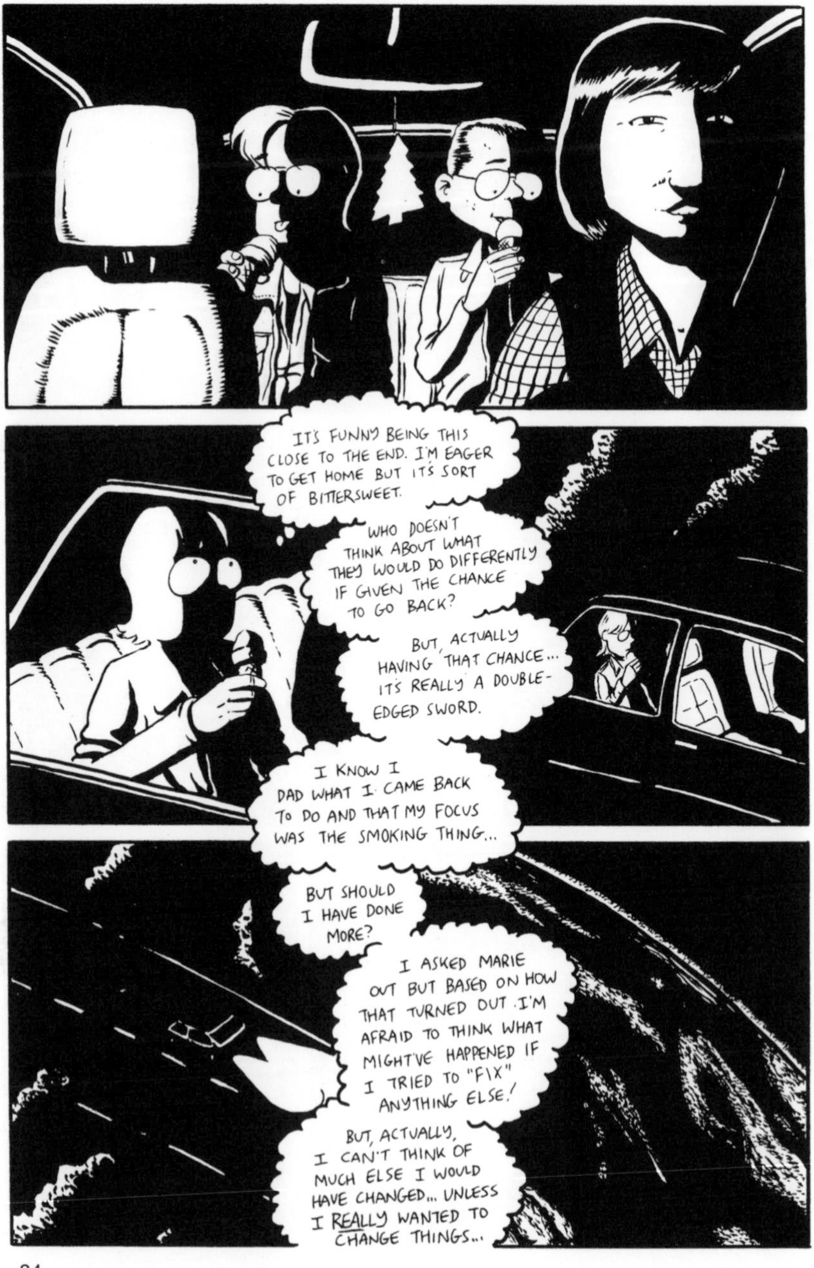

IT'S FUNNY BEING THIS CLOSE TO THE END. I'M EAGER TO GET HOME BUT IT'S SORT OF BITTERSWEET.
WHO DOESN'T THINK ABOUT WHAT THEY WOULD DO DIFFERENTLY IF GIVEN THE CHANCE TO GO BACK?
BUT, ACTUALLY HAVING THAT CHANCE... IT'S REALLY A DOUBLE-EDGED SWORD.
I KNOW I DAD WHAT I CAME BACK TO DO AND THAT MY FOCUS WAS THE SMOKING THING...
BUT SHOULD I HAVE DONE MORE?
I ASKED MARIE OUT BUT BASED ON HOW THAT TURNED OUT I'M AFRAID TO THINK WHAT MIGHT'VE HAPPENED IF I TRIED TO "FIX" ANYTHING ELSE!
BUT, ACTUALLY, I CAN'T THINK OF MUCH ELSE I WOULD HAVE CHANGED... UNLESS I REALLY WANTED TO CHANGE THINGS...

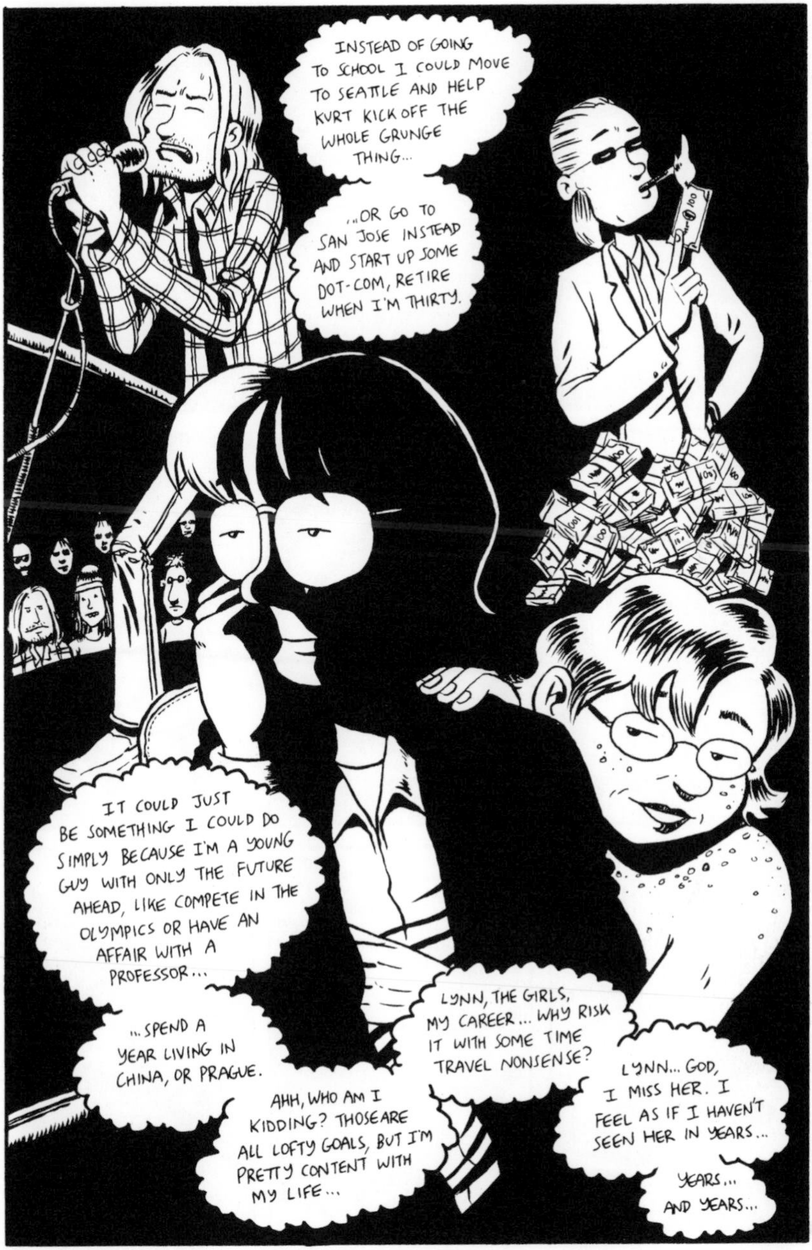
INSTEAD OF GOING TO SCHOOL I COULD MOVE TO SEATTLE AND HELP KURT KICK OFF THE WHOLE GRUNGE THING...
...OR GO TO SAN JOSE INSTEAD AND START UP SOME DOT-COM, RETIRE WHEN I'M THIRTY.
IT COULD JUST BE SOMETHING I COULD DO SIMPLY BECAUSE I'M A YOUNG GUY WITH ONLY THE FUTURE AHEAD, LIKE COMPETE IN THE OLYMPICS OR HAVE AN AFFAIR WITH A PROFESSOR...
...SPEND A YEAR LIVING IN CHINA, OR PRAGUE.
AHH, WHO AM I KIDDING? THOSEARE ALL LOFTY GOALS, BUT I'M PRETTY CONTENT WITH MY LIFE...
LYNN, THE GIRLS, MY CAREER... WHY RISK IT WITH SOME TIME TRAVEL NONSENSE?
LYNN... GOD, I MISS HER. I FEEL AS IF I HAVEN'T SEEN HER IN YEARS...
YEARS... AND YEARS...

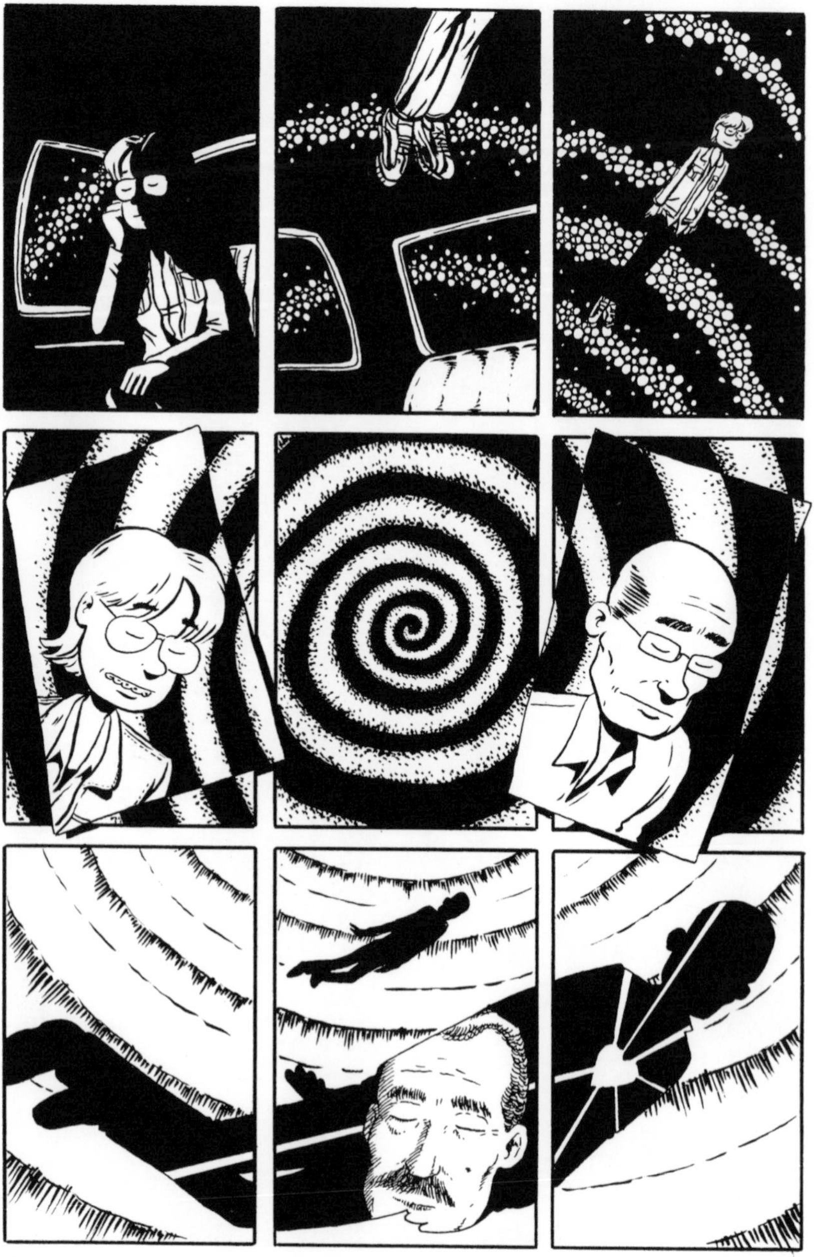

AND
WAK

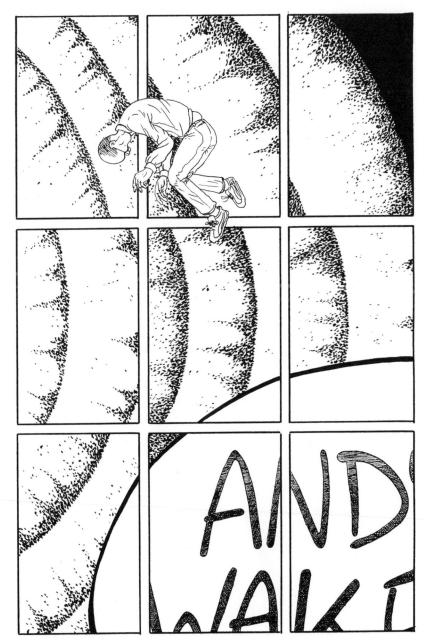

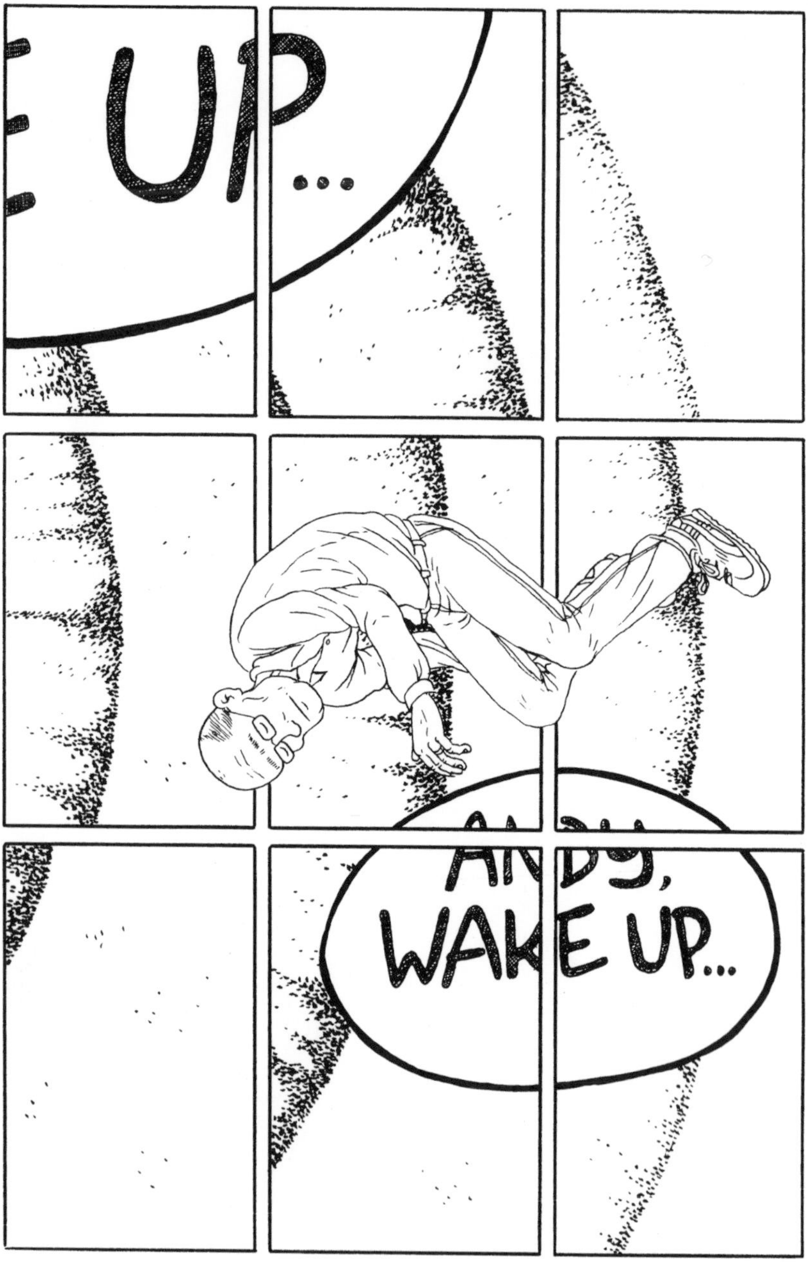
UP...
ANDY, WAKE UP...

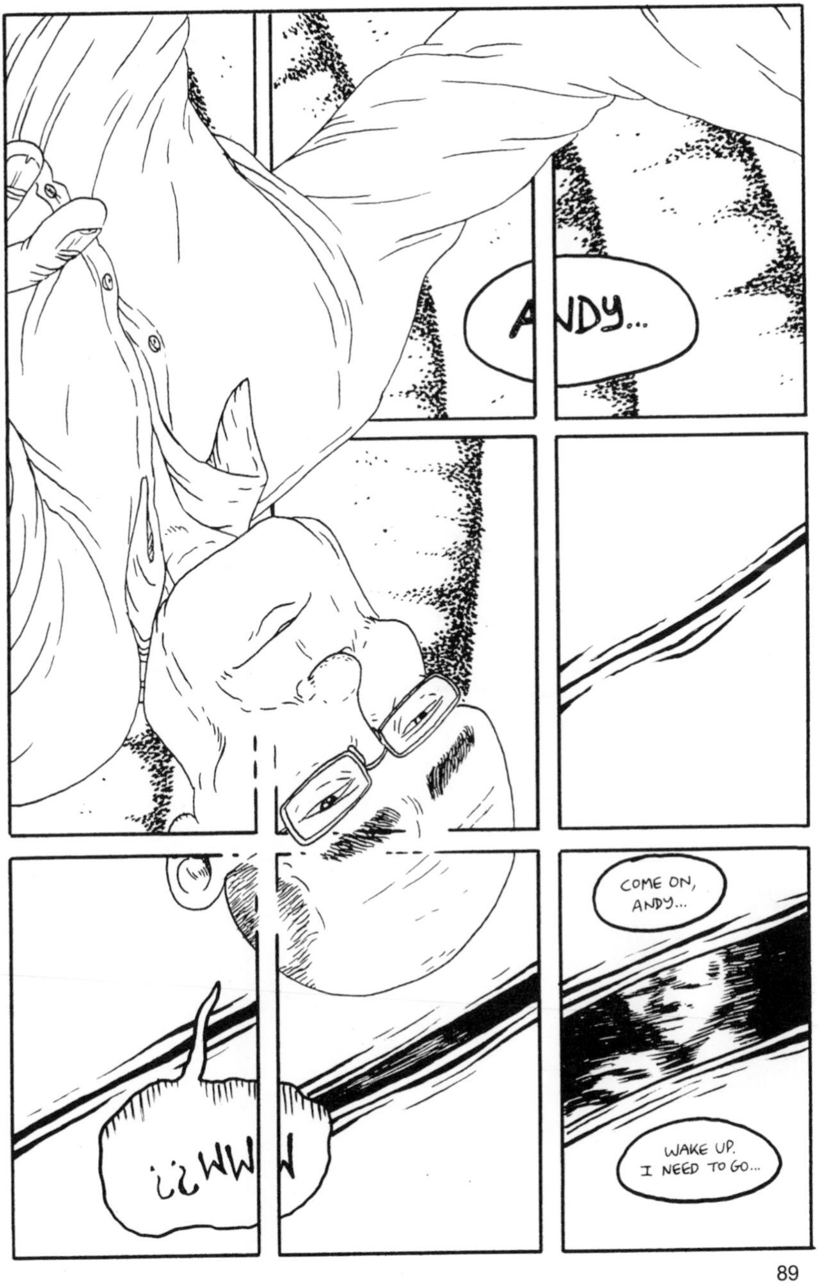
ANDY...
COME ON, ANDY...
WAKE UP. I NEED TO GO...
MMM??

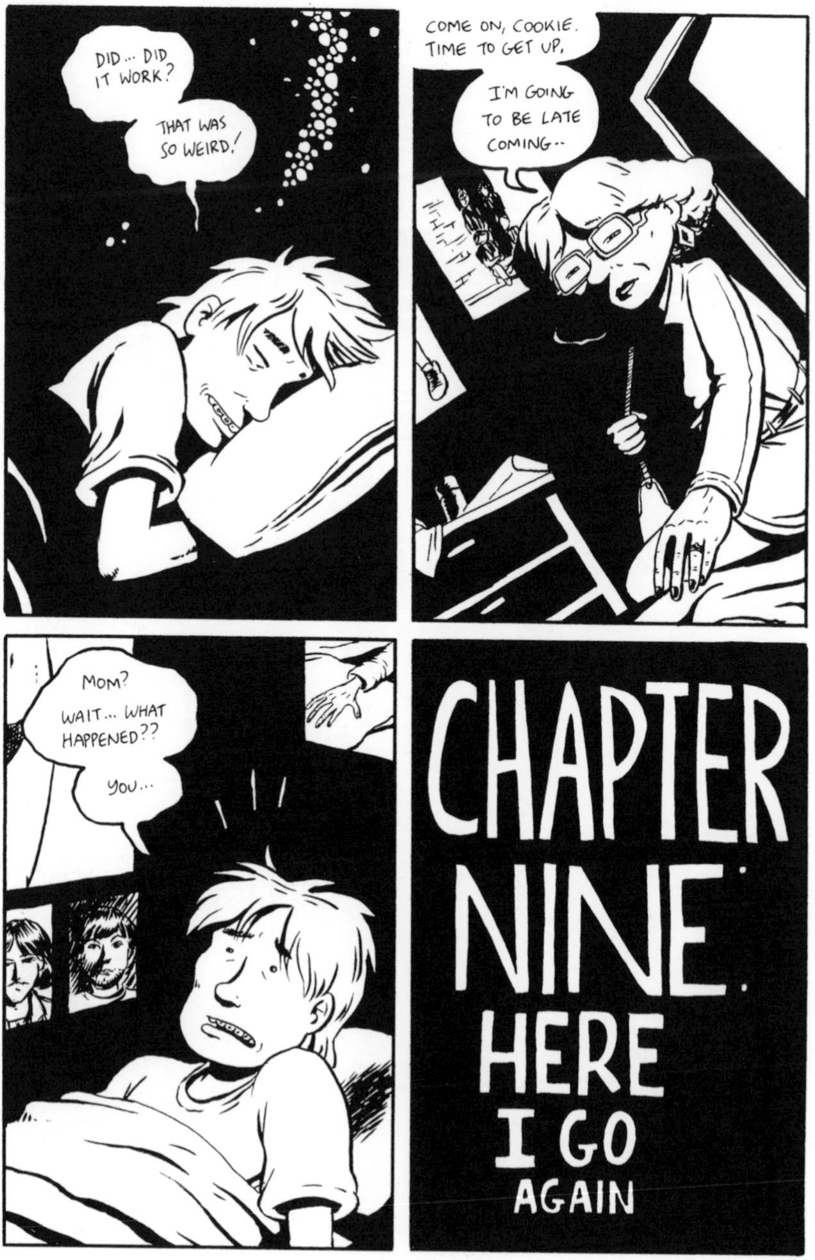
DID... DID IT WORK?
THAT WAS SO WEIRD!
COME ON, COOKIE. TIME TO GET UP,
I'M GOING TO BE LATE COMING..
MOM?
WAIT... WHAT HAPPENED??
YOU...
CHAPTER NINE:
HERE I GO AGAIN

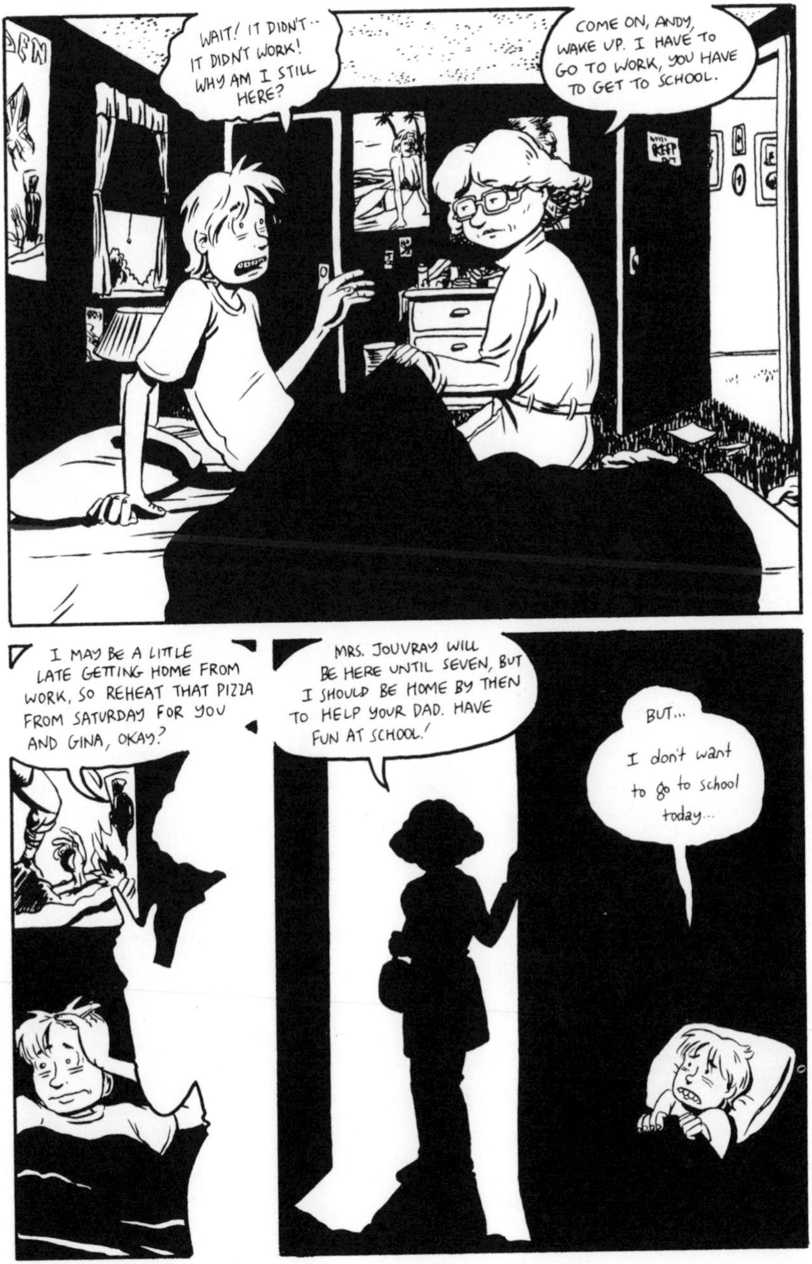
WAIT! IT DIDN'T... IT DIDN'T WORK! WHY AM I STILL HERE?
COME ON, ANDY, WAKE UP. I HAVE TO GO TO WORK, YOU HAVE TO GET TO SCHOOL.
I MAY BE A LITTLE LATE GETTING HOME FROM WORK, SO REHEAT THAT PIZZA FROM SATURDAY FOR YOU AND GINA, OKAY?
MRS. JOUVRAY WILL BE HERE UNTIL SEVEN, BUT I SHOULD BE HOME BY THEN TO HELP YOUR DAD. HAVE FUN AT SCHOOL!
BUT...
I don't want to go to school today...

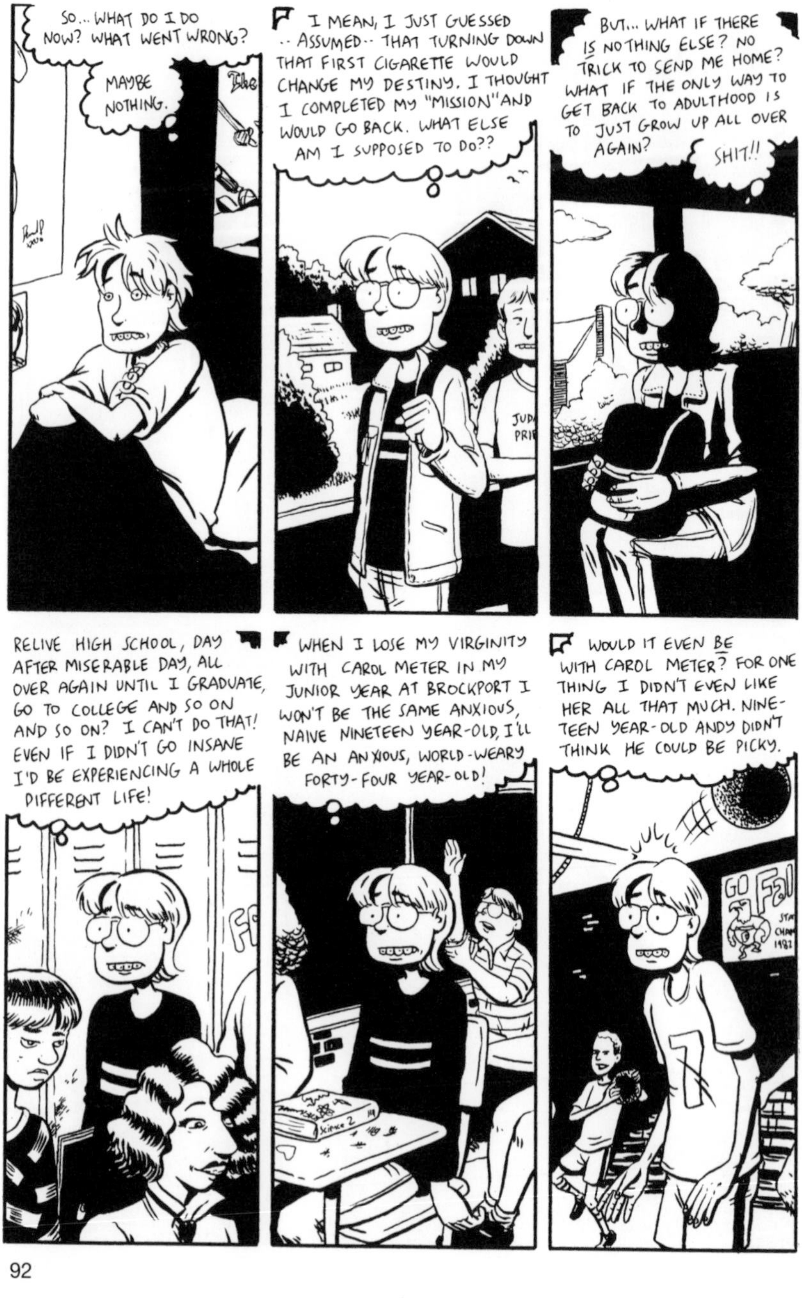
SO... WHAT DO I DO NOW? WHAT WENT WRONG?
MAYBE NOTHING.
I MEAN, I JUST GUESSED .. ASSUMED .. THAT TURNING DOWN THAT FIRST CIGARETTE WOULD CHANGE MY DESTINY. I THOUGHT I COMPLETED MY "MISSION" AND WOULD GO BACK. WHAT ELSE AM I SUPPOSED TO DO??
BUT... WHAT IF THERE IS NOTHING ELSE? NO TRICK TO SEND ME HOME? WHAT IF THE ONLY WAY TO GET BACK TO ADULTHOOD IS TO JUST GROW UP ALL OVER AGAIN?
SHIT!!
RELIVE HIGH SCHOOL, DAY AFTER MISERABLE DAY, ALL OVER AGAIN UNTIL I GRADUATE, GO TO COLLEGE AND SO ON AND SO ON? I CAN'T DO THAT! EVEN IF I DIDN'T GO INSANE I'D BE EXPERIENCING A WHOLE DIFFERENT LIFE!
WHEN I LOSE MY VIRGINITY WITH CAROL METER IN MY JUNIOR YEAR AT BROCKPORT I WON'T BE THE SAME ANXIOUS, NAIVE NINETEEN YEAR-OLD, I'LL BE AN ANXIOUS, WORLD-WEARY FORTY-FOUR YEAR-OLD!
WOULD IT EVEN BE WITH CAROL METER? FOR ONE THING I DIDN'T EVEN LIKE HER ALL THAT MUCH. NINETEEN YEAR-OLD ANDY DIDN'T THINK HE COULD BE PICKY.

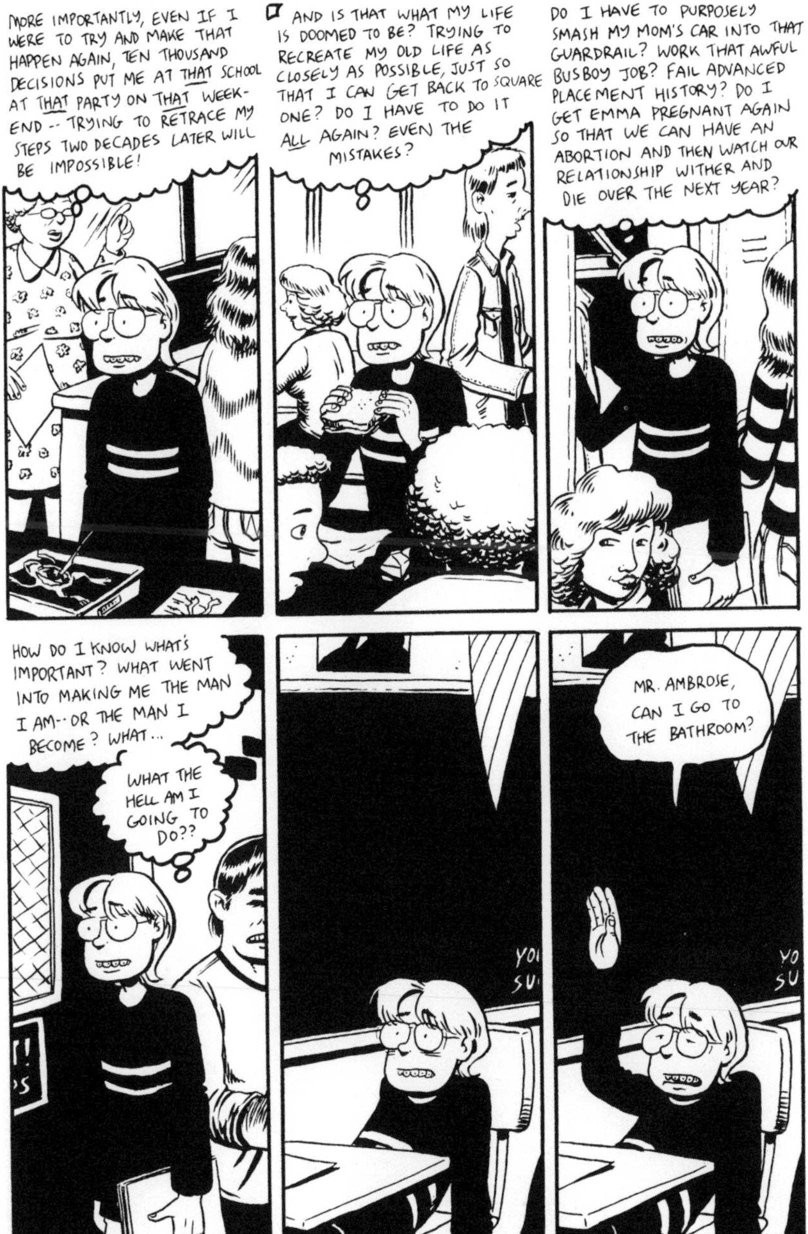
MORE IMPORTANTLY, EVEN IF I WERE TO TRY AND MAKE THAT HAPPEN AGAIN, TEN THOUSAND DECISIONS PUT ME AT THAT SCHOOL AT THAT PARTY ON THAT WEEK-END -- TRYING TO RETRACE MY STEPS TWO DECADES LATER WILL BE IMPOSSIBLE!
AND IS THAT WHAT MY LIFE IS DOOMED TO BE? TRYING TO RECREATE MY OLD LIFE AS CLOSELY AS POSSIBLE, JUST SO THAT I CAN GET BACK TO SQUARE ONE? DO I HAVE TO DO IT ALL AGAIN? EVEN THE MISTAKES?
DO I HAVE TO PURPOSELY SMASH MY MOM'S CAR INTO THAT GUARDRAIL? WORK THAT AWFUL BUSBOY JOB? FAIL ADVANCED PLACEMENT HISTORY? DO I GET EMMA PREGNANT AGAIN SO THAT WE CAN HAVE AN ABORTION AND THEN WATCH OUR RELATIONSHIP WITHER AND DIE OVER THE NEXT YEAR?
HOW DO I KNOW WHAT'S IMPORTANT? WHAT WENT INTO MAKING ME THE MAN I AM-- OR THE MAN I BECOME? WHAT...
WHAT THE HELL AM I GOING TO DO??
MR. AMBROSE, CAN I GO TO THE BATHROOM?

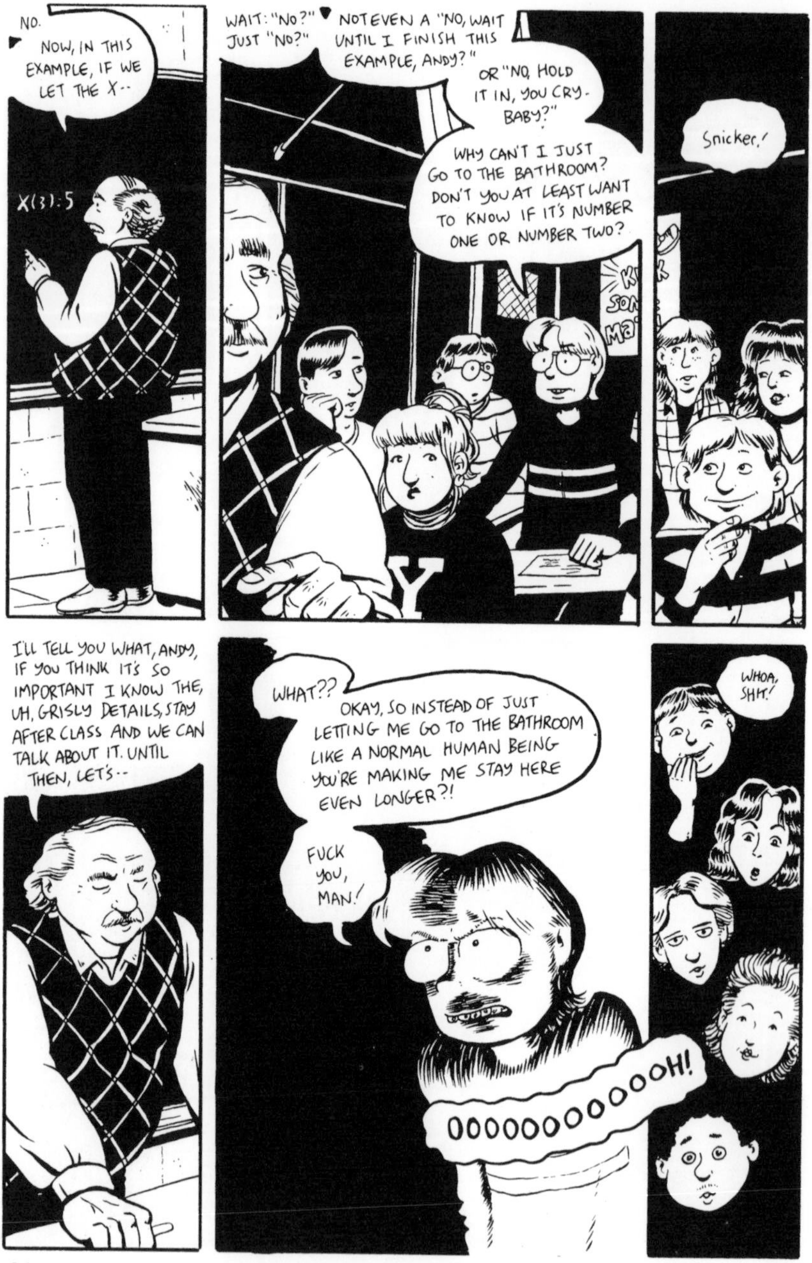
NO.
NOW, IN THIS EXAMPLE, IF WE LET THE X--
WAIT: "NO?" JUST "NO?"
NOT EVEN A "NO, WAIT UNTIL I FINISH THIS EXAMPLE, ANDY?"
OR "NO, HOLD IT IN, YOU CRY-BABY?"
WHY CAN'T I JUST GO TO THE BATHROOM? DON'T YOU AT LEAST WANT TO KNOW IF IT'S NUMBER ONE OR NUMBER TWO?
Snicker!
I'LL TELL YOU WHAT, ANDY, IF YOU THINK IT'S SO IMPORTANT I KNOW THE, UH, GRISLY DETAILS, STAY AFTER CLASS AND WE CAN TALK ABOUT IT. UNTIL THEN, LET'S--
WHAT??
OKAY, SO INSTEAD OF JUST LETTING ME GO TO THE BATHROOM LIKE A NORMAL HUMAN BEING YOU'RE MAKING ME STAY HERE EVEN LONGER?!
FUCK YOU, MAN!
WHOA, SHIT!
OOOOOOOOOOOOOH!

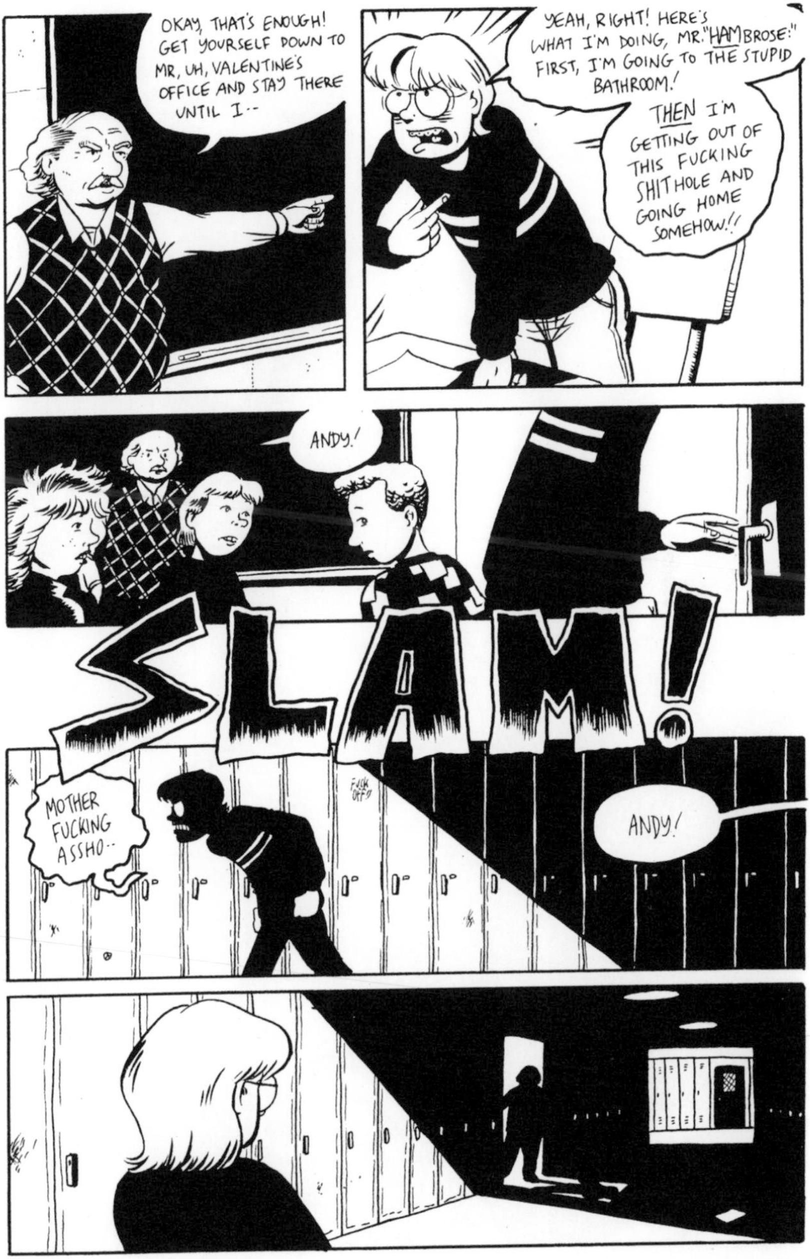
OKAY, THAT'S ENOUGH! GET YOURSELF DOWN TO MR, UH, VALENTINE'S OFFICE AND STAY THERE UNTIL I--
YEAH, RIGHT! HERE'S WHAT I'M DOING, MR. "HAMBROSE:" FIRST, I'M GOING TO THE STUPID BATHROOM!
THEN I'M GETTING OUT OF THIS FUCKING SHITHOLE AND GOING HOME SOMEHOW!!
ANDY!
SLAM!
MOTHER FUCKING ASSHO--
FUCK OFF!!
ANDY!

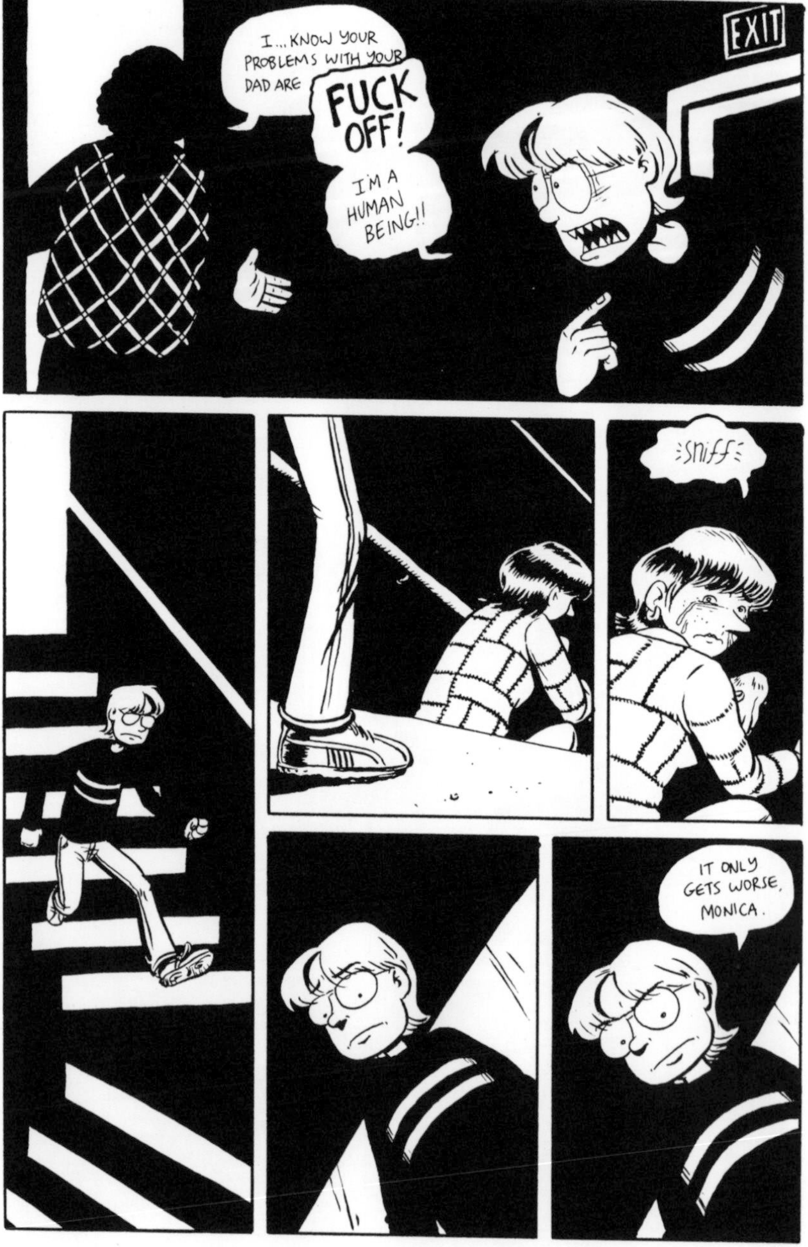
I... KNOW YOUR PROBLEMS WITH YOUR DAD ARE
FUCK OFF!
I'M A HUMAN BEING!!
EXIT
SNIFF
IT ONLY GETS WORSE, MONICA.

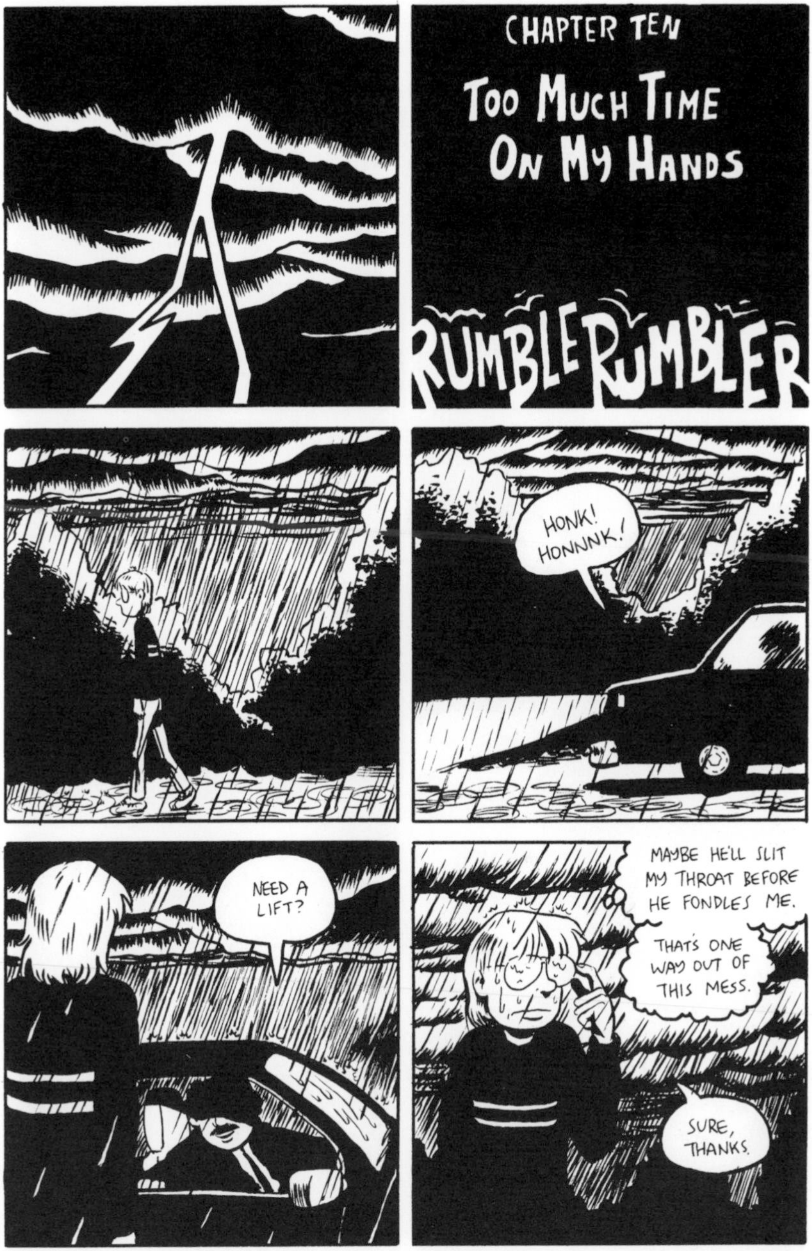
CHAPTER TEN
TOO MUCH TIME ON MY HANDS
RUMBLE RUMBLER
HONK! HONNNK!
NEED A LIFT?
MAYBE HE'LL SLIT MY THROAT BEFORE HE FONDLES ME.
THAT'S ONE WAY OUT OF THIS MESS.
SURE, THANKS.

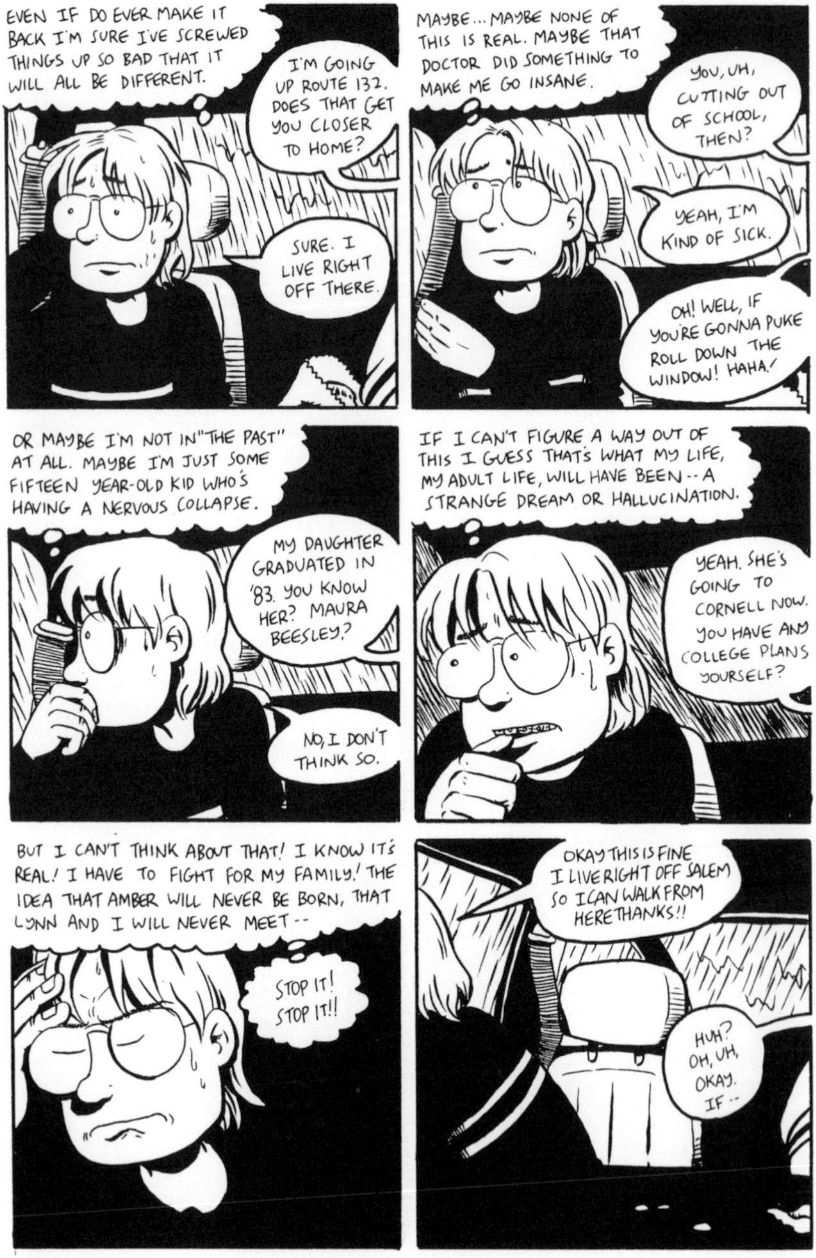
EVEN IF DO EVER MAKE IT BACK I'M SURE I'VE SCREWED THINGS UP SO BAD THAT IT WILL ALL BE DIFFERENT.
I'M GOING UP ROUTE 132. DOES THAT GET YOU CLOSER TO HOME?
SURE. I LIVE RIGHT OFF THERE.
MAYBE... MAYBE NONE OF THIS IS REAL. MAYBE THAT DOCTOR DID SOMETHING TO MAKE ME GO INSANE.
YOU, UH, CUTTING OUT OF SCHOOL, THEN?
YEAH, I'M KIND OF SICK.
OH! WELL, IF YOU'RE GONNA PUKE ROLL DOWN THE WINDOW! HAHA!
OR MAYBE I'M NOT IN "THE PAST" AT ALL. MAYBE I'M JUST SOME FIFTEEN YEAR-OLD KID WHO'S HAVING A NERVOUS COLLAPSE.
MY DAUGHTER GRADUATED IN '83. YOU KNOW HER? MAURA BEESLEY?
NO, I DON'T THINK SO.
IF I CAN'T FIGURE A WAY OUT OF THIS I GUESS THAT'S WHAT MY LIFE, MY ADULT LIFE, WILL HAVE BEEN -- A STRANGE DREAM OR HALLUCINATION.
YEAH. SHE'S GOING TO CORNELL NOW. YOU HAVE ANY COLLEGE PLANS YOURSELF?
BUT I CAN'T THINK ABOUT THAT! I KNOW IT'S REAL! I HAVE TO FIGHT FOR MY FAMILY! THE IDEA THAT AMBER WILL NEVER BE BORN, THAT LYNN AND I WILL NEVER MEET --
STOP IT! STOP IT!!
OKAY THIS IS FINE I LIVERIGHT OFF SALEM SO ICAN WALK FROM HERETHANKS!!
HUH? OH, UH, OKAY. IF --

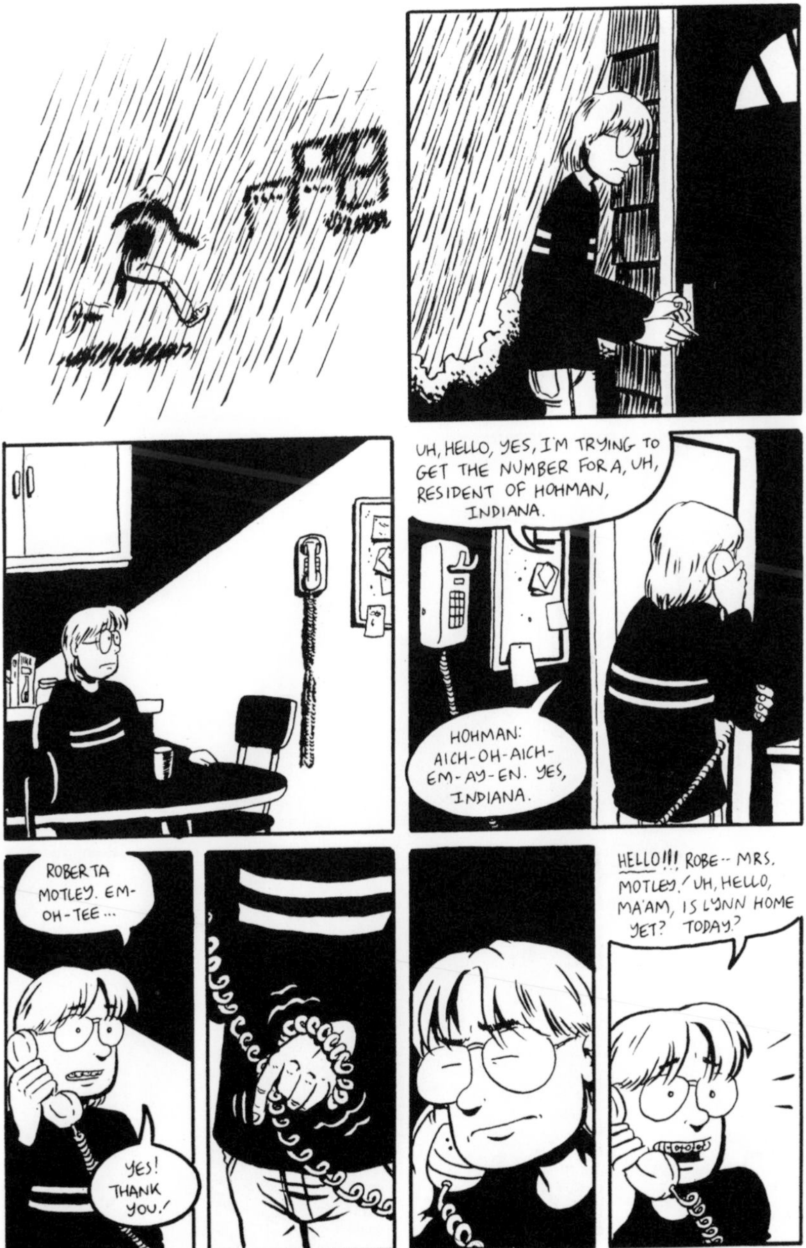
UH, HELLO, YES, I'M TRYING TO GET THE NUMBER FOR A, UH, RESIDENT OF HOHMAN, INDIANA.
HOHMAN: AICH-OH-AICH-EM-AY-EN. YES, INDIANA.
ROBERTA MOTLEY. EM-OH-TEE...
YES! THANK YOU.!
HELLO!!! ROBE-- MRS. MOTLEY.! UH, HELLO, MA'AM, IS LYNN HOME YET? TODAY.?

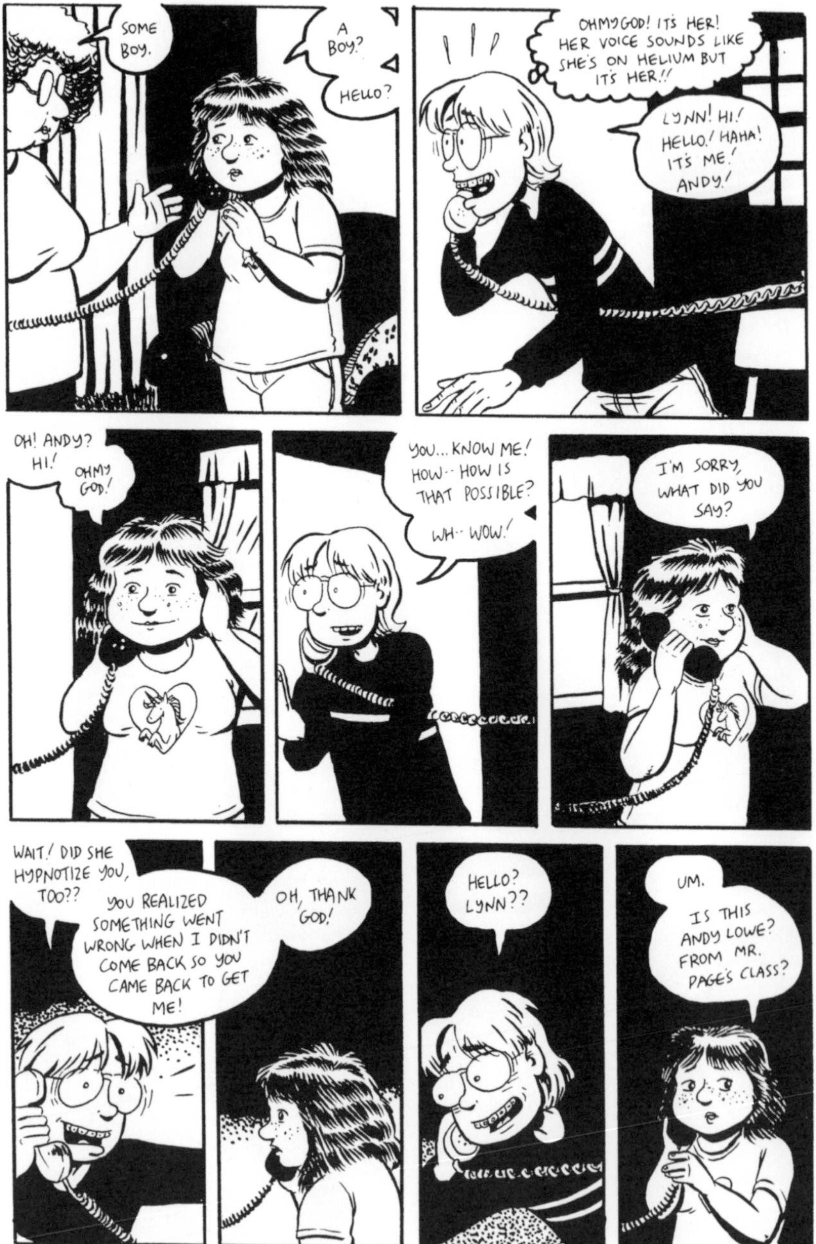
SOME BOY.
A BOY?
HELLO?
OHMYGOD! IT'S HER! HER VOICE SOUNDS LIKE SHE'S ON HELIUM BUT IT'S HER!!
LYNN! HI! HELLO! HAHA! IT'S ME! ANDY!
OH! ANDY? HI!
OHMY GOD!
YOU... KNOW ME! HOW-- HOW IS THAT POSSIBLE?
WH-- WOW!
I'M SORRY, WHAT DID YOU SAY?
WAIT! DID SHE HYPNOTIZE YOU, TOO??
YOU REALIZED SOMETHING WENT WRONG WHEN I DIDN'T COME BACK SO YOU CAME BACK TO GET ME!
OH, THANK GOD!
HELLO? LYNN??
UM.
IS THIS ANDY LOWE? FROM MR. PAGE'S CLASS?

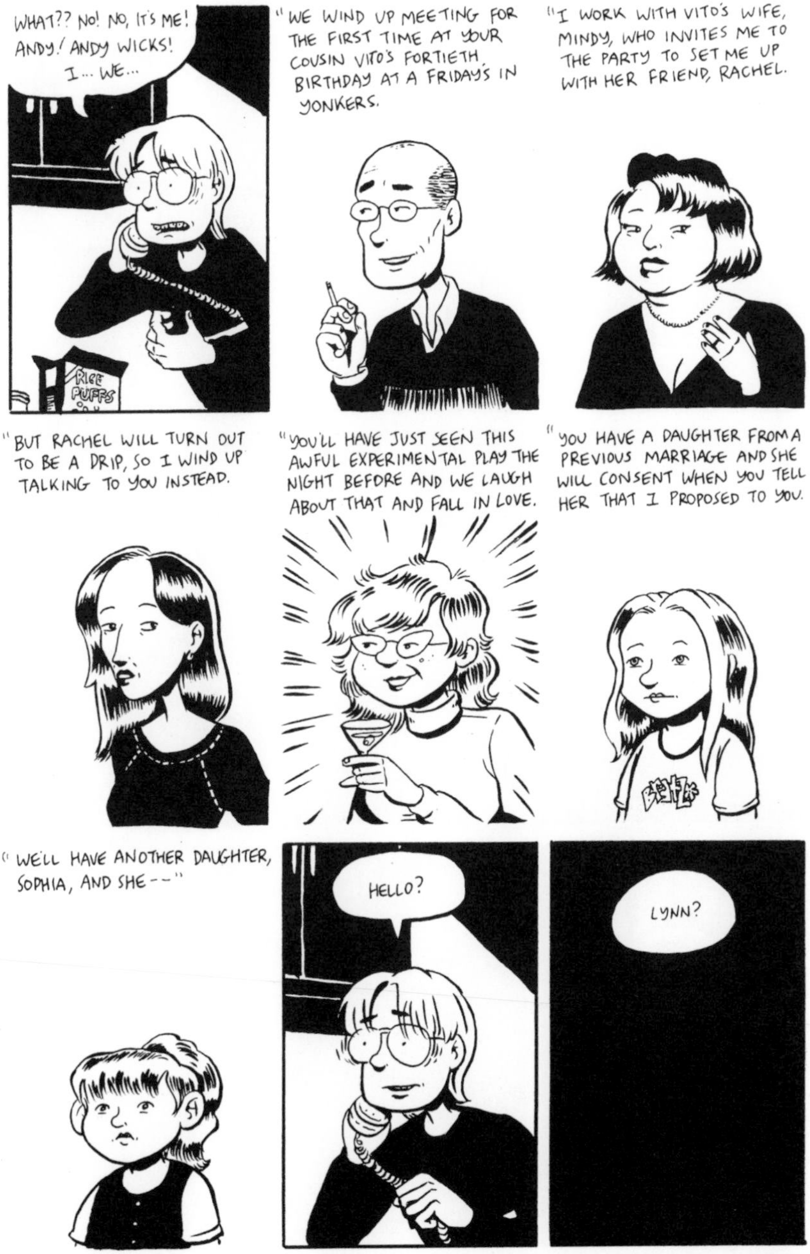
WHAT?? NO! NO, IT'S ME! ANDY! ANDY WICKS! I... WE...
RICE PUFFS
"WE WIND UP MEETING FOR THE FIRST TIME AT YOUR COUSIN VITO'S FORTIETH BIRTHDAY AT A FRIDAY'S IN YONKERS.
"I WORK WITH VITO'S WIFE, MINDY, WHO INVITES ME TO THE PARTY TO SET ME UP WITH HER FRIEND, RACHEL.
"BUT RACHEL WILL TURN OUT TO BE A DRIP, SO I WIND UP TALKING TO YOU INSTEAD.
"YOU'LL HAVE JUST SEEN THIS AWFUL EXPERIMENTAL PLAY THE NIGHT BEFORE AND WE LAUGH ABOUT THAT AND FALL IN LOVE.
"YOU HAVE A DAUGHTER FROM A PREVIOUS MARRIAGE AND SHE WILL CONSENT WHEN YOU TELL HER THAT I PROPOSED TO YOU.
"WE'LL HAVE ANOTHER DAUGHTER, SOPHIA, AND SHE--"
HELLO?
LYNN?

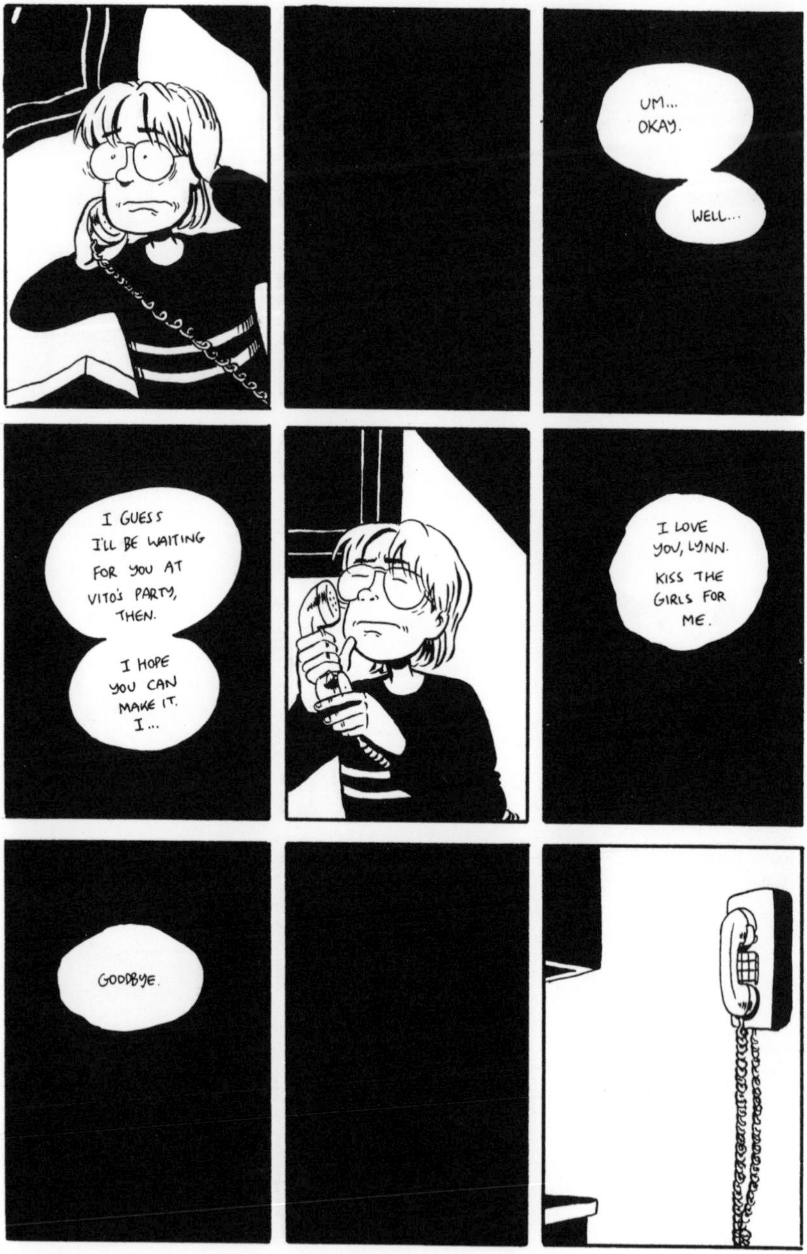
UM... OKAY.
WELL...
I GUESS I'LL BE WAITING FOR YOU AT VITO'S PARTY, THEN.
I HOPE YOU CAN MAKE IT. I...
I LOVE YOU, LYNN. KISS THE GIRLS FOR ME.
GOODBYE.

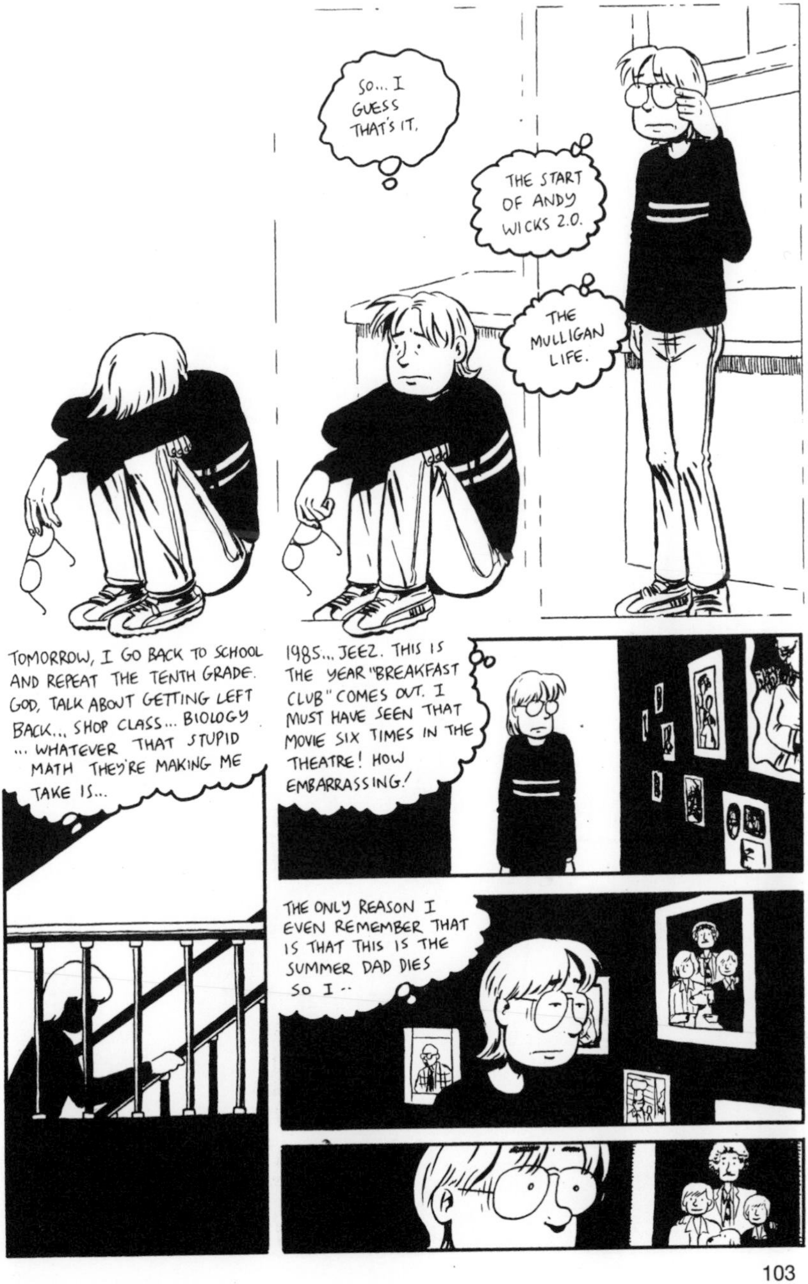
SO... I GUESS THAT'S IT.
THE START OF ANDY WICKS 2.0.
THE MULLIGAN LIFE.
TOMORROW, I GO BACK TO SCHOOL AND REPEAT THE TENTH GRADE. GOD, TALK ABOUT GETTING LEFT BACK... SHOP CLASS... BIOLOGY ... WHATEVER THAT STUPID MATH THEY'RE MAKING ME TAKE IS...
1985... JEEZ. THIS IS THE YEAR "BREAKFAST CLUB" COMES OUT. I MUST HAVE SEEN THAT MOVIE SIX TIMES IN THE THEATRE! HOW EMBARRASSING!
THE ONLY REASON I EVEN REMEMBER THAT IS THAT THIS IS THE SUMMER DAD DIES SO I--

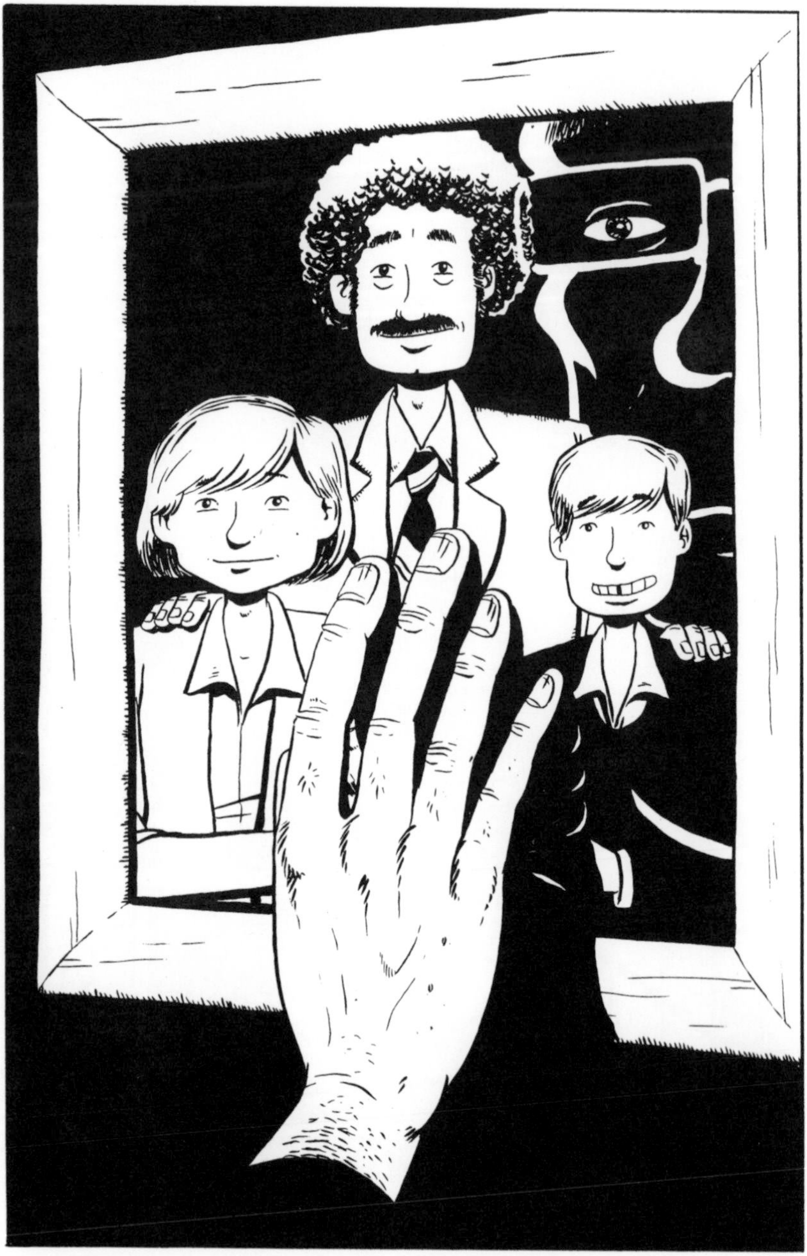

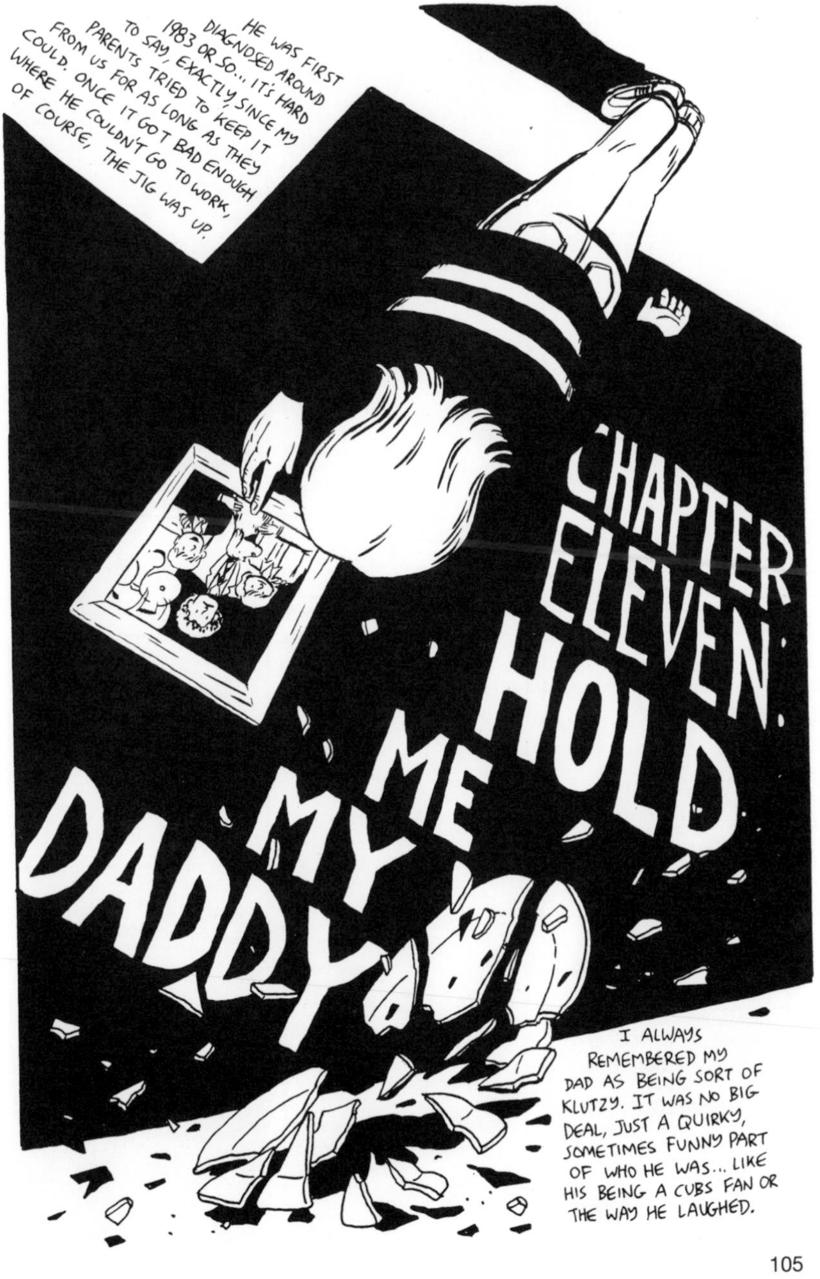
HE WAS FIRST DIAGNOSED AROUND 1983 OR SO... IT'S HARD TO SAY, EXACTLY, SINCE MY PARENTS TRIED TO KEEP IT FROM US FOR AS LONG AS THEY COULD. ONCE IT GOT BAD ENOUGH WHERE HE COULDN'T GO TO WORK, OF COURSE, THE JIG WAS UP.
CHAPTER ELEVEN: HOLD ME MY DADDY
I ALWAYS REMEMBERED MY DAD AS BEING SORT OF KLUTZY. IT WAS NO BIG DEAL, JUST A QUIRKY, SOMETIMES FUNNY PART OF WHO HE WAS... LIKE HIS BEING A CUBS FAN OR THE WAY HE LAUGHED.

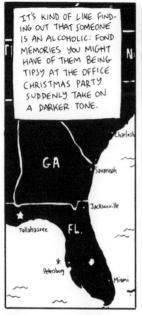

IT'S KIND OF LIKE FINDING OUT THAT SOMEONE IS AN ALCOHOLIC: FOND MEMORIES YOU MIGHT HAVE OF THEM BEING TIPSY AT THE OFFICE CHRISTMAS PARTY SUDDENLY TAKE ON A DARKER TONE.

GA

Charleston
Savannah
Jacksonville
FL.
Tallahassee
St. Petersburg
Miami

IN 1983 MY DAD'S KLUTZINESS TURNED INTO MY DAD'S A.L.S.— LOU GEHRIG'S DISEASE.

IT'S A HORRIBLE, HORRIBLE DISEASE FOR MANY REASONS, BUT ONE OF THE CRUELEST IS THAT, USUALLY, YOUR MIND IS UNAFFECTED.

IT'S YOUR BODY WHICH GIVES OUT— BETRAYS YOU.

THE CREEPING NUMBNESS GRADUALLY TOOK OVER HIS BODY, TURNING IT INTO A PRISON.

THE SUMMER OF 1985 WOULD SEE HIM DECLINE RAPIDLY. HE DIED OF RESPIRATORY FAILURE ON JULY 29, NINE DAYS SHY OF MY SIXTEENTH BIRTHDAY.

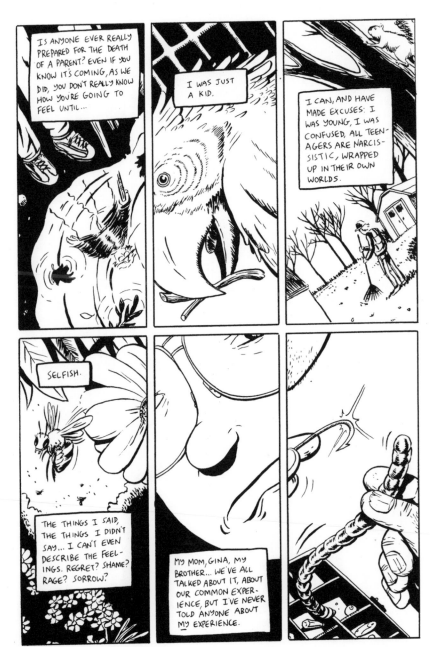

IS ANYONE EVER REALLY PREPARED FOR THE DEATH OF A PARENT? EVEN IF YOU KNOW IT'S COMING, AS WE DID, YOU DON'T REALLY KNOW HOW YOU'RE GOING TO FEEL UNTIL...

I WAS JUST A KID.

I CAN, AND HAVE MADE EXCUSES: I WAS YOUNG, I WAS CONFUSED, ALL TEEN-AGERS ARE NARCIS-SISTIC, WRAPPED UP IN THEIR OWN WORLDS.

SELFISH.

THE THINGS I SAID, THE THINGS I DIDN'T SAY... I CAN'T EVEN DESCRIBE THE FEEL-INGS. REGRET? SHAME? RAGE? SORROW?

MY MOM, GINA, MY BROTHER... WE'VE ALL TALKED ABOUT IT, ABOUT OUR COMMON EXPER-IENCE, BUT I'VE NEVER TOLD ANYONE ABOUT MY EXPERIENCE.

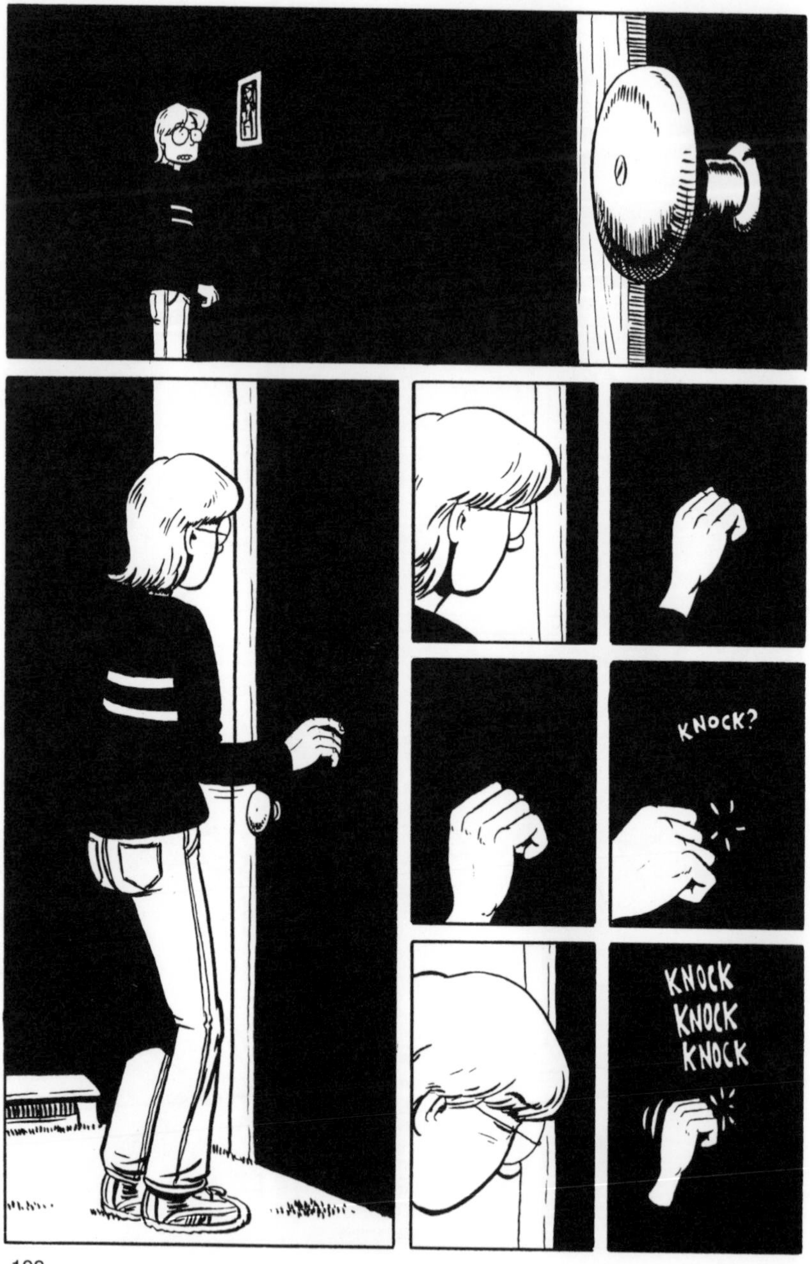
KNOCK?
KNOCK
KNOCK
KNOCK

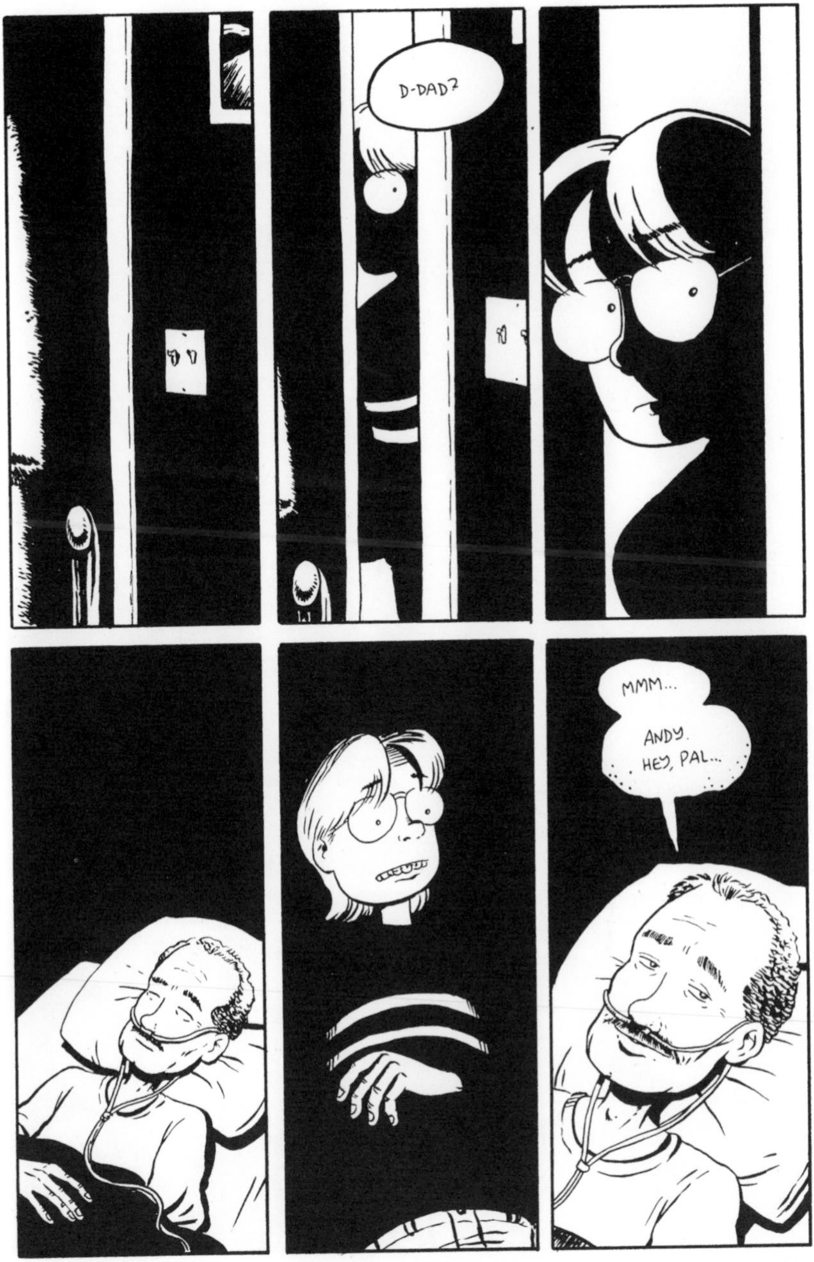
D-DAD?
MMM...
ANDY. HEY, PAL...

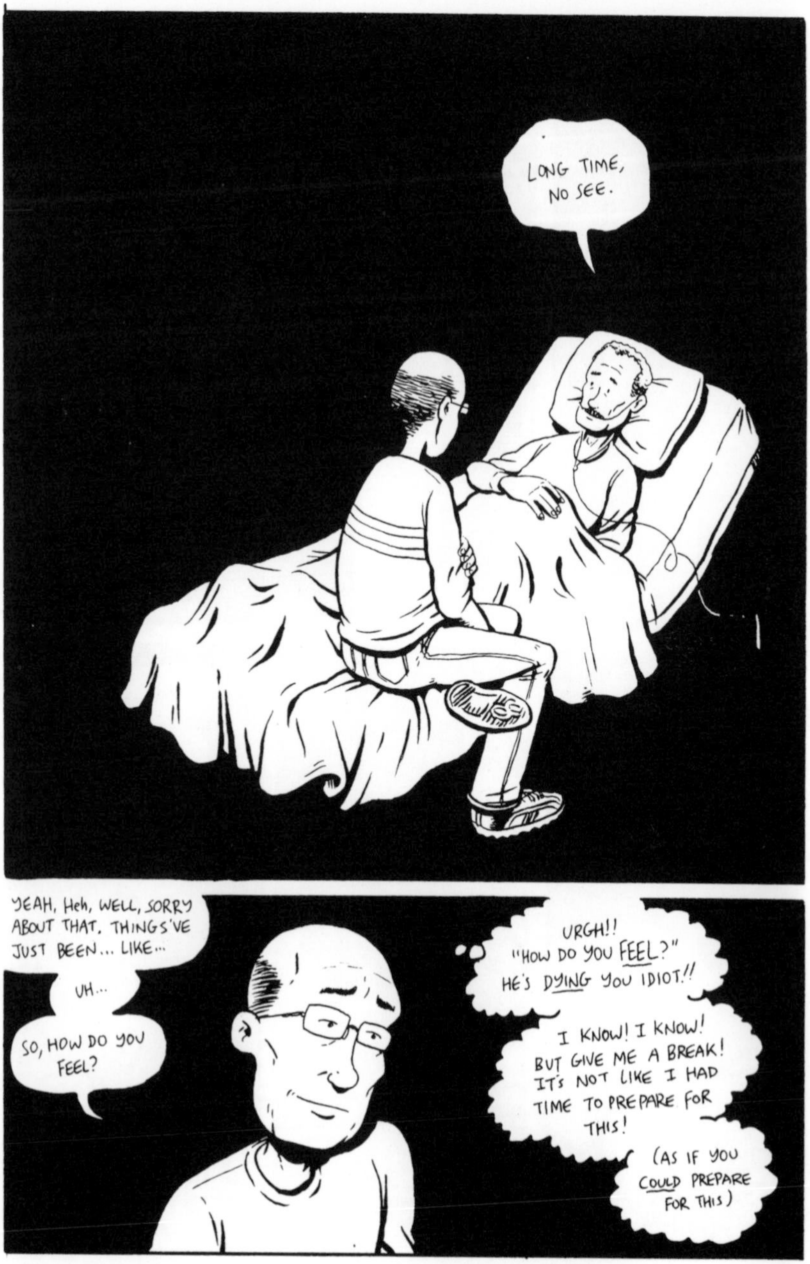

LONG TIME, NO SEE.
YEAH, Heh, WELL, SORRY ABOUT THAT. THINGS'VE JUST BEEN... LIKE...
UH...
SO, HOW DO YOU FEEL?
URGH!! "HOW DO YOU FEEL?" HE'S DYING YOU IDIOT!!
I KNOW! I KNOW! BUT GIVE ME A BREAK! IT'S NOT LIKE I HAD TIME TO PREPARE FOR THIS!
(AS IF YOU COULD PREPARE FOR THIS)

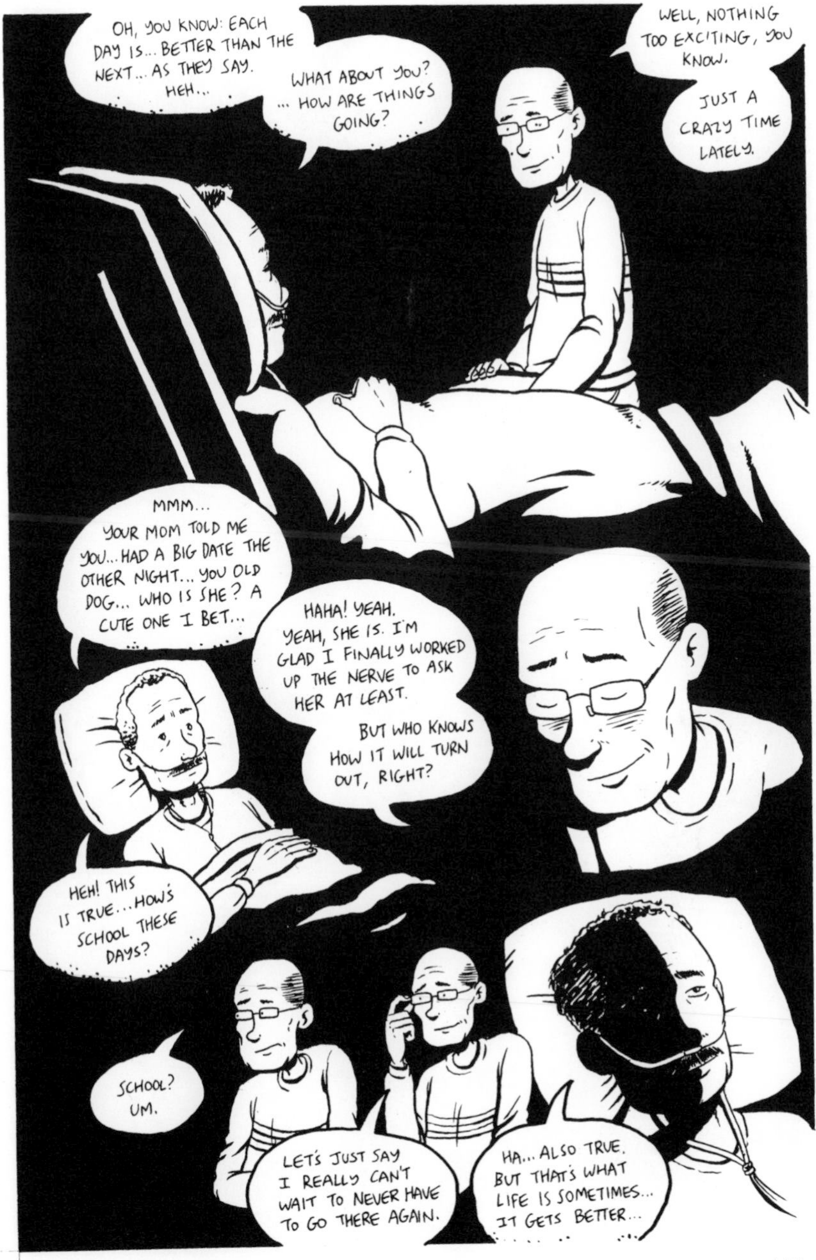
OH, YOU KNOW: EACH DAY IS... BETTER THAN THE NEXT... AS THEY SAY. HEH...
WHAT ABOUT YOU? ... HOW ARE THINGS GOING?
WELL, NOTHING TOO EXCITING, YOU KNOW.
JUST A CRAZY TIME LATELY.
MMM... YOUR MOM TOLD ME YOU... HAD A BIG DATE THE OTHER NIGHT... YOU OLD DOG... WHO IS SHE? A CUTE ONE I BET...
HAHA! YEAH. YEAH, SHE IS. I'M GLAD I FINALLY WORKED UP THE NERVE TO ASK HER AT LEAST.
BUT WHO KNOWS HOW IT WILL TURN OUT, RIGHT?
HEH! THIS IS TRUE... HOW'S SCHOOL THESE DAYS?
SCHOOL? UM.
LET'S JUST SAY I REALLY CAN'T WAIT TO NEVER HAVE TO GO THERE AGAIN.
HA... ALSO TRUE. BUT THAT'S WHAT LIFE IS SOMETIMES... IT GETS BETTER...

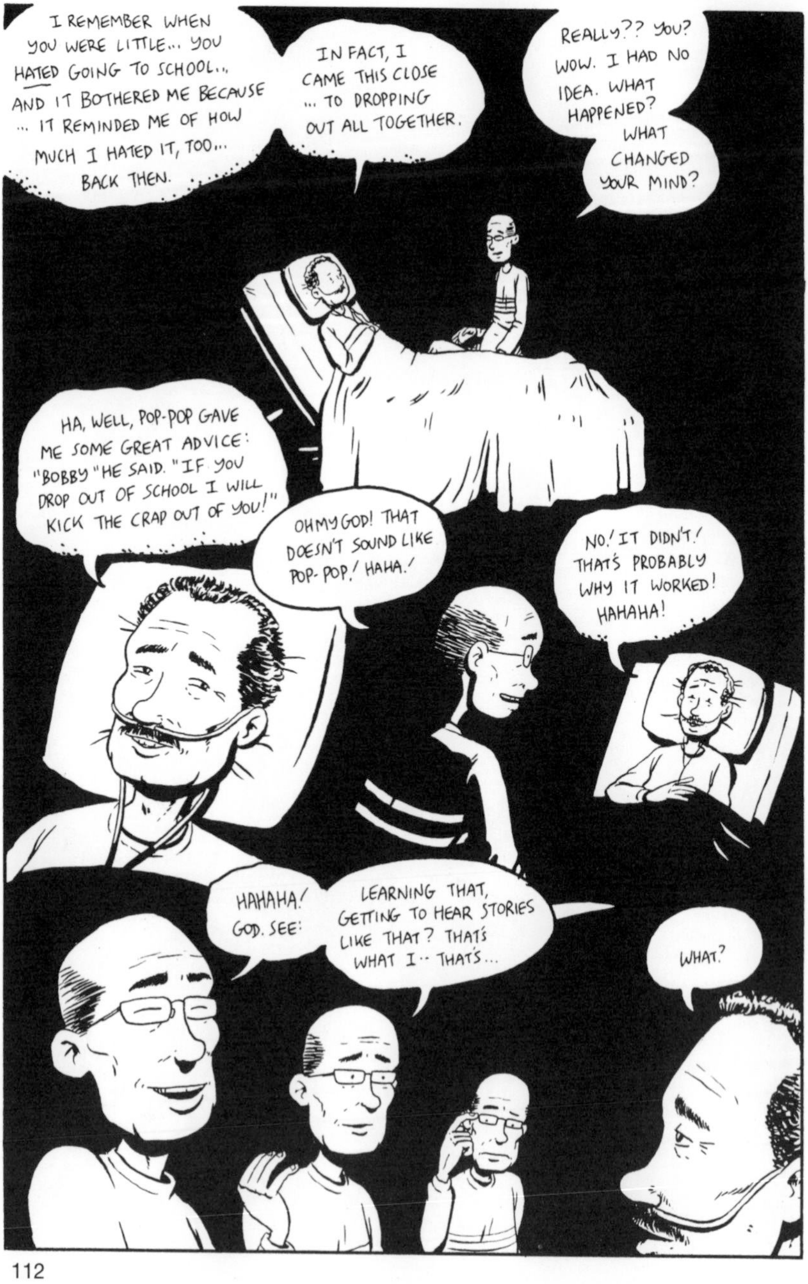
I REMEMBER WHEN YOU WERE LITTLE... YOU HATED GOING TO SCHOOL... AND IT BOTHERED ME BECAUSE ... IT REMINDED ME OF HOW MUCH I HATED IT, TOO... BACK THEN.
IN FACT, I CAME THIS CLOSE ... TO DROPPING OUT ALL TOGETHER.
REALLY?? YOU? WOW. I HAD NO IDEA. WHAT HAPPENED? WHAT CHANGED YOUR MIND?
HA, WELL, POP-POP GAVE ME SOME GREAT ADVICE: "BOBBY" HE SAID. "IF YOU DROP OUT OF SCHOOL I WILL KICK THE CRAP OUT OF YOU!"
OHMYGOD! THAT DOESN'T SOUND LIKE POP-POP! HAHA!
NO! IT DIDN'T! THAT'S PROBABLY WHY IT WORKED! HAHAHA!
HAHAHA! GOD. SEE:
LEARNING THAT, GETTING TO HEAR STORIES LIKE THAT? THAT'S WHAT I.. THAT'S...
WHAT?

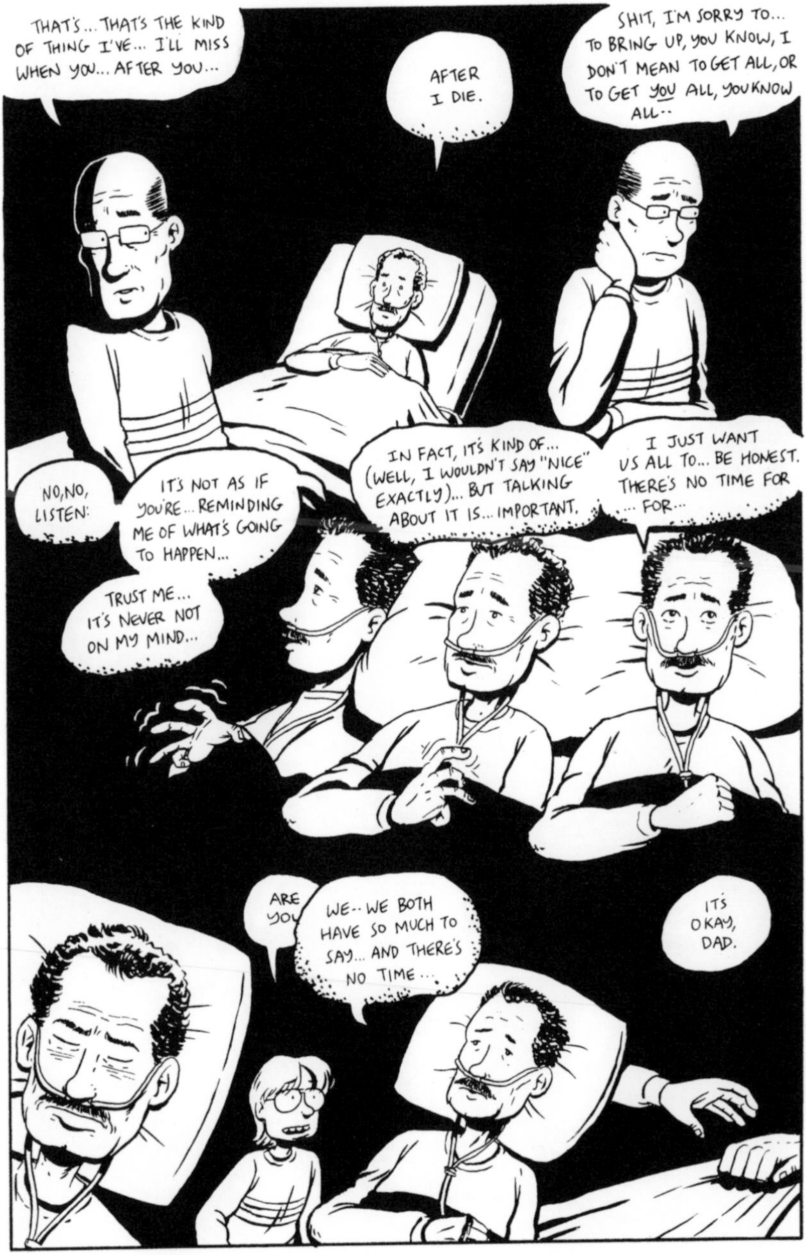
THAT'S... THAT'S THE KIND OF THING I'VE... I'LL MISS WHEN YOU... AFTER YOU...
AFTER I DIE.
SHIT, I'M SORRY TO... TO BRING UP, YOU KNOW, I DON'T MEAN TO GET ALL, OR TO GET YOU ALL, YOU KNOW ALL..
NO, NO, LISTEN:
IT'S NOT AS IF YOU'RE... REMINDING ME OF WHAT'S GOING TO HAPPEN...
TRUST ME... IT'S NEVER NOT ON MY MIND...
IN FACT, IT'S KIND OF... (WELL, I WOULDN'T SAY "NICE" EXACTLY)... BUT TALKING ABOUT IT IS... IMPORTANT.
I JUST WANT US ALL TO... BE HONEST. THERE'S NO TIME FOR ... FOR...
ARE YOU
WE.. WE BOTH HAVE SO MUCH TO SAY... AND THERE'S NO TIME...
IT'S OKAY, DAD.

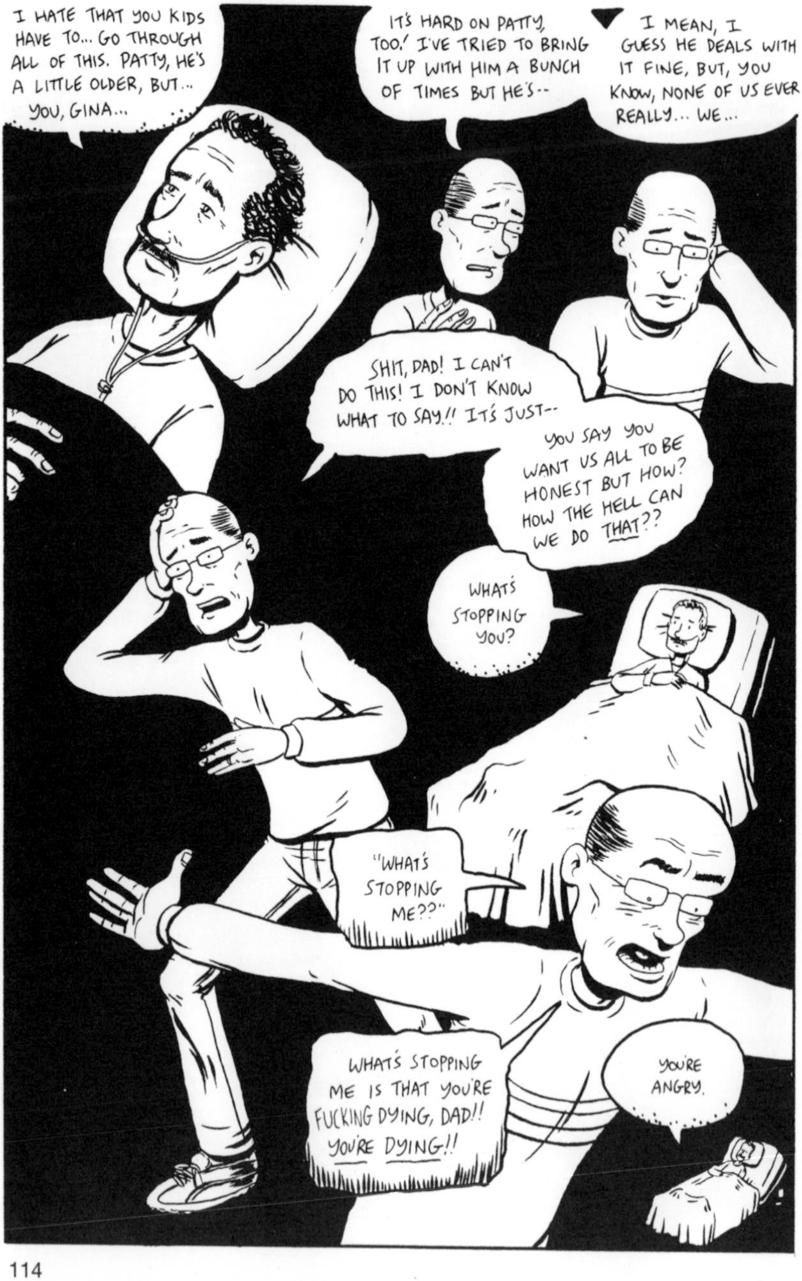
I HATE THAT YOU KIDS HAVE TO... GO THROUGH ALL OF THIS. PATTY, HE'S A LITTLE OLDER, BUT... YOU, GINA...
IT'S HARD ON PATTY, TOO.' I'VE TRIED TO BRING IT UP WITH HIM A BUNCH OF TIMES BUT HE'S--
I MEAN, I GUESS HE DEALS WITH IT FINE, BUT, YOU KNOW, NONE OF US EVER REALLY... WE...
SHIT, DAD! I CAN'T DO THIS! I DON'T KNOW WHAT TO SAY!! IT'S JUST--
YOU SAY YOU WANT US ALL TO BE HONEST BUT HOW? HOW THE HELL CAN WE DO THAT??
WHAT'S STOPPING YOU?
"WHAT'S STOPPING ME??"
WHAT'S STOPPING ME IS THAT YOU'RE FUCKING DYING, DAD!! YOU'RE DYING!!
YOU'RE ANGRY.

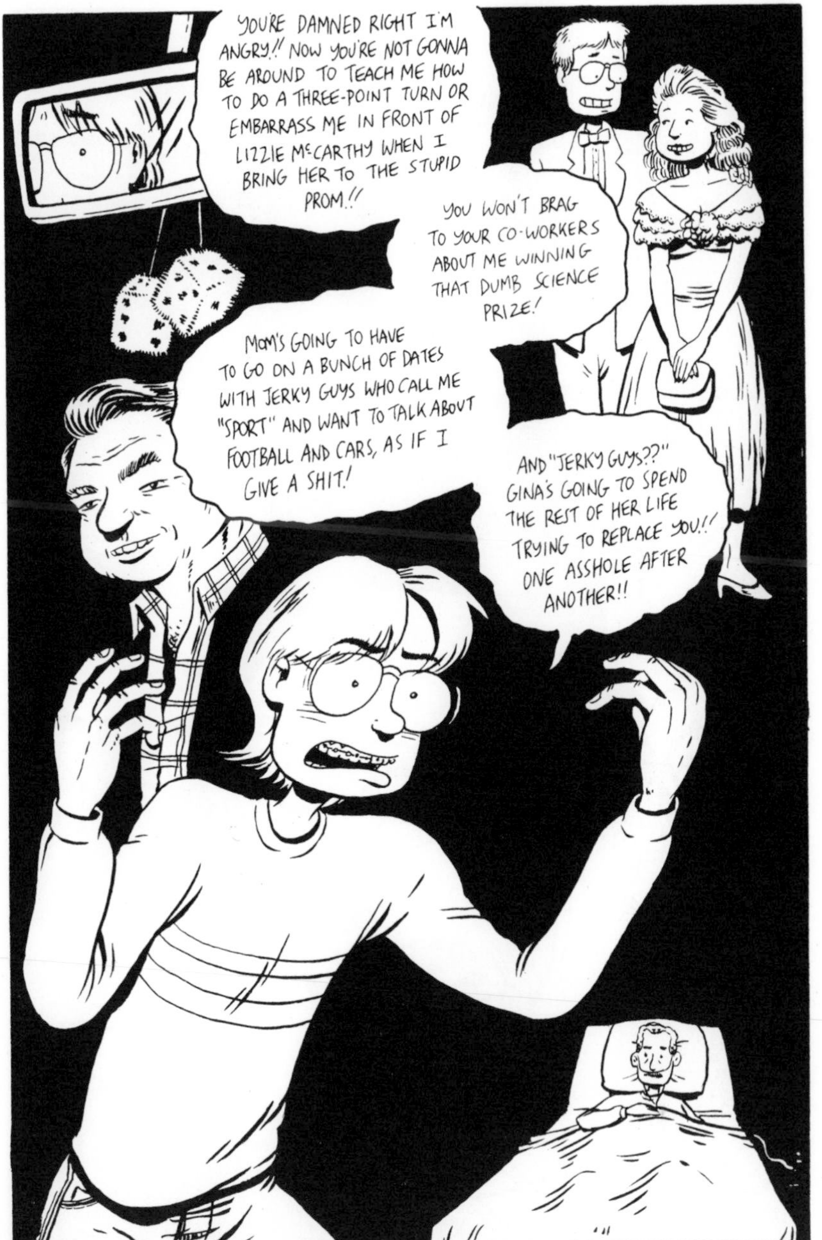
YOU'RE DAMNED RIGHT I'M ANGRY!! NOW YOU'RE NOT GONNA BE AROUND TO TEACH ME HOW TO DO A THREE-POINT TURN OR EMBARRASS ME IN FRONT OF LIZZIE McCARTHY WHEN I BRING HER TO THE STUPID PROM!!
YOU WON'T BRAG TO YOUR CO-WORKERS ABOUT ME WINNING THAT DUMB SCIENCE PRIZE!
MOM'S GOING TO HAVE TO GO ON A BUNCH OF DATES WITH JERKY GUYS WHO CALL ME "SPORT" AND WANT TO TALK ABOUT FOOTBALL AND CARS, AS IF I GIVE A SHIT!
AND "JERKY GUYS??" GINA'S GOING TO SPEND THE REST OF HER LIFE TRYING TO REPLACE YOU!! ONE ASSHOLE AFTER ANOTHER!!

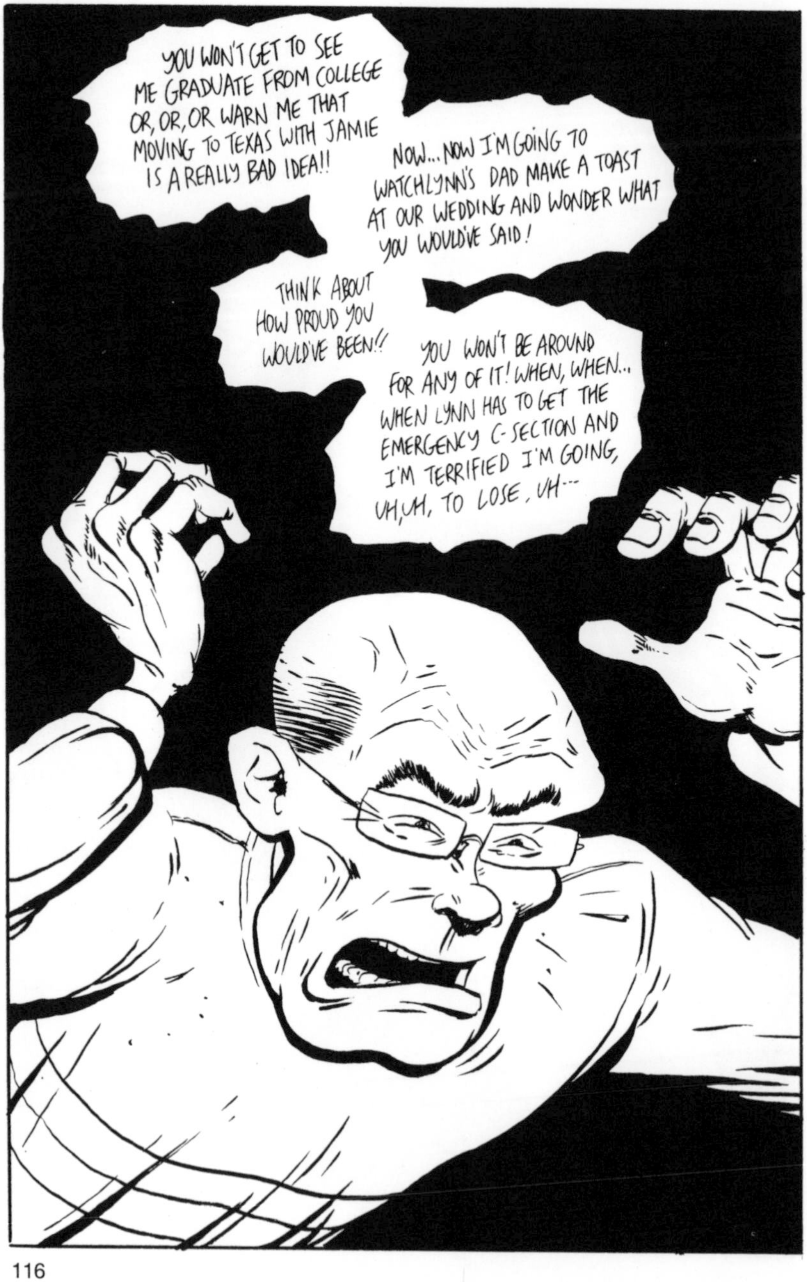
YOU WON'T GET TO SEE ME GRADUATE FROM COLLEGE OR, OR, OR WARN ME THAT MOVING TO TEXAS WITH JAMIE IS A REALLY BAD IDEA!!
NOW... NOW I'M GOING TO WATCH LYNN'S DAD MAKE A TOAST AT OUR WEDDING AND WONDER WHAT YOU WOULD'VE SAID!
THINK ABOUT HOW PROUD YOU WOULD'VE BEEN!!
YOU WON'T BE AROUND FOR ANY OF IT! WHEN, WHEN... WHEN LYNN HAS TO GET THE EMERGENCY C-SECTION AND I'M TERRIFIED I'M GOING, UH, UH, TO LOSE, UH---

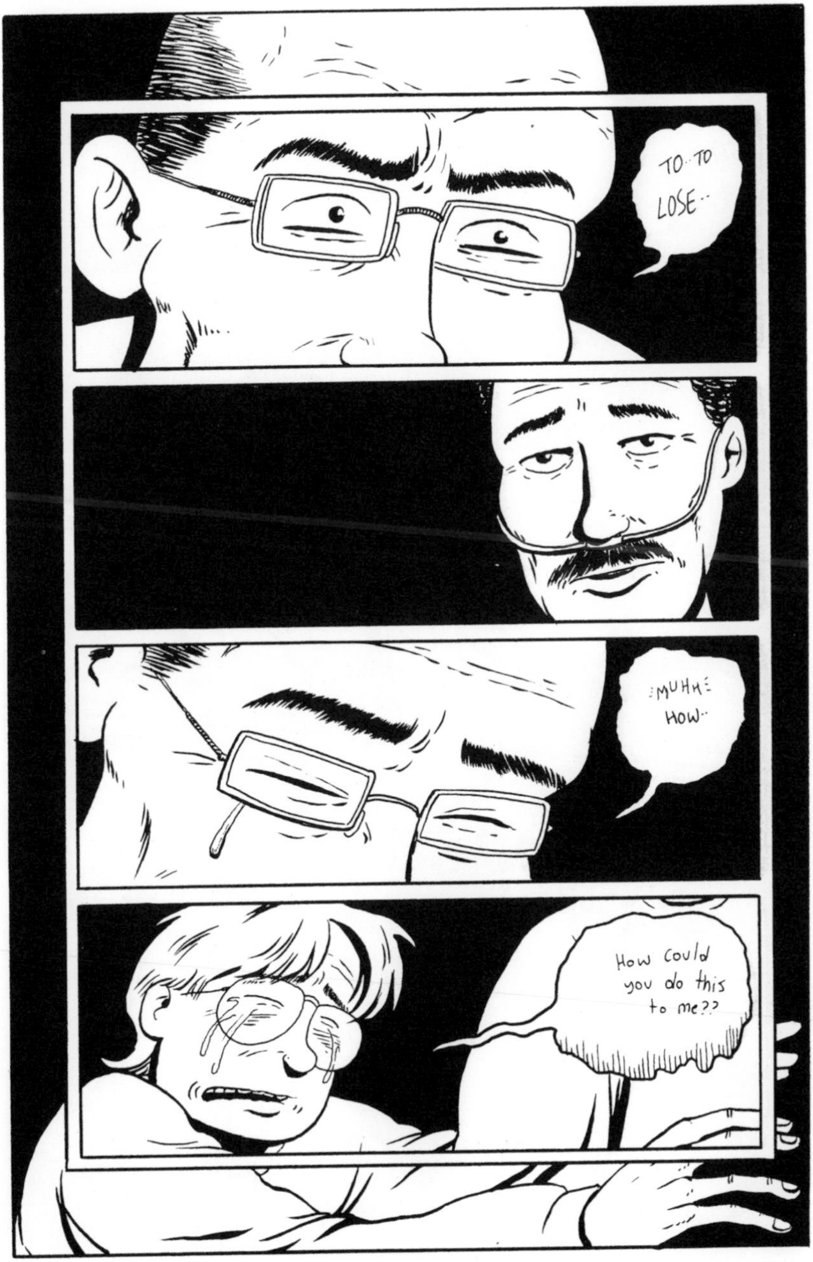
TO.. TO LOSE..
MUHH HOW..
How could you do this to me??

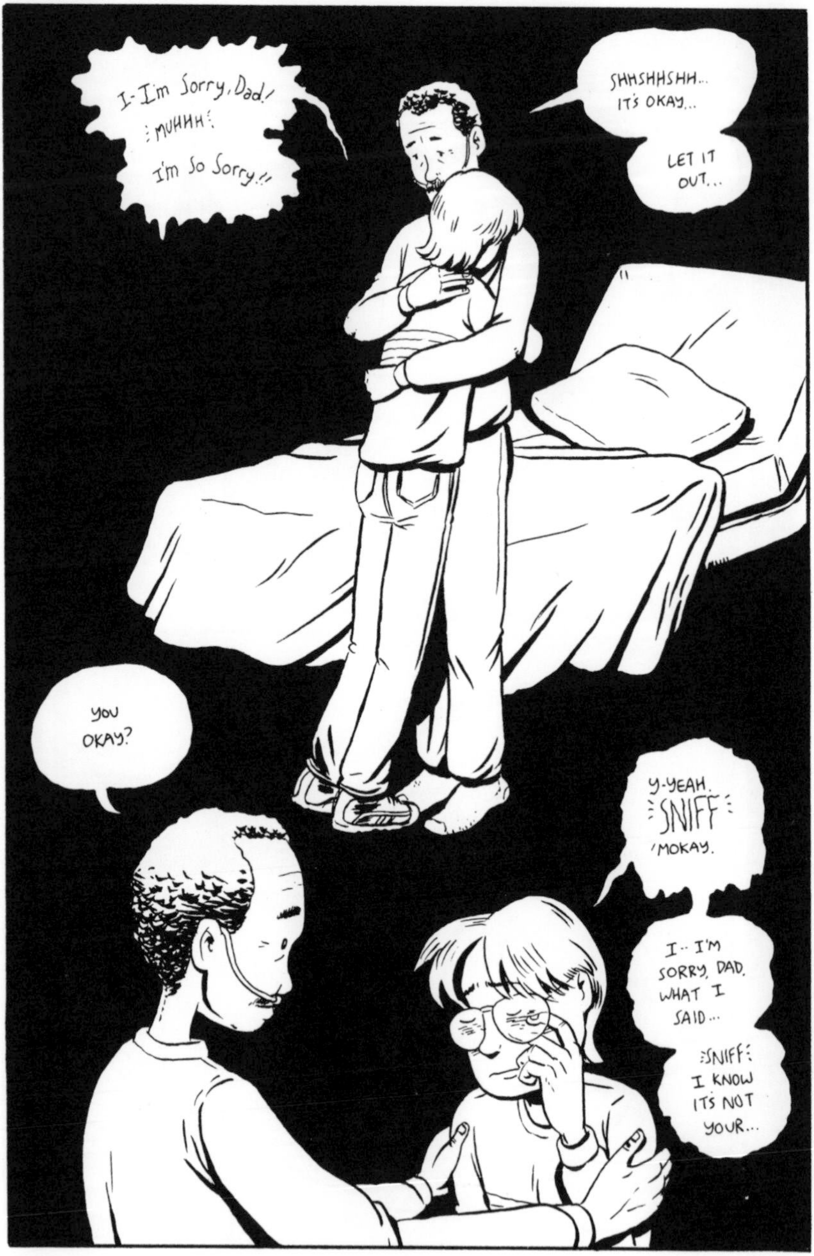
I-I'm Sorry, Dad!
MUHHH
I'm So Sorry!!
SHHSHHSHH... IT'S OKAY...
LET IT OUT...
YOU OKAY?
Y-YEAH.
SNIFF
'MOKAY.
I.. I'M SORRY, DAD. WHAT I SAID...
SNIFF
I KNOW IT'S NOT YOUR...

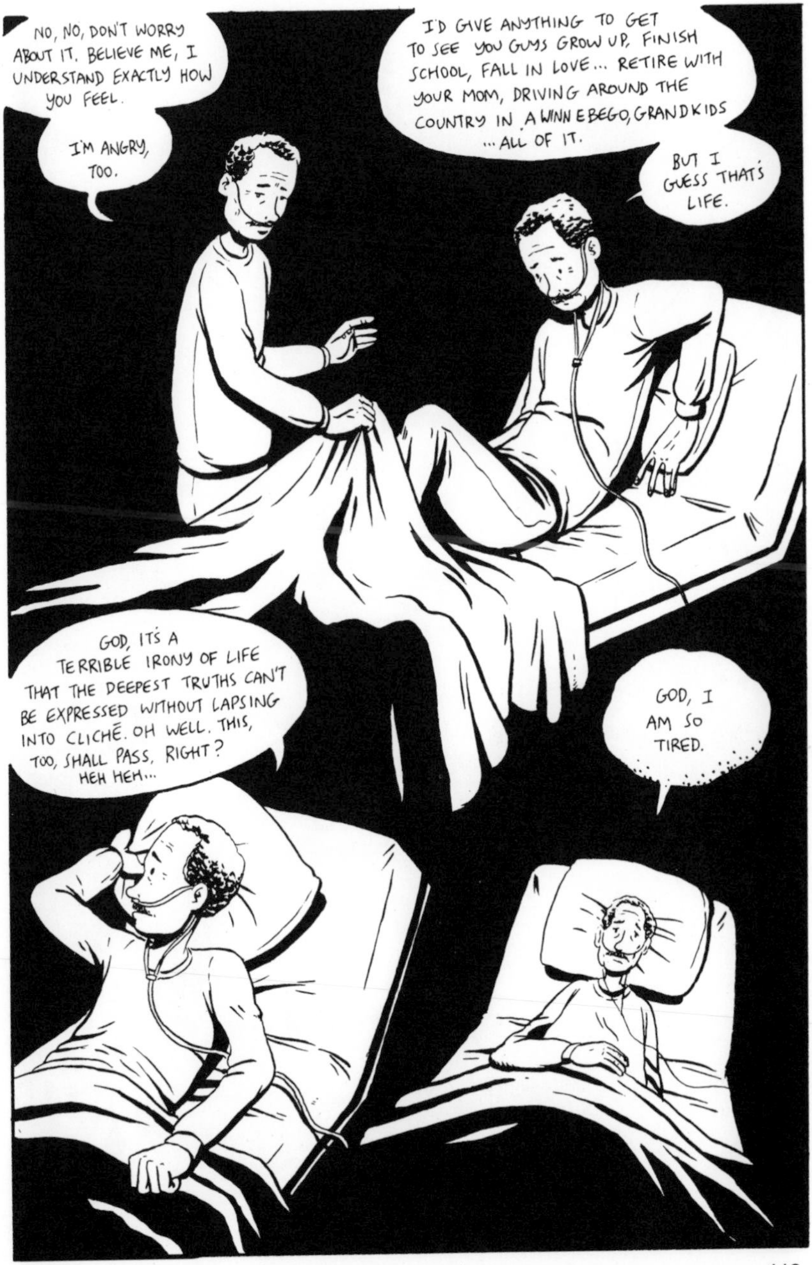
NO, NO, DON'T WORRY ABOUT IT. BELIEVE ME, I UNDERSTAND EXACTLY HOW YOU FEEL.
I'M ANGRY, TOO.
I'D GIVE ANYTHING TO GET TO SEE YOU GUYS GROW UP, FINISH SCHOOL, FALL IN LOVE... RETIRE WITH YOUR MOM, DRIVING AROUND THE COUNTRY IN A WINNEBEGO, GRANDKIDS ...ALL OF IT.
BUT I GUESS THAT'S LIFE.
GOD, IT'S A TERRIBLE IRONY OF LIFE THAT THE DEEPEST TRUTHS CAN'T BE EXPRESSED WITHOUT LAPSING INTO CLICHÉ. OH WELL. THIS, TOO, SHALL PASS, RIGHT? HEH HEH...
GOD, I AM SO TIRED.

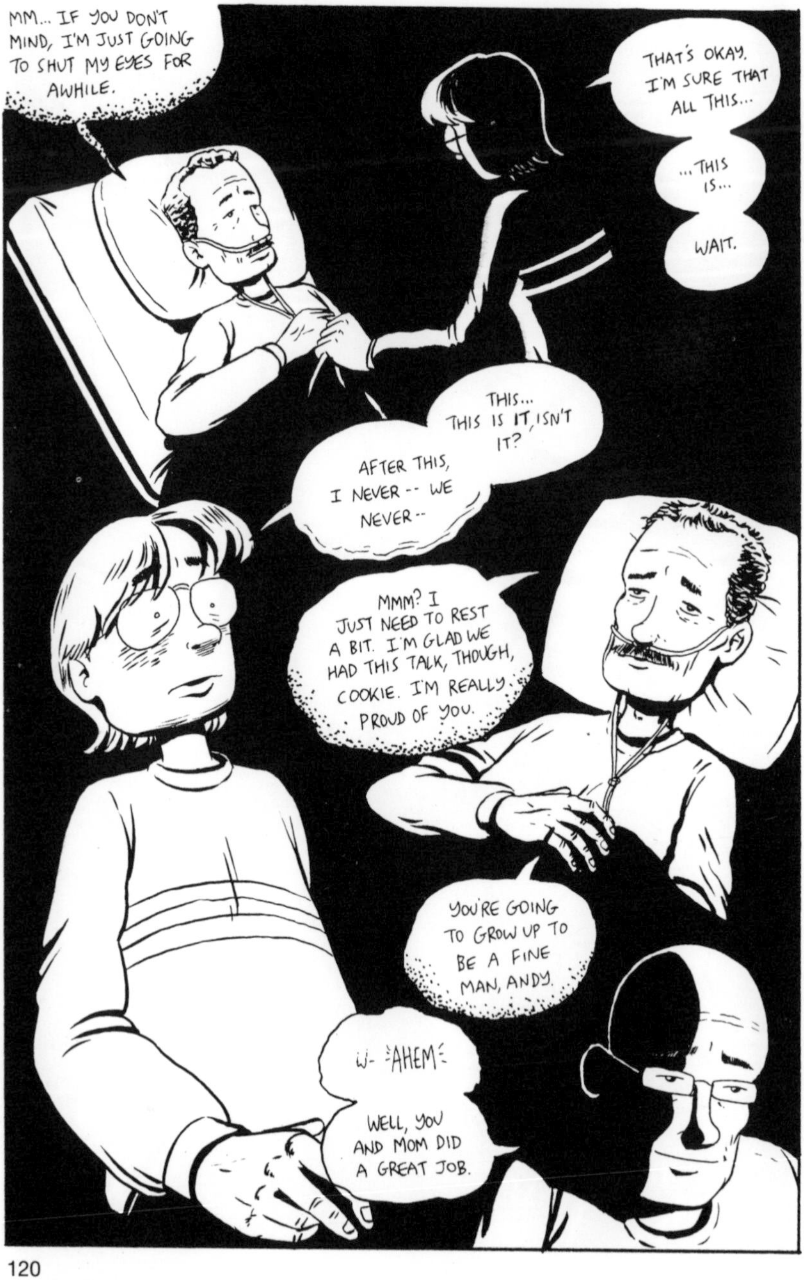
MM... IF YOU DON'T MIND, I'M JUST GOING TO SHUT MY EYES FOR AWHILE.
THAT'S OKAY. I'M SURE THAT ALL THIS...
...THIS IS...
WAIT.
THIS... THIS IS IT, ISN'T IT?
AFTER THIS, I NEVER -- WE NEVER --
MMM? I JUST NEED TO REST A BIT. I'M GLAD WE HAD THIS TALK, THOUGH, COOKIE. I'M REALLY PROUD OF YOU.
YOU'RE GOING TO GROW UP TO BE A FINE MAN, ANDY.
W- AHEM
WELL, YOU AND MOM DID A GREAT JOB.

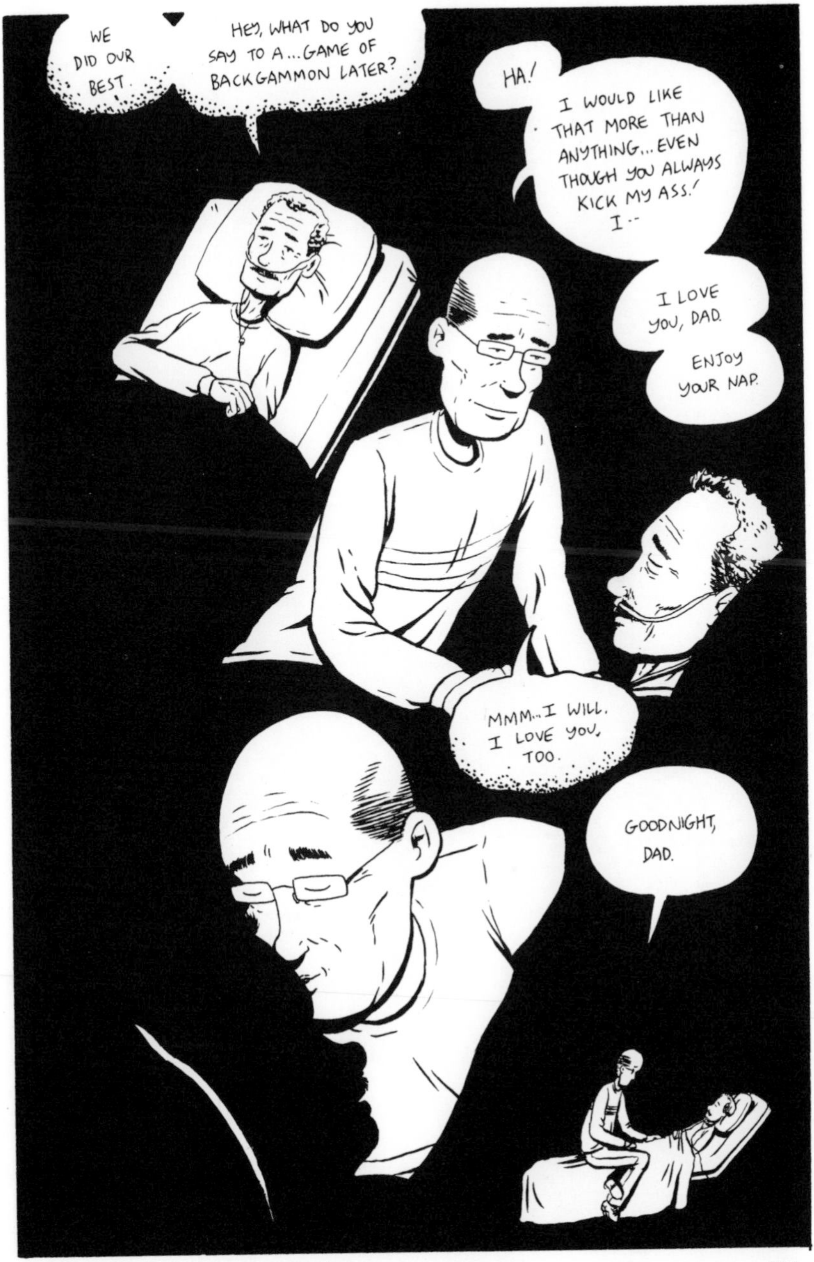
WE DID OUR BEST.
HEY, WHAT DO YOU SAY TO A... GAME OF BACKGAMMON LATER?
HA!
I WOULD LIKE THAT MORE THAN ANYTHING... EVEN THOUGH YOU ALWAYS KICK MY ASS! I--
I LOVE YOU, DAD.
ENJOY YOUR NAP.
MMM... I WILL. I LOVE YOU, TOO.
GOODNIGHT, DAD.

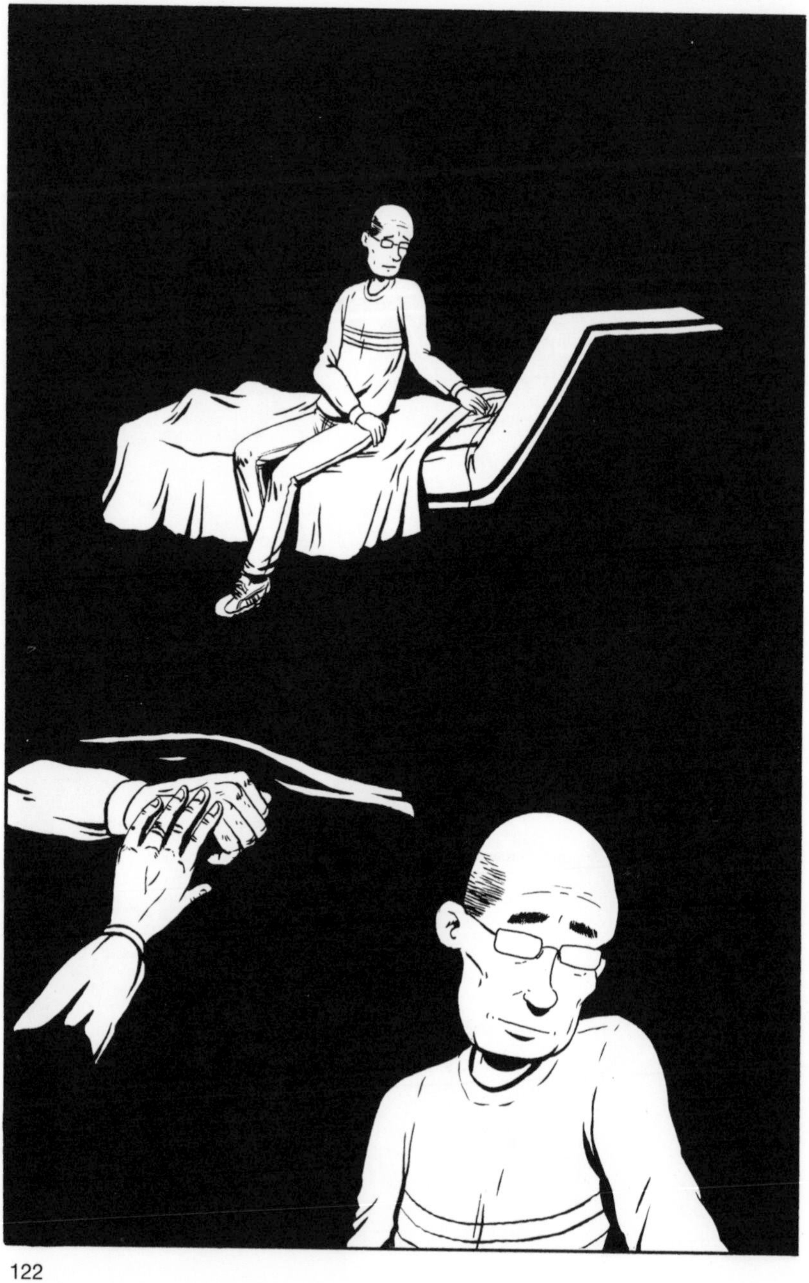

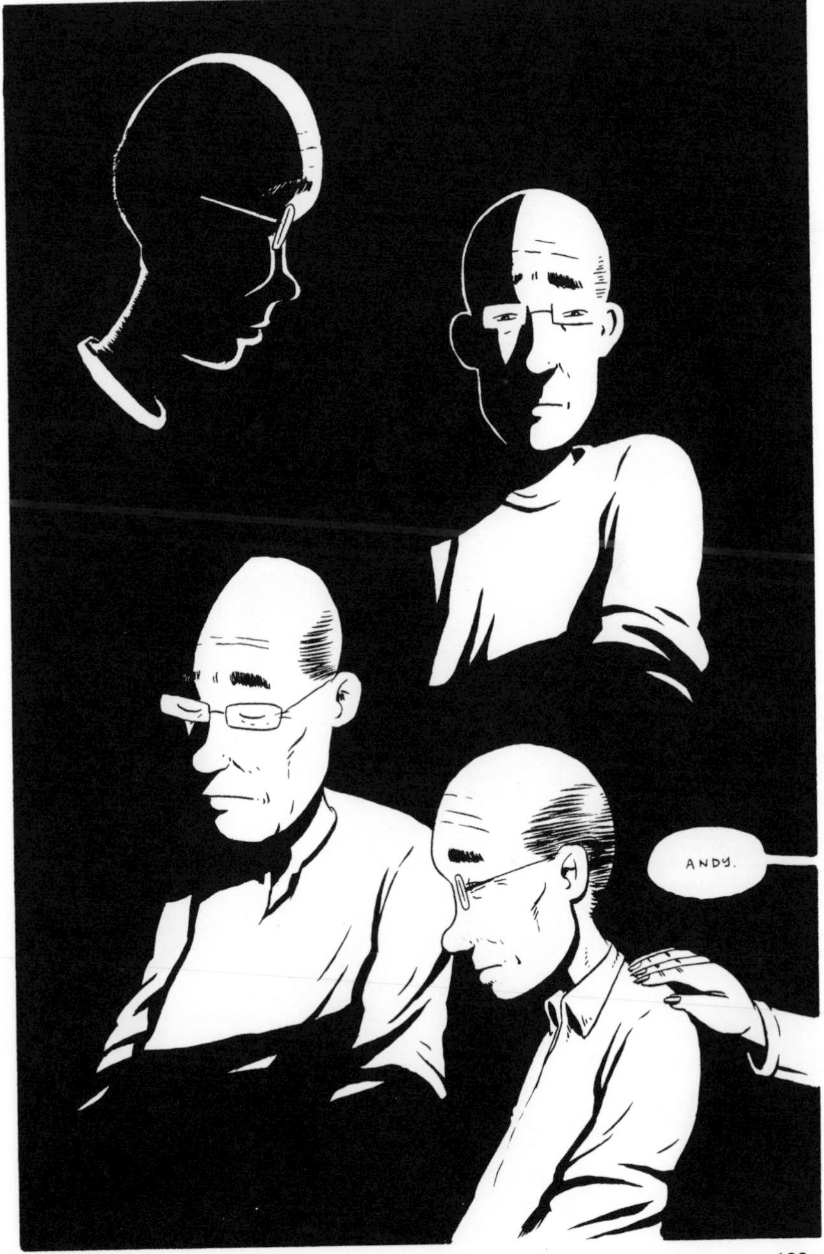
ANDY.

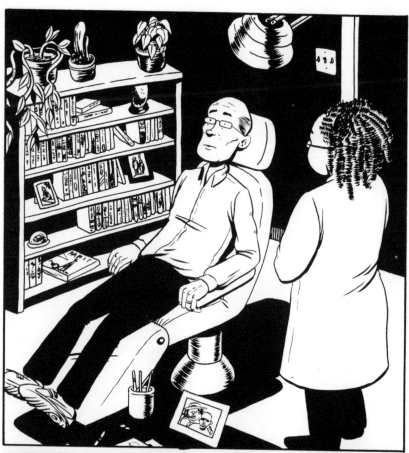

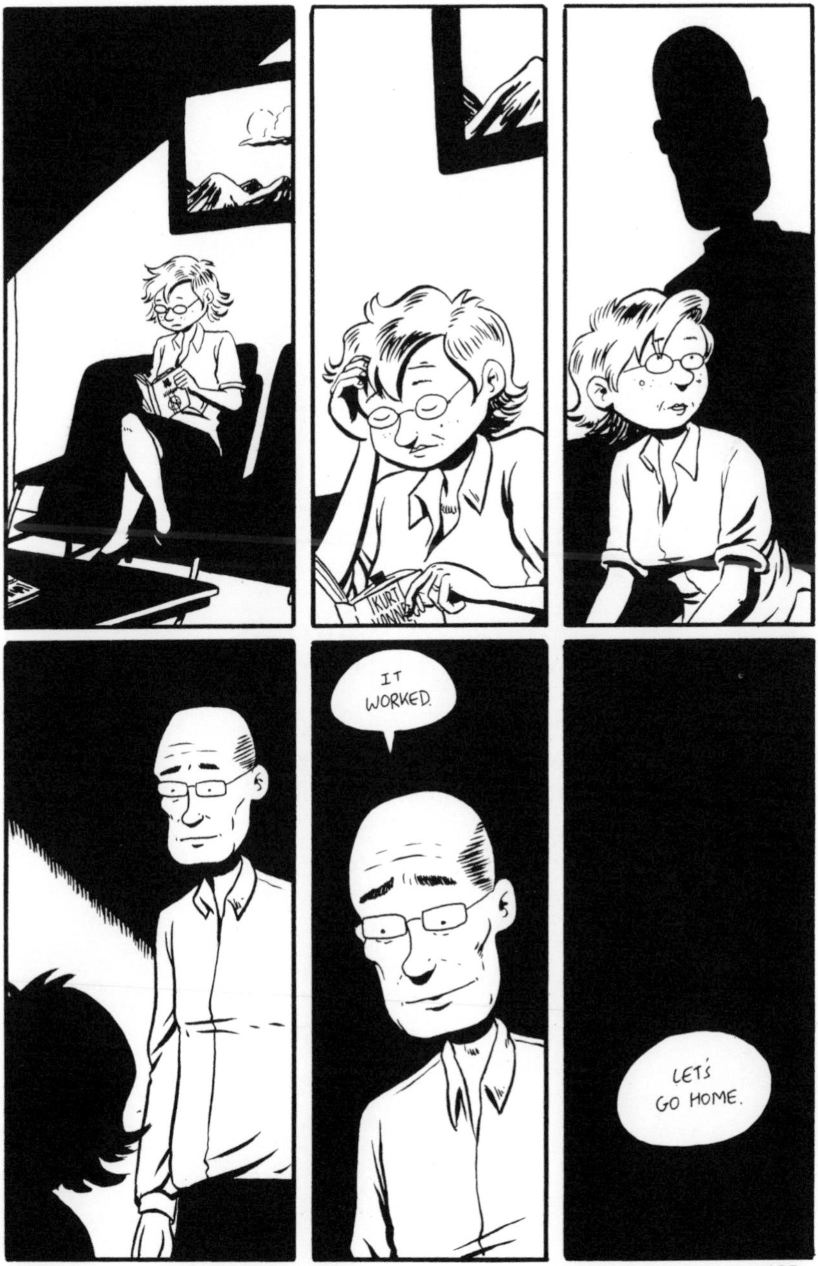
KURT VONNE
IT WORKED.
LET'S GO HOME.

Thanks to Al, Andrew, Bob, Burr,
Club, Dave, George, Ger, Howard,
Jeanine, Jeff, Jim, John, Kurt,
Larry, Mr. Baptiste, Paul, Ringo,
Robin, Roger and anyone else who
helped me serve out my time in
high school.

Thanks to Brett, Chris, Matt and
Rob, the Top Shelf crew who
helped put this book in your hands.

Thanks to Chris, Mike, Tim and
Tony, my Ink Panther brothers.

Thanks for Aliza and Vania, my
Pink Panther sisters, and Ruby the
littlest Panther (for now...).

Thanks to *Kristen*, for her
seemingly endless patience,
support and love.

Alex Robinson lives in New York City with his wife and their two cats. His other books, all available from Top Shelf Productions, are **Box Office Poison**, **BOP!**, **Tricked** and **Alex Robinson's Lower Regions**. He graduated from high school in 1987, and was voted *"Most Artistic"* by his classmates. He was not invited to the reunion.

www.comicbookalex.com

[Page 84 includes an error in which the protagonist, Mr. Wicks, thinks the word "Dad" instead of "Did." This will not be corrected in future editions, as it was intentional on the part of Mr. Robinson. The publishers and proofreaders wish to note their opposition to including such grammatically awkward and painfully heavy handed foreshadowing, but have let the issue rest out of respect for the author. We apologize if the author's stubborn refusal to listen to reason, demands or threats at all diminished your enjoyment of another otherwise entertaining Top Shelf product.]

ISBN 978-1-891830-98-3
1. Graphic Novels
2. Humor
3. Time-travel

Too Cool To Be Forgotten © 2008 *Alex Robinson*. Edited by Chris Staros.
Cover design by Matt Kindt.
Published by Top Shelf Productions,
PO Box 1282, Marietta, GA 30061-1282, USA.
Publishers: Brett Warnock and Chris Staros.

Visit our online catalog at *www.topshelfcomix.com*.

Visit *Alex Robinson* at
www.comicbookalex.com.

First Printing, July 2008. Printed in China.